EVE AND HENRY JAMES

EVE
and Henry James

PORTRAITS OF WOMEN AND GIRLS
IN HIS FICTION

by Edward Wagenknecht

UNIVERSITY OF OKLAHOMA PRESS
NORMAN

RECENT BOOKS BY EDWARD WAGENKNECHT

Nathaniel Hawthorne: Man and Writer (New York, 1961)
Mark Twain: The Man and His Work (Norman, 1961, 1967)
Washington Irving: Moderation Displayed (New York, 1962)
The Movies in the Age of Innocence (Norman, 1962)
Edgar Allan Poe: The Man Behind the Legend (New York, 1963)
Chicago (Norman, 1964)
Seven Daughters of the Theater (Norman, 1964)
Harriet Beecher Stowe: The Known and the Unknown (New York, 1965)
Dickens and the Scandalmongers: Essays in Criticism (Norman, 1966)
The Man Charles Dickens: A Victorian Portrait (Norman, 1966)
Henry Wadsworth Longfellow: Portrait of an American Humanist (New York, 1966)
Merely Players (Norman, 1966)
John Greenleaf Whittier: A Portrait in Paradox (New York, 1967)
The Personality of Chaucer (Norman, 1968)
As Far as Yesterday: Memories and Reflections (Norman, 1968)
The Supernaturalism of New England, by John Greenleaf Whittier (editor)
    (Norman, 1969)
William Dean Howells: The Friendly Eye (New York, 1969)
The Personality of Milton (Norman, 1970)
James Russell Lowell: Portrait of a Many-sided Man (New York, 1971)
The Personality of Shakespeare (Norman, 1972)
Ambassadors for Christ: Seven American Preachers (New York, 1972)
Ralph Waldo Emerson: Portrait of a Balanced Soul (New York, 1974)
The Letters of James Branch Cabell (editor) (Norman,1975)
The Films of D. W. Griffith (with Anthony Slide) (New York, 1975)
A Pictorial History of New England (New York, 1976)

Library of Congress Cataloguing in Publication Data

Wagenknecht, Edward Charles, 1900–
    Eve and Henry James.

    Includes bibliographical references.
    1. James, Henry, 1843–1916 — Character — Women.
2.   Women in literature.   I.   Title.

PS2127.W6W3   813'.4   77–18613
ISBN 0–8061–1422–3

For my granddaughter
CAROLINE THERESE WAGENKNECHT
who will not be reading James for some time

CONTENTS

PREFACE

WHEN A WRITER has published nearly sixty books, he may, I suppose, safely be regarded as having had his public "say" upon a fairly large proportion of the things that are important to him. But though more than half a century has gone by since my great teacher Edith Rickert made both a Chaucerian and a Jacobean of me, I have hitherto written of Henry James at any length only in the chapter devoted to him in my *Cavalcade of the American Novel.*

It might seem that the most natural way for me to treat James would have been to produce a psychograph of him to stand beside my studies of his only peers among American writers of fiction in the late nineteenth and early twentieth centuries—Mark Twain and William Dean Howells. But since not all the material necessary for such a study is even yet available, I decided instead to try to paint the portraits of some of his characters. This project interested me, first of all, because I thought it might provide an interesting variation of my usual methods and technique, and I decided to do women rather than men because of the fairly general impression which prevails to the effect that, with few exceptions, James's female characters are more interesting than the male.

As everybody knows, there have been plenty of books about Shakespeare's characters, and in 1901, Howells himself published two substantial volumes on *Heroines of Fic-*

tion, in which James was represented by Daisy Miller. The immediate suggestion for my book, however, came from Richard Curle's *Joseph Conrad and his Characters* (Essential Books, 1958). At first I thought in terms of a general comprehensive study of all James's female characters, classifying them by type; I even went so far as to divide them under

    I.   Innocents
   II.   Harpies
  III.   Ficelles
   IV.   Problems
    V.   Heroines

Further consideration soon convinced me, however, that this must result in either an enormous book or else a painfully superficial treatment; I decided therefore to choose a limited number of what are to me the most interesting characters.

Gamaliel Bradford once wrote:

> The most real of all human figures are the creations of the imagination. The nearest approach to earthly immortality, to an existence that is not shattered or imperiled by failure or decay, belongs to spirits that have never lived in the flesh, but have been embodied by great artists in dream shapes that have taken an enduring hold upon the fancy and memory of humanity. Helen, Hector, and Achilles, Dido and Aeneas, Hamlet, Lear, Rosiland and Portia, live and will live, when millions who have known and loved them have been buried and forgotten.

James's characters have not yet had a chance to demonstrate their command of the kind of earthly immortality that has been achieved by those Bradford mentions, but their vitality is undeniable, and while working on this book, I have at times found myself surprised by how strongly one can react to them, even to the extent of indignation over what seem like unjust or ungenerous interpretations of them by uncomprehending critics. From my previous readings of

Roderick Hudson and *The Princess Casamassima* I had supposed that I disliked Christina Light, but when I came to
study her in detail, I found myself much more sympathetic
toward her. Obviously, though the great novelists always
try to convince us of the "reality" of their characters, these
can never be "real" except in a special sense; if we write
about them as if they had lived in the flesh, we so hopelessly
confuse art and life that we really understand neither. On
the other hand, we must never forget that the human being
who created them *was* real and that when we make discoveries about them we are discovering him also; hence the kind
of enterprise that is undertaken in such a book as this acquires a double interest.

So far from being intended as anything approximating a
James "bibliography," my footnotes do not even add up to a
complete record of my reading concerning the works under
consideration, being intended only to identify my references
to other writers, to treat subordinate matters, and in some
cases to tell the reader where he can find fuller discussion
of the points I raise and different interpretations of them.
I have, however, taken the opportunity afforded by a final
review of the manuscript before a somewhat delayed going
to press to take notice of a number of books and articles
which have appeared since I finished my work.

All quotations from Jamesian texts are from the New
York Edition by kind permission of the authorized publishers, Charles Scribner's Sons.

EDWARD WAGENKNECHT

West Newton, Massachusetts

No other novelist has approached Mr. James in his appreciation of women, and in his ability to suggest the charm which is never wholly absent from women, whether they are good, bad or indifferent in looks and behavior. Take all the other men that have written novels in English and match their women with his, and they seem not to have written of women at all.

W. D. Howells

EVE AND HENRY JAMES

The following abbreviations are employed in the notes for publishers and periodicals frequently cited:

AI	*American Imago*
AL	*American Literature*
AQ	*American Quarterly*
CE	*College English*
CoUP	Cornell University Press
CUP	Cambridge University Press
EIC	*Essays in Criticism*
ELH	*ELH: English Literary History*
HM	Houghton Mifflin Company
HUP	Harvard University Press
Li	J. B. Lippincott Company
MFS	*Modern Fiction Studies*
MLN	*Modern Language Notes*
NEQ	*New England Quarterly*
NCF	*Nineteenth Century Fiction*
NQ	*Notes and Queries*
OUP	Oxford University Press
PMLA	*PMLA: Publications of the Modern Language Association*
PQ	*Philological Quarterly*
PUP	Princeton University Press
RUP	Rutgers University Press
SR	*Sewanee Review*
SSF	*Studies in Short Fiction*
TSLL	*Texas Studies in Language and Literature*
UCP	University of Chicago Press
UKCR	*University of Kansas City Review*
UNCP	University of North Carolina Press
UNP	University of Nebraska Press
WHR	*Western Humanities Review*
YUP	Yale University Press

I. INNOCENCE ABROAD

DAISY MILLER

IN LATER YEARS Henry James disliked being thought of as "the author of *Daisy Miller*" for much the same reasons that Rachmaninoff objected to being tagged as the composer of "Prelude in C-Sharp Minor." Modern criticism regards so much of James's later work as more important that it is hard for us to remember that so great a novelist should only this once, in 1878, have achieved something of a literary sensation. And if it was, in a measure, only a *succès de scandale,* this should not greatly surprise us who live in a society which has always been more interested in scandal than in literature.

Daisy was a singularly innocent anticipation of the flapper or gamine type of heroine who has become so popular in American fiction since her time, and it is not the least of the ironies associated with her that she should have been created by the most fastidious of American writers. There are of course plenty of vulgar women and girls in the Jamesian novel world, but the point about this little piece of "pure poetry," as James himself calls her, is that she manifests his "incurable prejudice in favor of grace" and that her creator loves her. If we do not understand that, we shall understand nothing about her, nor much, I fear, about him. In other words, James himself passes the test which the frosty Winterbourne of the tale fails (thus contributing his bit toward cropping the little inland daisy), and it is suitable, in a story crammed with subtle ironies, both that Giovanelli, who was not quite a gentleman, should have passed it too and that James should not have shrunk from making the Italian his own spokesman at the end, permitting him to utter the definitive, touching verdict on the dead girl: "She was the most beautiful young lady I ever saw, and the most amiable. Also— naturally!—the most innocent." But it is equally important to remember that James overlooks none of Daisy's faults or limitations: he would, I think, have no sympathy with those who would see her as a Christian martyr, a high priestess of American Transcendentalism, or even a Milly Theale.[1] The basic objection to all this is that it blurs distinctions; accepting it, we prove ourselves incapable of loving the girl James created and substituting something of an abstraction for her.

In his Preface to *Daisy Miller* in the New York Edition, James attributes the origin of the story to an anecdote he heard in Rome in 1877 about how an American girl had created scandal by "picking up" and going about with "a good-looking Roman, of vague identity." This may not completely cover the case, however. In 1934 the great New Testament scholar Edgar J. Goodspeed recorded how he had read *Daisy Miller* as his first grown-up story when he was about ten years old and been greatly impressed by it. "In it Henry James seems to have discovered the American girl, in all her directness, independence, sincerity and charm." That was why she had been discussed like a real person, inspiring disagreement quite as real people do. But Goodspeed had not been able to reconcile himself to her death. "It is so abrupt, so uncalled-for, so out of key. From the lightest of banter, one passes

---

[1] James Kraft, *The Early Tales of Henry James* (Southern Illinois University Press, 1969), calls Daisy a mystic because she embodies "an essential element of the American experience that transcends the immediate encounter and touches upon elements common to us all." Similarly, Ihab Hassan, *Radical Innocence: Studies in the Contemporary American Novel* (PUP, 1961), sees her affirming "her faith in the autonomy of candor, in the rights of the individual against those of the group, in Protestant conscience against Catholic form. She is, in short, a rebel, and the price of her rebellion is death." Hassan adds, however, that James was quite aware that, if initiation into the world can be tragic, so can the refusal to be initiated.

suddenly into grim tragedy." He had continued to be puzzled by the matter until 1933, when W. W. Norton published the *Diary* of Julia Newberry, a Chicago girl who died in Rome in April, 1876, and was buried in the American Cemetery there. But Dr. Goodspeed apparently did not know that as early as 1873 James had been moved by the pathos of finding a girl's grave in Rome, as he reported in an article in *The Nation.*

In 1938, in her highly speculative biography of Louisa May Alcott, Katharine Anthony suggested another possible source in "Louisa's adventures with her Polish youth in Vevey and Paris; they were to have met in Rome, but never did." Miss Alcott, says Katharine Anthony, disliked *Daisy Miller* and warned American girls against it in a story which the biographer did not identify. "As Louisa seldom mentioned the works of her contemporaries in her diaries, this reference to a story of the day in a piece of fiction is rather surprising." It may not be wholly irrelevant to note that James himself reviewed Miss Alcott's adult novel, *Moods*, very severely; apparently he was even shocked by it.

Ten years later, Violet Dunbar pointed out the relevance to *Daisy Miller* of a novel, *Paule Méré,* by the Swiss novelist Victor Cherbuliez (1829–99), now forgotten but once popular in English translation in the United States as well as in Europe. In 1950, Edward Stone showed that there were more parallels between *Paule Méré* and *Daisy Miller* than Violet Dunbar had suggested, and in 1969, Cherbuliez was accepted by Motley Deakin, who also found Turgenev, George Sand, and Madame de Staël heroines in Daisy Miller, thus somewhat shifting the emphasis from her innocence to her independence. James himself had given these critics a long-overlooked clue when, in the story itself, he had had Mrs. Costello ask Winterbourne to bring her a copy of *Paule Méré*; the irony here is that she obviously does not recognize that Cherbuliez directs his satire not against Daisy Miller-people but Costello-people. James also referred to *Paule Méré,* though not by name, in a magazine article of 1872; in 1875, however, he called the heroine "not absolutely natural."[2]

However all this may be, James wrote *Daisy Miller* in London in the spring of 1878 and sent it to *Lippincott's Magazine*, whose editor, John Foster Kirk, promptly rejected it without explanation ("a friend" explained to the puzzled author that it had probably been regarded as "an outrage on American girlhood"), but Virginia Woolf's father, Leslie Stephen, gladly accepted it for the *Cornhill*. After its appearance there, it was promptly pirated in America by both *Littell's Living Age* and *The Home Journal,* and Harpers brought it out in their twenty-five-cent Half-Hour Series, where it sold widely but yielded James only two hundred dollars in royalties. If the critical reception was somewhat less severe than has sometimes been suggested,[3] it is still clear that it displeased many readers and, as William Dean Howells said,[4] divided society between Daisy Millerites and anti-Daisy Millerites, so that we hear of one young lady who,

[2] Edgar J. Goodspeed, "A Footnote to *Daisy Miller,*" *Atlantic Monthly*, CLIII (1934), 252–53; Katharine Anthony, *Louisa May Alcott* (Knopf, 1938); Violet Dunbar, "A Note of the Genesis of *Daisy Miller,*" *PQ*, XXVII (1948), 184–87; Edward Stone, "A Further Note on *Daisy Miller* and Cherbuliez," *PQ*, XXIX (1950), 213–16 — see also his book, *The Battle and the Books: Some Aspects of Henry James* (Ohio State University Press, 1964); Motley F. Deakin, "Daisy Miller, Tradition, and the European Heroine," *SSF*, VI (1969), 45–59. Tristram P. Coffin, "Daisy Miller, Western Hero," *Western Folklore*, XVII (1958), 273–75, sees Daisy as "really little more than a Western hero with parasol and bank account," though he adds that she was not created with the West in mind. James's review of *Moods*, in *The North American Review*, 1865, is reprinted in Pierre de Chaignon la Rose, *Notes and Reviews by Henry James* (Dunster House, 1921).

[3] See Edmund L. Volpe, "The Reception of *Daisy Miller,*" *Boston Public Library Quarterly*, X (1958), 55–59.

[4] Howells' paper on Daisy in his *Heroines of Fiction* (Harper, 1901) is still the best-known essay she has inspired, but George Monteiro has shown convincingly that the first of the two pieces attributed to him by William T. Stafford and others (from "The Contributors' Club" in the *Atlantic*, February, 1879) was actually written by Constance Fenimore Woolson and the second (March, 1879) by John Hay. See

when she heard James was returning to America, wondered if he was coming in search of more *"raw* material," while another hated him with all her heart and longed to see him married to "a perfect Daisy Miller."

James, who was indifferent to many aspects of the American scene, believed that "small female fry," as he called them, greatly mattered, but he also believed that where a light lamp would do it was no use to carry a heavy one, and he obviously took pains not to pile upon Daisy's slim shoulders more weight than they could carry. When the story was first published, it was subtitled "A Study," though he dropped the tag when reprinting in the New York Edition. The effect was to suggest that the thing had not been completely "done" (he himself speaks of the "flatness" of his heroine, as well as her "shy incongruous charm") and perhaps also that it suggests a type or a problem.

We should not be surprised, then, that, although Daisy's death at the end is not wholly unprepared for, James is careful not to make a full-fledged tragedy of it. Less than two pages are devoted to her whole illness, while one curt sentence reports her actual passing. Winterbourne, whom she loves, and who might have loved her if he had had more insight and less priggishness, gives her up at last when he finds her visiting the Colosseum at night with her Italian "gentleman friend," Giovanelli. For himself Winterbourne makes this relinquishment with a certain sense of relief: the "riddle" has now become "easy to read," and he can have the comfort of dismissing it from his overburdened mind, but he treats Daisy so coldly that she exclaims, "I don't care whether I have Roman fever or not!" This, however, is more prepara-

Monteiro, "William Dean Howells: Two Mistaken Attributions," *Papers of the Bibliographical Society of America*, LVI (1962), 254–57—also his book, *Henry James and John Hay: The Record of a Friendship* (Brown University Press, 1965), and see further Stafford, *James's* Daisy Miller: *The Story, The Play, The Critics* (Scribners, 1963). This useful "research anthology" extracts a number of critical writings not listed separately in my notes.

tion than motivation. We have all said such things without really meaning them, and Daisy has also just remarked, "I never was sick, and I don't mean to be! I don't look like much, but I'm healthy."

Her final interview with Winterbourne certainly does not make her ordeal easier (the message she sends him from her deathbed shows that), but in the last analysis what kills her is not cruelty but malaria, and she contracts malaria through recklessly visiting the Colosseum at night because she wishes to see it by moonlight and is accustomed to having her own way regardless of consequences. Daisy does not really defy society but only disregards it, and if there is an element of heroism involved in carrying personal independence to such lengths, her behavior is still more unadvised than ill-advised and too spontaneous to permit the reader to posit any calculated choice or predetermination. J. A. Ward is as cruel as Winterbourne when he accuses her of having no moral or aesthetic consciousness and calls her "a person on whom everything is lost,"[5] but Bret Harte was certainly right when he long ago observed that "she might have gone in a conventionally proper way to the Colosseum, and yet caught the malarial fever and died."[6]

Whether Harte was also right in finding her fate "almost absurdly illogical" ("You cannot believe her dying for love,

[5] *The Imagination of Disaster: Evil in the Fiction of Henry James* (UNP, 1961).

[6] In the unacted *Daisy Miller, A Comedy in Three Acts*, which James R. Osgood published in 1884, after it had been serialized in the *Atlantic*, James keeps Daisy alive for a final mating with Winterbourne, but this hardly counts. One of the mysteries of literary history is how a man could write such good novels as Henry James and such bad plays. If he had designed the latter merely as potboilers, there would be no great problem, but he thought they were good. The *Daisy Miller* comedy reads not like an adaptation made by the author himself but like a dramatization effected by a Hollywood scenarist or a popular playwright of very mild literary pretensions. It runs over with the intrigues which abounded in popular nineteenth-century drama, the most important being the conspiracy between Giovanelli and the Miller courier Eugenio to marry Giovanelli to Daisy, for which Eugenio is to receive a commission! But these are not the only characters who are

any more than you can believe the cold-blooded hero, who notices all her defects, as a lover, or a creature such as a girl could love"), every reader must decide for himself. Though *Daisy Miller* is not written in the first person, James does tell the story from Winterbourne's point of view, and what Winterbourne does not understand about Daisy is very large. Some may well find the focus of the story blurred on this account, while others will judge the method of narration to have contributed to the ironies and ambiguities with which the tale bristles. None of this, however, can reasonably be taken to justify us in seeing *Daisy Miller* as "a comedy" or arguing that the real subject is not Daisy Miller but the effect she has on others or that Winterbourne, not Daisy, is the principal character. "We don't find out much about Daisy," writes one critic, "but we do find out what Winterbourne is like." But do we really care very much about that? In the one hundred years that the story has now been in existence, has a single human being ever read it not because he was interested in Daisy but because he was interested in Winterbourne? I doubt it very much. Certainly James's addiction to the use of a reflecting consciousness does not involve his always having been more interested in the reflector than the reflected. Winterbourne was created to wonder and worry (as our surrogate) about Daisy, and if she is not worth worrying about, then he has no excuse for being. "Daisy," wrote Cornelia P. Kelley long ago, "even though she is looked at

---

cheapened. In the very first act Daisy tells Winterbourne that "you're the first gentleman who has been at all attentive" and "the first I've cared anything about!" and when Mrs. Costello wonders whether he is going to wait until she invites him to her room before he makes up his mind that she has been making advances, he laughingly replies, "I shall not have to wait very long"! Parenthetically it is interesting to look at Edith Wharton's neatly ironic story "Roman Fever" (included in *The World Over*, 1936), in which a girl brings back from a midnight tryst in the Colosseum not malaria but the seed of a child! Though there are no other echoes of *Daisy Miller* in "Roman Fever," Mrs. Wharton's relationship to James being what it was, she could not possibly have written it without mental reference to his work.

through Winterbourne, is the whole of her story. She is the focal point throughout."[7]

What he worries about is, to put it simply and bluntly, whether or not Daisy is a "nice" girl. The question is posed by the contrast between the breeziness of her manners (or lack of them) and the freshness and daintiness of her personality, what Howells called "her wilding charm" and her "flowerlike purity." There is no denying, I think, that this does introduce an element of "vulgarity" into the story; in a sense any nosing out of sexual corruption is vulgar; that, I suppose, is why most normal people instinctively sympathize with the exposed rather than the exposers, even when they recognize that the exposure needs to be made. Indeed, if it is true, as Sir Thomas Overbury wrote, and as Longfellow liked to quote, that

He comes too near, that comes to be denied,

then it must also be true that one cannot even defend one's reputation without admitting that it has been blown upon. The nosing out of corruption plays an important part in some of James's later stories, and in *The Sacred Fount*, many of whose readers find it difficult to breathe comfortably in a kind of sexual miasma, it virtually takes over.

Winterbourne's first question about Daisy, when he encounters her, with her *enfant terrible* of a brother,[8] in the garden at Vevey, is "Was she simply a pretty girl from New

[7] *The Early Development of Henry James*, first published in *Illinois Studies in Language and Literature*, XV, Nos. 1–2 (1930), reprinted University of Illinois Press, 1965. For other matters discussed in this paragraph, see Christof Wegelin, *The Image of Europe in Henry James* (Southern Methodist University Press, 1968); James E. Gargano, "*Daisy Miller*: An Abortive Quest for Innocence," *South Atlantic Quarterly*, LIX (1961), 114–20; John H. Randall III, "The Genteel Reader and *Daisy Miller*," *AQ*, XVII (1965), 568–81; Peter Buitenhaus, "From Daisy Miller to Julia Bride: A Whole Panorama of Intellectual History," *AQ*, XI (1959), 136–46. Both Wegelin and Gargano are extracted in Stafford, *op. cit.* In "Frederick Winterbourne: The Good Bad Boy in Daisy Miller," *Arizona Quarterly*, XXIX (1973), 139–50, Ian Kennedy takes a hypercritical and supersubtle view of that character.

York State—were they all like that, the pretty girls who had had a good deal of gentlemen's society? Or was she also a designing, an audacious, in short an expert young person?" He gets his first delighted shock from her when, at their first informal meeting, she accepts his only half-extended invitation to take her to the Château de Chillon (he had supposed at first that her mother would go too). At their second meeting she asks him, in that vapid creature's presence, to take her for a row on the lake at eleven o'clock at night. "I'm sure Mr. Winterbourne wants to *take* me," she says. "He's so awfully devoted!" But she is pleased when he offers "formally," for she "likes a gentleman to be formal." When they go to Chillon, she finds him as solemn on the way as if he were taking her to a prayer meeting or a funeral and calls him "a queer mixture." She often tells him he is "too stiff," and when she hears he is returning to Geneva, she not only calls him "horrid" but accuses him of hurrying back there to a "charmer." "Does she never allow you more than three days at a time?" When she meets him again in Rome, she tells him he was "awfully mean" to her at Vevey.

Winterbourne defends Daisy against his snobbish aunt, Mrs. Costello, who declines to meet either her or her mother on the ground that it is the duty of cultivated Americans not to encourage such vulgarians. Mrs. Costello's exclusiveness attracts Daisy, however, because she would like to be exclusive herself. As a matter of fact, both she and Mrs. Miller are exclusive: "We don't speak to any one—or they don't speak to us. I suppose it's about the same thing." But when she gathers from the embarrassed nephew that Mrs. Costello does not wish to meet her, she not only blurts it right out but

---

[8]Only Leon Edel and Muriel G. Shine have been able to find any charity in their hearts for Randolph C. Miller, both seeing him as a victim of the American permissiveness which we know James deplored. See Shine, *The Fictional Children of Henry James* (UNCP, 1969), Chapter IV, "The Spoiled Child," especially pp. 41–43. At the age of nine Randolph must be "persuaded" to go to bed; he prefers to sit up half the night in the hotel. In the play he begs cigars, but in the story he contents himself by destroying his teeth with candy and lumps of sugar.

even "crows" over it: "Why should she want to know me?" Winterbourne admits that Daisy and her family are "very ignorant—very innocent only, and utterly uncivilized," but denies that they are bad. " 'Common' she might be, as Mrs. Costello had pronounced her; yet what provision was made by that epithet for her queer little native grace?" To which Mrs. Costello replies coldly that "whether or no being hopelessly vulgar is being 'bad' is a question for the metaphysicians." And metaphysics could not well be expected to mean much to a perfect lady who lives quite correctly by forms, upon the surface of life.

For the rest of the story, until he finally makes up his mind (and makes the wrong decision), Winterbourne oscillates uneasily between Millerism and Costelloism, seeing Daisy an "an inscrutable combination of audacity and innocence." When she makes a spectacle of herself by going unattended about Rome, at all hours, with a young Italian who is not even quite a gentleman, it hurts him "because it was painful to see so much that was pretty and undefended and natural sink so low in human estimation," until at last believing in her becomes "more and more but a matter of gallantry too fine-spun for use." She ought to have a built-in fineness which would warn her automatically against Giovanelli's shortcomings, and it soils her in his regard that she has not. At last, in the Colosseum, the "once questionable quantity" loses all its shades to become "a mere little black blot," and he even feels ashamed of "all his tender little scruples and all his witless little mercies."

The author, on the other hand, commits himself to Daisy Miller quite as uncompromisingly as, at the end, Giovanelli is committed, not only in the Preface to the late New York Edition, where he calls her "pure poetry" and avers his own "incurable prejudice in favor of grace" (thus making it pretty clear that he held no brief for the real "Daisy Millers," as they were coming to be called—breezy, uncultivated American girls who were making themselves conspicuous in Europe by the freedom of their manners) but, even more clearly, in a letter to Mrs. Lynn Linton,[9] written in response to her specific queries, about 1880, where both complete innocence and complete lack of calculation are ascribed to Daisy —"a light, thin, natural, unsuspecting creature" who is "sacrificed as it were to a rumpus that went on quite over her head." It is true that he calls her a "flirt" and that she herself assumes this label in the course of the story, but it is not employed pejoratively. In the language of the tale, a girl who "flirts" only plays with her "gentlemen friends," never compromising her honor or encouraging them to become serious. In the same way, it must be understood that the term "vulgar" can be applied to Daisy only in a qualified sense. She has an extremely graceful, refined prettiness, she is not in any way rough or coarse, and her every movement is charming. Her manner is quiet and tranquil and her voice soft, slender, and agreeable. Even Mrs. Costello admits that she dresses beautifully and always in perfect taste.

But she has no "form." Her "bright sweet superficial little visage" expresses neither mockery nor irony; she lacks finish and makes no point. She chatters, addressing Winterbourne upon their first meeting as if she had known him for years. "Well, I guess you'd better be quiet," she tells her terrible little brother, and "Well, I guess you'd better leave it somewhere," and to Winterbourne she adds, "He don't like Europe." She herself misses society in Europe. "There ain't any society—or if there is I don't know where it keeps itself."[10] Though she lives in Schenectady, where her father,

---

[9] This letter, first published by George Somes Layard, *Mrs. Lynn Linton* (Methuen, 1901) has been reprinted by Bruce R. McElderry, Jr., "The 'Shy, Incongruous Charm' of *Daisy Miller*," *NCF*, X (1955–56), 162–65; by Leon Edel, *Selected Letters of Henry James* (Farrar, Straus, 1955); and by Stafford, *op. cit.*

[10] In fairness to Daisy, I am not sure her *ain'ts* ought to count too much against her. James seems very fond of this contraction and often uses it where we should hardly expect to find it.

Ezra B. Miller,[11] is even now engaged in earning more money for his wife and children to spend abroad, she has always had "a great deal of gentlemen's society." It is true that the consternation the Millers awaken among the snobbish American contingent in Rome by being friendly with their courier may well strike us today as more to their credit than to that of their critics (was Emerson vulgar when he proposed to his servants, who rejected the suggestion, that they should take their meals with the family?), but there is no denying that, no matter how generous the discount we take for such things, acquaintance with the Millers might still well pose a problem.

Daisy makes much of the fact that she has never allowed gentlemen to tell her what to do. She has not allowed anybody else either or had much occasion to. Her mother is too much of a fool to try, and her father is a cipher so far as the story is concerned. The one person who does try is Mrs. Walker, who, cruel though she is at the end, still differs notably from Mrs. Costello. Mrs. Costello refuses to meet Daisy at all, but Mrs. Walker not only takes her up but actually goes in her carriage to rescue her from the Pincian Gardens, where she is making a spectacle of herself by walking with Giovanelli. She wishes to drive Daisy about for half an hour, "so that the world may see she's not running absolutely wild—and then take her safely home." From Mrs. Walker's point of view, and that of the American colony, this is a considerable gesture. Daisy of course refuses to be rescued, and it is not until afterwards that we learn her most creditable reason: she could not bear to hurt Giovanelli's feelings by leaving him unceremoniously and robbing him of the pleasure he had been looking forward to. What she tells Mrs. Walker is that she is more than five years old; that if she could not walk, she would die; and that if what she is doing is not the custom in Rome, it ought to be. But her most

[11]Daisy's own proper name, as her brother informs Winterbourne, is Annie P. Miller, and her mother sometimes uses it when her vague placidity is momentarily disturbed.

revealing remark, and the one most conclusive as to her innocence, is her wondering, "Talked about? What do you mean?" and when Mrs. Walker replies, "Come into my carriage and I'll tell you," Daisy is quite serious in saying, "I don't think I want to know what you mean. I don't think I should like it."

Actually she does not know, not in the sense of any real or emotional realization. Of course, I do not mean that she is altogether a stranger and pilgrim in the world. She has heard enough about European society so that when Winterbourne tells her that flirting is not understood there, she replies, "I thought they understood nothing else." "Not in young unmarried women," he tells her, and her response is intended to testify not only to her innocence but to the superiority of American over European moral standards: "It seems to me much more proper in young unmarried than in old married ones." But she shows still more penetration when she says, "They're only pretending to be shocked. They don't really care a straw what I do." A girl as young as Daisy who has already learned that society cares very little about corruption but a great deal about conformity is not exactly a fool.

Out of her own experience, however, Daisy has no real knowledge of corruption. She has always been treated with respect. Depending upon the angle from which it is viewed, the European system of chaperonage "protects" young people or insults them by assuming that they will not do right unless they are watched. There is no question where Daisy stands. She has staked out a kind of American extraterritoriality with reference to sexual mores in Rome, for she is doing there what she has always done without question of scandal at home under the freer, perhaps more naïve, American system. When Winterbourne finds her with Giovanelli in the Colosseum, he is so disgusted that he tries to deny himself "the small, fine anguish of looking at her," but all she is concerned about is whether he believes her to be engaged to Giovanelli, and this is important to her only because she cares for Winterbourne. James writes specifically that she seemed "not in the least embarrassed." From her own point of view, she had no reason to be. Unless she should be raped or otherwise manhandled against her will, Daisy was perfectly safe from anything except gossip's tongue anywhere in Rome, for the simple reason that she was in no danger from being tempted by her own nature. Yet I think Motley Deakin is inclined to make too much of her resemblance to the heroines of Turgenev and other European writers (he himself recognizes that there is a note of self-conscious rebellion in these girls which poor little Daisy altogether lacks), and it is difficult to see how he can draw the conclusion that, in the light of these possible sources or influences, her death became "a social and symbolic necessity," marking James's adherence to a European tradition from which Howells departed. Innocence is not commitment; in an adult it is rather a failure to respond to experience. Daisy is no martyr, no saint, and no rebel, except that, like a child, she insists upon her own way. On the intellectual level, it has never occurred to her that she has anything to rebel against. One of the last heirs of the romantic tradition, she is a child of nature and a comparatively undifferentiated society who simply follows the lead of a pure and uncorrupted heart.

From the point of view of American society in Rome it was different, and Mrs. Walker (though with exaggeration) sums up the indictment against Daisy. She flirts with any man she can pick up; she sits in corners with mysterious Italians; she dances all evening with the same partners; she receives visitors alone at eleven o'clock at night. From the moment she is rebuffed in the Pincian Gardens, Mrs. Walker is through with her, but Daisy of course does not realize it, having no cause to do so, and she has one last moment of triumph when, in one of James's most richly charged scenes (any decent young actress would give her eyeteeth for a chance to play it), she sails in late at Mrs. Walker's party, rustling forward "in radiant loveliness, smiling and chattering, carrying a large bouquet and attended by Mr. Giovanelli." "I'm afraid you thought I was never coming," she

coos; she has been coaching Giovanelli, who "sings beautifully," in some songs she wants him to do for the company,
and she actually succeeds in bringing this off before Mrs.
Walker both literally and figuratively turns her back on her
and thus ends her social career in Rome. After that there is
only the Colosseum and the Roman fever.[12]

Though James may never have equaled in kind what he
himself called Daisy's "shy incongruous charm," she does
not stand quite alone among his heroines. In the Preface to
The Reverberator, he himself remarks that "in the heavy
light of 'Europe' thirty or forty years ago, there were more
of the Francie Dossons and the Daisy Millers and the Bessie
Aldens and the Pandora Days than of all the other attested
American objects put together," a statement not perhaps
entirely reconcilable with his detachment of her "pure poetry" from the actual international scene elsewhere. Other writers have invoked additionally Gertrude Wentworth, Grace
Mavis, and others, while Howells and other novelists have
also been drawn into the consideration.[13]

---

[12] Carol Ohman, "*Daisy Miller*: A Study of Changing Intentions," *AL*, XXXVI
(1964–65), 3–11, argues that "James began writing *Daisy Miller* as a comedy of
manners and finished it as a symbolic presentation of a metaphysical ideal. He
began by criticizing Daisy in certain ways and ended simply by praising her."
Though this point of view may gain some support from Viola R. Dunbar's demonstration, in "The Revision of Daisy Miller," *MLN*, LXV (1950), 311–17, that in the
New York Edition James judges Daisy much more gently than in the original version,
and her critics more severely. I am not convinced that this cannot be accounted
for without postulating changing intentions. (I might add, however, that I think
James's complete consistency in his portrait of Giovanelli might reasonably be
questioned.) John B. Humma, "The 'Engagement' of Daisy Miller," *Research Studies
Washington State University*, XXXIX (1971), 154–55, is useful on Daisy's innocence,
but Donald E. Houghton seems wide of the mark when, in "Attitude and Illness in
Daisy Miller," *Literature and Psychology*, XIX (1969), 51–60, he not only finds all
the Millers sick but also decides that their ill-health is caused by the wrong attitudes
they take up toward Europe.

[13] David H. Hirsch, "William Dean Howells and Daisy Miller," *English Language Notes*, I (1963–64), 123–28, has some interesting comparisons between Daisy
and Howells' girls, but the other aspects of his interpretation are questionable.
See also Annette Kar, "Archetypes of American Innocence: Lydia Blood and
Daisy Miller," *AQ*, V (1953), 31–38.

It does not seem necessary to consider all these girls here. Julia Bride in the story of the same title (1908) is the one that has been studied most closely, but, except for her triumphant prettiness, she suggests Daisy only by contrast. Citing as evidence the *Harper's Bazaar* articles on "The Manners of American Women" which James intended for the second, never-to-be-written volume of *The American Scene,* Mr. Buitenhaus sees Julia Bride as James's attempt to show the deterioration of the American girl since Daisy's time. Julia is the daughter of a thrice-divorced mother, and she herself has six broken engagements on her record (she kept all the rings). Having now the chance to make an advantageous marriage, she is, when we meet her, driven to the desperate expedient of appealing to one of her former step-fathers and one of her own discarded suitors to testify to her respectability, and this does not work out quite as she had planned. James does not commit himself about the exact degree of Julia's purity or lack of it, but it is clear that her indiscretions have been much more serious than Diasy's.

Even so, Julia Bride is a far more charming girl than the heroine of "Pandora" (1884), who was "not fast, nor emancipated, nor crude, nor loud, and there wasn't in her, of necessity at least, a grain of the stuff of which adventuresses are made." She was "much more serious and strenuous" than Daisy and more cultured too, though her culture was "perhaps a little too restless and obvious." But her respectability is as cold as ice, and she allows nothing, not even the President of the United States, to stand in the way of what she wants for herself and her lover. Pandora is James's companion portrait to Daisy Miller, but she is the new "self-made girl," just coming up into society, and again the comparison becomes a contrast. The juxtaposition is more inescapable here than with any of the other stories, for the unnamed novel which Count Vogelstein reads on shipboard is unmistakably *Daisy Miller* itself; Pandora too is equipped with a family, and the differences and resemblances between her situation and Daisy's are carefully drawn.

The story which most profitably rewards scrutiny in connection with *Daisy Miller* is, however, *The Reverberator* (1888). Though Francie Dosson's family is far from being the horror that is Daisy Miller's, it is quite bad enough from the point of view of the Proberts, South Carolinian in origin but now more Parisian than the aristocratic French themselves, whose son wishes to marry the American girl. If one may judge by her effect upon the other characters, Francie is even more attractive than Daisy, being indeed "exceedingly, extraordinarily pretty," with "a slow sweetness" and "a still scattered radiance," quite without "emphasis" or "point," plus "a weak pipe of a voice and inconceivabilities of ignorance." From the beginning she is sure that sooner or later she will, "in perfect innocence," do something that the Proberts will consider monstrous, which is a safe enough bet with a family whose teeth she has already set on edge by calling their city "Parus." What she does, however, is bad enough. Out of naïve gratitude to the vulgar American journalist Flack, a discarded suitor who set in motion the train of events which brought Gaston Probert into her orbit, she babbles a rather overextensive catalogue of Probert family secrets with which one would hardly have expected her to be familiar at this time and which he promptly spreads over the international scandal sheet that he edits! For the "perfect flower of plasticity" that the admiring artist Waterlow calls her, I am bound to say I think Francie takes it rather coolly; for once the Proberts have a just complaint (however ridiculous their extreme reaction to it), and she shows little understanding of their point of view.

This, however, is not the essential point. Gaston takes Francie as she is, risking a break with his family to remain faithful to his love, and James makes it quite clear that this is just what he ought to have done. If only poor Daisy had met him instead of Winterbourne!

In other words, although Henry James is, in a sense, a novelist of manners, he sees good manners and values them only as the outward sign of an inward spiritual grace. Where this is absent, the manners alone take on the sound of clanging cymbals; both *The Reverberator* and *The American* show that our author had no illusions about the skeletons in "good" family closets. At their worst, as with Daisy Miller's enemies and those of Grace Mavis, manners in the narrower sense may even be destructive of human values and of life itself. And, on the other hand, when the heart is right, though one may still deplore the absence of certain convenient externalities, one must show oneself enough of a connoisseur of values to be able to manage without them.

I have spoken of Grace Mavis. "The Patagonia" (1889) is a minor piece by any standard, but it is of value here as helping to set up a criterion to differentiate clearly between mere ignorance and carelessness and the cold selfishness which is evil intent. Like *Daisy Miller* it ends in death, this time by suicide, over the side of an ocean liner. Grace Mavis is a Boston girl from the South End, without social position, on her way to Europe to marry a man she no longer loves, in the care of the fashionable Mrs. Nettlepoint, of Beacon Street. She is fascinated and, to the scandal of the ship, hopelessly compromised by Mrs. Nettlepoint's worthless son. Grace is a dark and comparatively dull heroine compared with either Francie or Daisy, but the important consideration is that Jasper, who does not love her, has complicated her already difficult position to the point of despair for no better reason than to beguile the tedium of an ocean voyage and that his mother's "maternal immorality" has caused her to compound his felony. And if these things are evil, evil too are the observations of the vicious Mrs. Peck, prime spokesman for the outraged passengers, a creature compared to whom Mrs. Costello was charity itself, and one bad enough to tempt any decent person to abjure respectability forever.

II. THE VICTIM
MADAME DE MAUVES

ALTHOUGH "Madame de Mauves" is probably the most carefully wrought of James's earlier tales, he professed in later years to be able to recall nothing about its origin and composition save that the latter had occurred, in the summer of 1873, in "a dampish, dusky, unsunned room, cool, however, to the relief of the fevered muse," in an old inn at Bad Homburg. The story appeared first in *The Galaxy* in February and March, 1874. When in 1905 Auguste Monod requested permission to translate both it and "The Siege of London" for publication in a French periodical, James refused, calling "Madame de Mauves" "a very early and meagre performance" which had "no great sense." Both it and "The Siege of London" were "primitive," he thought, and he did not plan to include them in the New York Edition. He must later have changed his mind, for they are both there; possibly upon rereading them, he found that they were better than he had remembered. He added that he was not eager to be translated, especially into French, and that he thought his characteristic note likely to be lost in the process, but he softened the blow by offering to send some later stories if Monod was keen on translating him.[1]

There are no clearly established sources for "Madame de Mauves," either in James's reading or in his own life ex-

[1] E. F. Benson, ed., *Henry James: Letters to A. C. Benson and Auguste Monod . . .* (Scribners, n. d.), 97–98.

perience, though Flaubert's *Madame Bovary* and the early (1678) French novel by Madame de La Fayette, *The Princess of Clèves,* have often been invoked. Madame de Mauves certainly resembles Madame Bovary in the contrast which develops between what her girlish, unrealistic daydreams had led her to expect from marriage and what she finds, but the two women are otherwise quite dissimilar. There are more resemblances between the James story and *The Princess of Clèves* (the maiden name of Madame de Mauves was Euphemia Cleve, and Auvergne figures in both stories), but we have no positive evidence of indebtedness.[2] *The Scarlet Letter* has also been mentioned;[3] about the only foundation for this is Madame Clairin's suggestion that Madame de Mauves is "shutting herself up to read free-thinking books." But the only author whom we are actually told she read is Wordsworth, and there is no reason to suppose that she read such books as interested Hester Prynne or that they had a comparable effect upon her. If she could have solved her problems by taking a lover, as some of her critics seem to feel, Hester had done that long ago,and before she had read anything. As for the autobiographical approach, Albert Mordell takes literally James's statement that "the gentle Euphemia" visited him at Bad Homburg, honoring him with her confidence yet putting "twenty questions by" (I suppose it is natural that writers who find deep hidden meanings in everything that is straightforwardly literal should make up for this, as it were, by treating everything which is obviously

[2] See, especially, Benjamin C. Rountree, "James's *Madame de Mauves* and Madame de Lafayette's *Princesse de Clèves,*" *SSF,* I (1963–64), 264–71; and John Kenneth Simon, "A Study of Classical Gesture: Henry James and Madame de Lafayette," *Comparative Literature Studies,* III (1966), 273–83. Also consult James Kraft, " 'Madame de Mauves' and *Roderick Hudson*: The Development of James's International Style," *Texas Quarterly,* XI, Nos. 3–4 (1968), 143–60; and cf. his book, *The Early Tales of Henry James* (Southern Illinois University Press, 1969).

[3] Cf. Robert F. Gleckner, "James's *Madame de Mauves* and Hawthorne's *The Scarlet Letter,*" *MLN,* LXXIII (1958), 580–86.

figurative as actuality), and Leon Edel is not much more convincing when he sees the story influenced by Henry James's friendship, under very different circumstances from those which prevail in the story, with Sarah Butler Wister, daughter of Fanny Kemble and mother of the author of *The Virginian.*[4]

James uses Longmore as a reflecting consciousness to bring the reader his vision of Madame de Mauves, much as he was to use Winterbourne in *Daisy Miller,* but he adds considerable material by the omniscient author, especially with reference to the heroine's past life. She is introduced almost casually by her friend Mrs. Draper, whom Longmore already knows, both to him and to the reader, being seen characteristically "through the thickening twilight," which deepens as the scene proceeds and seems somehow to provide a fitting atmosphere for her; even at the end, Longmore would see her "for the last time at the hour of long shadows and pale reflected amber lights, as he had almost always seen her." She is slight, fair, naturally pale though now slightly flushed; she has beautiful, gentle, almost languid gray eyes, a high forehead, thick brown hair, a slender throat, and a mouth "all expression and intention," whatever we may choose to read into that. She seems, as she soon proves herself, friendly, in the innocent American fashion; though no woman could be more unlike Daisy Miller, her manners, on their own more refined and sophisticated level, quite as clearly betray her heritage. So she had conducted herself, it seems, before her marriage, toward Richard de Mauves; perhaps this was what had impelled him to propose to her in what was, in his milieu, a highly unconventional manner. Mrs. Draper rouses Longmore's (and the reader's) interest in her by postponing to a later occasion her reply to his query about her, but we are not kept in suspense long.

[4] Albert Mordell, ed., *Literary Reviews and Essays by Henry James on American, English, and French Literature* (Twayne, 1957), "Appendix"; Leon Edel, *Henry James: The Conquest of London, 1870–1884* (Li, 1962), 113–22.

Euphemia Cleve had been a rich, French convent-bred (but a non-Catholic) American girl, whose views of love and marriage had been nurtured upon "various Ultramontane works of fiction—the only ones admitted to the convent library." Though her mother was under the impression that she had brought her up with care, it is difficult to perceive how, beyond paying her bills at the convent, she had brought her up at all. When she heard that the girl had engaged herself to M. de Mauves, she had promptly ordered her back there, but it had taken her three weeks to arrive from Nice, and beyond insisting upon a two-year delay and the coming of M. de Mauves to the United States, so that the betrothal and marriage might be conducted with all due regard to form, she had done little to prevent a union which she knew might well be disastrous. The Count's grandmother had known that too; at first she had cynically urged Euphemia to avoid agony by learning to take life not as a fifty years' mass but rather as a game of skill, but later she came to love her enough so that she urged her to forget such "worldly rubbish" and "to remain your own sincere little self only, charming in your own serious little way." The chief engineer of the marriage had been the Count's sister (later Madame Clairin—Longmore's "that dreadful woman—that awful woman"), whom Euphemia met at the convent school and who established a hold over her through being "very positive, very shrewd, very ironical, very French—everything that Euphemia felt herself unpardonable for not being," and who was, in intent at least, quite as corrupt as her brother. After her husband's death, she both makes a play for Longmore herself and supports the Count's idea that Madame de Mauves ought to restore domestic harmony by falling into line, as she expresses it, through modeling her sexual conduct upon his own.

The motive for the marriage on the de Mauves side, is of course money, and James is very careful to prevent us from rejecting Euphemia because she mistakes a rake and wastrel for a fairy prince. The bride is as much a fool as you like, but since her foolishness is that of innocence and inexperience, it is intended to awaken pity and sympathy, not contempt. Rank for its own sake means nothing to her, and the idea that she could relish lording it over others has never crossed her mind. Her visit to the de Mauves *castel,* which was neither cheerful nor luxurious, did not disillusion her, and Richard de Mauves himself differed from the "rather grim Quixotic ideal" in her mind only in being rather more handsome. To her "the fact of birth" was simply "the direct guarantee of an ideal delicacy of feeling."

Romances [says James] are rarely worked out in such transcendent good faith, and Euphemia's excuse was the prime purity of her moral vision. She was essentially incorruptible, and she took this pernicious conceit to her bosom very much as if it had been a dogma revealed by a white-winged angel.

She saw her husband, in other words, as "an historic masterpiece," to be apprehended mystically, and it is absurd to blame her for not perceiving that he was evil, for there had been nothing in either her nature or her experience to qualify her to recognize that. James knew that the impulse to worship must be judged by the purity of the worshiper and not by the worthiness of the object of adoration.

By the time Longmore meets Madame de Mauves, she has all this behind her. Her mother had warned her (it seems to have been the only sweet maternal contribution she made to her marriage) that though her husband would never beat her, there would be times when she would wish he would. Politeness is indeed the one good quality that never fails M. de Mauves; his "manners were perfect, his discretion irreproachable, and he seemed never to address his companion but, sentimentally speaking, hat in hand." But he believes in nothing and has no ethics whatever. A lecher and a cheat who fulfills his obligations to neither his women nor his creditors, he had indeed "subdued" his own early "violence" before meeting Euphemia, but this apparently was the only spiritual victory he was ever to achieve. Whether he had ever "loved" his wife, even as he was capable of loving, must remain speculative. She was Christian, he pagan; he thought her morbid, and it is clear that it was a strain for him to be with her. "She was too dim, too delicate, too modest; she had too few arts, too little coquetry, too much charity." The Count liked plenty of spice, in both women and art, and the creature Longmore accidentally sees with him in a Paris restaurant must have been much more to his taste than Euphemia. He would have liked her to learn how to bend without breaking; perhaps he would have liked to see her take a lover, not only because this would make it easier for him to pursue his own infidelities but also because he could be much more comfortable if he thought she had descended to his level. As with Cassio and Iago, she has a daily beauty in her life that makes him ugly. But his politeness itself becomes monstrous when he urges this upon her; his sister says that "he came in with the gravity of an ambassador, and I'm sure that when he made his *demande en mariage* his manner wasn't more respectful."[5]

By the time the story opens, Madame de Mauves has been sufficiently disillusioned so that "her whole being was pitched in a lower key than harmonious Nature had designed; she was like a powerful singer who had lost her high notes," and her new friend sees her as, sooner or later, "calling vainly for help." She does nothing of the kind, however, even when he musters up courage to ask her about her situation directly; instead she indicates merely that she had retreated from a miserable actuality to "a nameless and doubtless not at all remarkable, little country" in her own mind. Thus the situa-

[5] H. A. Bouraoui, "Henry James and the French Mind: The International Theme in 'Madame de Mauves,' " *Novel*, IV (1970–71), 69–76, attributes subtleties to M. de Mauves for which I find no warrant in the text (he also discusses both *Bovary* and *Clèves*). Whether James is fair to the French point of view in sexual and other matters, in this story and elsewhere, is a fair question, but it is certainly true that he had not himself made terms with French attitudes at the time he wrote "Madame de Mauves," if, indeed, he was ever to do so. There is plenty of evidence in *Transatlantic Sketches* and elsewhere that French sexual standards shocked him.

tion stands substantially until after Longmore has returned to Saint-Germain from Paris, simply because, having innocently surprised her husband there at his illicit rendezvous, he found it impossible to stay away. Madame de Mauves greets him kindly but "with no pleasure," he thinks, and asks him point-blank why he came back, but it is clear to him that there has been a crisis in her relations with her husband, for "grief and agitation" have replaced the "self-contained melancholy" he had previously observed in her. She now sees clearly the limitations of her previous romanticism and has begun to view men and women as "very poor creatures" and to read life in terms of "hard prose" in place of the glowing verse in which she had formerly seen it written. Generalizing upon her own experience, she has even come to believe that life for many people is only "a conscious compromise." As for her, she has nothing left on earth except "a dogged obstinate clinging conscience" which may prevent her "from doing anything very base" but will probably also keep her from everything very fine.

Here it is essentially that she sets up her Ebenezer and thereafter defends it consistently, with what Longmore calls "horrible and unnatural lucidity," even after her husband and her sister-in-law have brought all the pressure in their power to bear upon both him and her. When she asks him to leave her at last, it is for his sake as well as her own. *"Don't disappoint me,"* she cries, and she adds that "if I were to find you selfish where I thought you generous, narrow where I thought you large, vulgar where I thought you rare, I should think worse of human nature." And so he passes out of her life.

That Madame de Mauves exemplifies a type of moral intransigence which it is easier to admire than to emulate goes without saying, but I am not aware that, in James's own time, any responsible reader doubted that she was intended to be admired. Of late years, however, a number of writers have rebelled against this view with sufficient passion to suggest that they may share M. de Mauves's lack of comfort in her presence:

Both the Princesse de Clèves and Madame de Mauves [writes James Kraft] act from the principle of duty and in the process kill their husbands, deny their lovers, and end senselessly hidden from the life they desire, one in a convent and the other deep in the country. Both works are subtly conceived moralistic attacks upon a corrupt society, *but both condemn the virtuous woman as much as the corrupt society* [italics mine].

J. A. Ward is in agreement when he equates Madame de Mauves with her corrupt sister-in-law, Madame Clairin, because both "act in much the same way," one being guided by "the absolute law of conscience" and the other by her native tradition, but each imposing upon experience "a single, narrow rule," and Louise Dauner sees even Euphemia's garden as a symbol of her emotional and spiritual frigidity, while Robert C. McLean, who can usually be counted upon to take the part of the devil's advocate toward Jamesian characters, takes a dim view of both Euphemia and Longmore.[6]

Madame de Mauves's enemies (who are also, of course, Longmore's enemies) weaken their position by never spelling out, however, just what they think the two ought to have done. Do they believe that Euphemia ought to have divorced her husband and then, after a decent interval, married Longmore? Ought they simply to have tossed their caps over the windmill and run off together? Or should Madame de Mauves have followed her husband's suggestion, preserving the form of her marriage by discreetly accepting Longmore as her lover and leaving monsieur free to follow his own ways? These

[6] Ward, "Structural Irony in 'Madame de Mauves,' " *SSF*, II (1964–65), 170–82; Dauner, "Henry James and the Garden of Death," *UKCR*, XIX (1952–53), 137–43; McLean, "The 'Disappointed Observer' of 'Madame de Mauves,' " *Research Studies Washington State University*, XXXIII (1965), 181–96. In another article, "The Completed Vision: A Study of 'Madame de Mauves' and *The Ambassadors*," *Modern Language Quarterly*, XXXVIII (1967), 446–61, McLean sees the later work as a reworking and elaboration of themes first adumbrated in "Madame de Mauves."

three lines of action do not all occupy the same ethical standing ground, and it would be quite possible to accept one and reject another. Parenthetically I may add that, at an earlier period or in a different type of story, Longmore might have abducted the lady, as, it was said, the Earl of Bothwell abducted Mary, Queen of Scots, but so far as I know, nobody has suggested this as a conceivable possibility here. As a matter of fact, divorce and remarriage was, at the time the story was written, equally impossible. Between 1816 and 1884 the only possibility available under French law for disunited couples was legal separation (*séparation de corps*), and this ruled out the possibility of another marriage for either party.[7]

There is an austerity about Madame de Mauves which perhaps surpasses that of even such later James heroines as come closest to her type, but this is probably to be attributed to the young author's limitations as an artist rather than to deliberate intention on his part. In the opening chapters she says very little, and James relies mainly upon his own narrative of past events to qualify the reader to understand her. When she speaks her tone is formal, not particularly lifelike, more like that of the heroine of a costume drama than a story of modern life. When Longmore contemplates a trip to Flanders, she tells him that she is very fond of the Dutch painters, but he doubts this, and I think we may doubt it with him. Her enemies have made much of her dislike of tragedy (at the end of Chapter III) as indicating a failure to confront life foursquare: "I'm a dreadful coward about having to suffer or to bleed. I've always tried to believe that—without base concessions—such extremities may always be somehow dodged or indefinitely postponed." But this statement will not carry the weight which some critics have sought to impose upon it. In its context it hardly means more than that Madame de Mauves does not wish to make a fuss about the

---

[7]Thanks to my friend Sylvère Monod, who consulted the proper authorities on my behalf, I speak authoritatively on this matter.

situation in which she finds herself, and she never does do that. Uncompromisingly and at all times she rejects the cult of feeling that is now so popular. Ernest Hemingway once expressed his idea of morality by saying that that is moral which makes you feel good after doing it, and this point of view has now been so widely accepted that there are bumper stickers available to proclaim to an attentive world: "IF IT FEELS GOOD, DO IT!" Longmore presents this idea to Madame de Mauves in a much less blatant form when he says, "The only thing for one's mind to be fair to is the thing one *feels!*" but she only replies, "If that were so it would be a weary world."

Two special considerations arise in this connection. The first is the charming country interval in Chapter VII (culminating in an allegorical-erotic dream which sends all the Freudian critics into ecstasy), in which Longmore watches and half-envies the pretty Claudine and her painter-lover. The other is the story's enigmatic ending, reporting the suicide of M. de Mauves.

When he sees the young painter and the girl going off together, Longmore, who at first supposes them to be man and wife, is tempted to think of them as having recovered Eden, but he soon learns from the landlady that they are not married and that their union, such as it is, will probably not be permanent. Marius Bewley is tempted to interpret this episode in the light of the much more famous scene in *The Ambassadors* in which Strether observes Chad and Madame de Vionnet on the river, from which Bewley proceeds to find in the artist and his lover "a reproach to the moral characters of the American woman and her French sister-in-law: as much to the festering righteousness of the American as to the more amiable corruption of Madame Clairin" (note the carefully chosen perversity of the adjectives "festering" and "amiable").[8] Actually, James uses the lovers merely to raise ques-

    [8] "Henry James and 'Life,' " *Hudson Review*, XI (1958–59), 167–85, reprinted in his book *The Eccentric Design* (Columbia University Press, 1959).

tions in Longmore's mind, and even Bewley admits this—
"I do not mean that James absolutely commits himself to
them as the ideal embodiment of what he believes in"—but,
having made the admission, he at once proceeds to disregard
it. Claudine and her lover do not merely occupy a different
social status from Longmore and Madame de Mauves; they
also stand on a different level of human development. In its
own way what they have is "good," and Longmore can admire
it and in a sense long for it, without really wishing to emulate
them, much as a queen might say, "Sometimes I wish I were
the wife of an ordinary man," or as Melville defended the
morality of the South Seas as good in itself because it had
developed in response to the needs of those who practiced
it, without ever dreaming of advocating it for himself or for
his America. Bewley also thinks that the natural speech
rhythms of the country lovers, as contrasted to the more formal rhetorical character of Madame de Mauves's own speech,
was intended to reflect upon her, but this too seems extremely doubtful. It would have been very difficult indeed to make
Claudine rhetorical, but the James of the 1870's was not able
to avoid it with so dignified a figure as Madame de Mauves.

The ambivalent ending, which is really an epilogue to
the story, is more puzzling. In two paragraphs we are told
that Longmore had heard nothing more about Madame de
Mauves for two years after his return to America. Then Mrs.
Draper had come home with some startling news. After Longmore's departure, Madame de Mauve had left Saint-Germain
and gone to live, apparently alone, in the country. A year of
silence had succeeded some correspondence between the
two ladies, after which Mrs. Draper had encountered at Vichy
"a clever young Frenchman whom I accidentally learned to
be a friend of that charming sister of the Count's, Madame
Clairin," and who reported that M. de Mauves had repented
of his sins, amended his way of life, and begged his wife's
forgiveness, which she had refused. "She was stone, she was
ice, she was outraged virtue." And the Count, now madly in
love with her, had taken this repudiation so much to heart

that he had gone into seclusion, lost his health, and finally killed himself. To which James (not the young Frenchman, not Mrs. Draper) adds that, though Longmore's first impulse, upon hearing the news, was to go to Madame de Mauves, he had not done so. "The truth is that, in the midst of all the ardent tenderness of his memory of Madame de Mauves, he has become conscious of a singular feeling—a feeling of wonder, of uncertainty, of awe." And these are the last words in the story.

Most commentators have taken this report at face value, important exceptions including Rountree and Charles Kaplan.[9] Ward says that "the reason for such an indirect account of the suicide is probably narrative economy." I can think of others, such as a deliberate attempt to create ambiguity, thus forcing the reader to think and ponder, or (more probably) an attempt to get over something James knew was unconvincing by treating it as succinctly as possible and presenting it only as a *fait accompli.* The story comes to us at the third remove, and the source, like everything connected with Madame Clairin, is highly suspect. Mrs. Draper's view of this lady as the Count's "charming" sister does not testify to her penetration, and the wild extravagance of the "young Frenchman's" reference to Madame de Mauves—"That's the terrible little woman who killed her husband"—may have been intended to put us on guard.[10] The suicide itself I do not find incredible. It takes us by surprise, but that is what suicide always does in life, and one can easily conceive of a man who lived like the Count being swallowed up at last by disgust. Other elements in the story are more difficult, however. On

[9] "James's 'Madame de Mauves,' " *Explicator*, XIX (1961), Item 32; see also Rountree's n. 11 on p. 267 of his article, cited in note 2 above.

[10] At least one critic, laboring the resemblance between Madame de Mauves and Madame Clairin, makes the point that they both "killed" their husbands. Madame Clairin has enough sins to answer for; we need not, I think, charge murder to her account. Her husband kills himself because of his own cowardice and folly. His refusal to go home after he had gambled all his money away because "I'm afraid of my wife" was not the decisive factor.

the assumption that we have had an accurate account of what happened, I would agree that a woman who confronted true repentance with stone and ice and outraged virtue must have failed in the Christianity that James had previously credited her with, but I would still have to say that I had seen nothing in the Count which could cause me to believe him capable of either the repentance or the love here postulated. As for Longmore's inaction, as Ward says, he has always been uncertain about Euphemia. This is not the first time he has experienced awe in connection with the thought of her, and this might well reflect his own modesty or sense of unworthiness, the uncertainty in such matters not uncharacteristic of James's heroes (or, even, for that matter, the author's own ambivalent attitude toward love and marriage)[11] without having been intended to suggest monstrosity in Madame de Mauves. Or, again, it may be that Longmore is only clear-sighted, realizing that Euphemia cannot or will not love again ("He who thinks he has loved twice," wrote Ambrose Bierce, "has not loved once").

It was all immensely sad, almost as sad for Longmore as for Madame de Mauves. He has not been considered for his own sake here, for this is a book about James's heroines, not his heroes. But they would have made a good pair, for they were both idealistic and capable of devotion, and both were better equipped to endure than to do. Only, for that very reason he did not qualify in any distinguished fashion to deliver her from whatever it was she may have needed to be delivered from. Instead he turned to her for guidance and allowed her to set his tone. If she had thrown herself at his head, who can doubt that he would have taken her? But she was stronger than he was; so he followed her lead, and when she was no longer at his side to guide him, he did nothing. For all that, we must not forget that there was a great deal

[11] Watching the artist in the country, Longmore had wondered, "was it his work . . . that made him so happy?" It wasn't. But this may have been James's own answer, nevertheless.

in him that fought on her side. In a very real sense, she *was* his higher self, and her penetration was keen when she perceived that if she were to betray herself she must necessarily betray him also. It is even possible that if she had permitted him to persuade her he would ultimately have made her pay for it, though this would certainly not have been intentional on his part.

While it was still touch and go, he had asked himself whether renunciation was "all that youth and longing and ardor were meant for? Was experience to be muffled and mutilated like an indecent picture?" Though it did not seem enough, it was about all he could have expected with Madame de Mauves unless they had been two other people. In the end she had a conscience which had not been wholly negativistic in its operations, and he, besides his hesitations, the consolation, whatever it might be worth to him, of not having soiled his love.[12]

[12]John O. McCormick's article, "The Rough and Lurid Vision: Henry James, Graham Greene and the International Theme," *Jahrbuch für Amerikastudien*, II (1957), 158–67, is pro-Euphemia; Rebecca Patterson's "Two Portraits of a Lady," *Midwest Quarterly*, I (1960), 343–61, is not. Krishna Baldev Vaid's discussion in *Technique in the Tales of Henry James* (HUP, 1964) concentrates, of course, on the tale's manner of telling. Other studies include E. Bruce Kirkham, "A Study of Henry James's 'Madame de Mauves,' " *Ball State University Forum*, XII, 2 (1971), 63–69, and Ora Segal's chapter in *The Lucid Reflector: The Observer in Henry James's Fiction* (YUP, 1969). Millicent Bell, *Edith Wharton and Henry James: The Story of Their Friendship* (George Braziller, 1965), 250–51, compares "Madame de Mauves" with Mrs. Wharton's story "Madame de Treymes."

III.   DESTINY "AFFRONTED"
ISABEL ARCHER

THOUGH THERE IS a sense in which the female protagonist of any work of fiction may be called its "heroine," the term seems quite appropriate only when applied to characters of a certain stability and integrity. *The Portrait of a Lady* was James's first "big" novel, and there can be no doubt that Isabel Archer is one of his important heroines. Yet she has grave limitations and displays a lack of judgment which brings almost fatal consequences upon her. Not only does she not achieve her full stature until nearly the end of the novel, but there is some doubt about what the ending is and whether the decision Isabel makes even then is the right one.

Isabel was the "intellectual superior" among the three Archer girls of Albany (neither the "beauty" nor the "practical one") and a great trial to her brother-in-law, who disliked "originals," found her written in a foreign language, and hoped she would not "develop" more. She loved Browning, George Eliot, and Gounod. When her aunt, Mrs. Touchett, discovered her and carried her off to England, she judged her "a clever girl" who had a strong will, a high temper, and "no idea of being bored." She was indeed "very fond of my liberty," did not consider herself a candidate for adoption, and would not promise to do everything she was told even to be taken to Europe. She took herself seriously, tried very hard to do right, and was intensely humiliated whenever she felt she had put herself in the wrong or become ridiculous.

She was idealistic and for the most part ignorant of the evil she condemned or disdained. Her cousin, Ralph Touchett, thought her too conscientious and urged her to keep her conscience for great occasions ("Don't try so much to form your character—it's like trying to pull open a tight, tender young rose"). In the manner of the girls of the young American republic, Isabel had been encouraged to self-expression from her youth. She disdained timidity and conventionality as unprofitable luxuries and believed that to judge wrongly was less disgraceful than not to attempt judgment at all. Theoretically she recognized the danger of pride and struggled against it, but she accepted the unique value of her own individuality and was unwilling to be expressed by anything outside of herself. When she reached England, the whole country and its people went on trial before her. She wanted to see life, but she was very fastidious in her choice of experiences, and she did not wish to suffer for nothing. She did not like to have everything settled beforehand (sometimes she thought her idea of happiness was a swift carriage rattling through a dark night over an unseen road), but she would accept having things settled for her if they were settled as she liked.

Isabel has been plausibly related to Dorothea Brooke and less plausibly to another George Eliot heroine, Gwendolen Harleth;[1] at one point or another, it sometimes seems, every heroine of fiction who has ever shown a modicum of spunk has been considered in connection with her. The influence of Turgenev, which James himself acknowledges in another connection in the Preface to the *Lady* in the New York Edition, is one of the more reasonable suggestions; another is Oscar Cargill's reference to George Sand's *Indiana*.[2] One critic has called Isabel an Emersonian Becky Sharp; another, an Emersonian Saint Joan. She is neither. She is no Becky Sharp because she is neither an adventuress

[1] See George Levine, "Isabel, Gwendolyn, and Dorothea," *ELH*, XXX (1963), 244–57.

nor an exploiter, and she is no Saint Joan because she has no mission. One might think that having her an Emersonian Isabel Archer might be enough.

This she unquestionably is. To have found her reading Emerson's *Essays* when Mrs. Touchett comes upon her at her home in Albany would have been to give a more direct hint than James was capable of, but he suggests the same idea obliquely by having her turn over the pages of a history of German philosophy, so important for the Concord Transcendentalists. "You must be our crazy Aunt Lydia" is her greeting to Mrs. Touchett; no wonder that lady's first observation concerning her is that she is very independent. This is not the only time she gives an impression of bluntness,[3] self-esteem, or girlish caprice, but in her position it would be difficult for any young girl, essentially ignorant of the world and untutored in its ways, to avoid this, and allowances must

[2] *The Novels of Henry James* (Macmillan, 1961), 80. Blair Gates Kenney, "The Two Isabels: A Study in Distortion," *Victorian Newsletter*, No. 25 (1964), 15–17, sees Trollope's *The Duke's Children* as a source for *The Portrait of a Lady* and finds Trollope both more subtle and more human. Robert L. Gale, "A Possible Source for Elements in *The Portrait of a Lady*," *Studi Americani*, XI (1965), 137–41, suggests comparisons between characters and situations in *Lady* and the lives of the sculptor Thomas Crawford; his wife, Louisa Ward; and her second husband, Luther Terry. The comparisons between *Lady* and both *The Scarlet Letter* and Lockhart's *Life of Mr. Adam Blair* made by Laurence Bedwell Holland, *The Expense of Vision: Essays on the Craft of Henry James* (PUP, 1964) are interesting but rather finespun.

[3] At one point James says of Isabel that "her accent had put her slightly in the wrong." She declines to let Ralph Touchett dine with her "because I don't care for it," and when he suggests that she must be tired of him, she replies, "I shall be an hour hence." It seems cruelly unnecessary that in discussing his suit for Pansy with Ned Rosier she should tell him that, if he had proposed to her, she would have refused him on the spot. James cannot have employed such material without intending it to have some meaning for characterization, but its usefulness is weakened by the fact that everybody in the book talks very much the same way. Thus Madame Merle tells Isabel to her face that though she is exquisite she is no "*parti*" in the marriage market, and the Countess Gemini tells Madame Merle that she and Osmond together are "dangerous—like some chemical combination." Caspar tells Isabel he would rather see her dead than married to another man, and when, at Isabel's suggestion, he offers to take the dying Ralph home to Gardencourt, and Ralph thanks him for his kindness, he replies bluntly that he only intends being kind to Isabel! This seems a curious element of vulgarity in a very refined novel.

be made for her inexperience. Isabel's notion of freedom may be romantic and impractical, but her ideal is never merely to do as she likes. She wishes to be free so that she may devote her life to the highest conceivable values, achieving maximum development for herself at the same time that she performs maximum service to others and to the cosmos, and when the Touchett inheritance suddenly and unexpectedly makes her a rich woman, she welcomes her wealth because she believes it must increase her power to do these things. Nothing, surely, could be more Emersonian than this.

Isabel had at least one important nonliterary source in James's cousin, Mary (Minny) Temple (1845–70). Neither as a man nor as an artist did he ever forget her; many years later she was to supply him with Milly Theale in *The Wings of the Dove*. There is probably less of her in Isabel, but James himself admits that in some sense he had her in mind. Milly is allowed to die, as Minny had died, but James spares Isabel to live as his cousin's surrogate. There has been much speculation whether James ever loved Minny. In some sense of that capacious word he certainly did; in some sense, too, she loved him, and though there were never any love passages or any kind of understanding between them, the least we can say is that you can make a better case for her as "the starved romance of my life" than for any other woman. As a matter of fact, there are no other candidates.[4]

Whether or not James loved Minny Temple, however, he certainly loved Isabel Archer, and if we allow his awareness of all her little gaucheries to blind us to his affection, we shall go utterly astray.[5] Though it is not consistently centered in her consciousness, as James suggests, *The Portrait of a Lady* was built around her—a "frail vessel," the "mere

[4]See Robert C. Le Clair, "Henry James and Minny Temple," *AL*, XXI (1949–50), 35–48; also Dorothea Krook on "The Sexual Theme of *The Portrait of a Lady*" in *The Ordeal of Consciousness in Henry James* (CUP, 1962); and, of course, Leon Edel, *Henry James: The Untried Years, 1843–1870* (Li, 1963) and James's own comments on Minny's death at the end of *Notes of a Son and Brother*.

slim shade," complex as she is, "of an intelligent and presumptuous girl." The key passages to support this reading occur early in the novel, the first in Chapter VI, where we are told of her that "she would be an easy victim of scientific criticism if she were not intended to awaken on the reader's part an impulse more tender and more purely expectant," and the second in Chapter XII, where we read that

she was a person of great good faith, and if there was a great deal of folly in her wisdom those who judge her severely may have the satisfaction of finding that, later, she became consistently wise only at the cost of an amount of folly which will constitute almost a direct appeal to charity.

The ordeal she undergoes is carefully prepared for. She is told at the outset that she will never be able to see the Gardencourt ghost until she has suffered, to which she replies that people suffer too easily, that we were not made to suffer, and that the great point is to be as happy as possible. Mr. Touchett has no doubt that there is "room" for her in England but fears that she may have to pay too much for it. In making her a rich woman, Ralph and his father take a calculated risk, well knowing that her wealth will make her more attractive to the fortune hunters, and Henrietta Stackpole thinks it may well prove a curse in disguise. And when her marriage to Gilbert Osmond is under consideration, practically everybody, including Osmond's own sister, fears the worst for her. I do not say that all this is subtly or masterfully done; much of it seems to me anything but that. But the intent is therefore no less plain.

I have said that Isabel Archer is neither an exploiter nor a missioned spirit; one thing more should be noted. She is

[5]Like William Bysshe Stein, for example, in "*The Portrait of a Lady*: Vis Inertia," *WHR*, XIII (1959), 177–90, and Marjorie Perloff in "Cinderella Becomes the Wicked Stepmother: *The Portrait of a Lady* as an Ironic Fairy Tale," *NCF*, XXIII (1968–69), 413–33. Both grotesquely exaggerate Isabel's faults and James's judgment of them.

no artist, and she has no talent but merely a desire to make her life itself a beautiful thing.[6] Her problem therefore, is considerably more complicated than that, say, of the actress Miriam Rooth in *The Tragic Muse,* and this greatly increases James's difficulty in portraying her. Today artistic power is the only kind that many writers trust, wherefore the only characters they are capable of portraying meaningfully must themselves be artists. But whatever moral problems may be involved in the grand old ideal of self-cultivation, the Gospel of Art has, in the long run, as great shortcomings as the Gospel of Work. That a man keeps busy may be either good or bad, the answer depending wholly upon the value of what he produces. And surely if life has any meaning, it must be an end in itself, not merely a means toward an end, even if that end be the creation of a beautiful work of art. How can it be worth while to write about a triumphant life if such a life is not worth living? And how can the portrait of a beautiful woman be of more value than the woman herself? If it be the sole function of either work or art to keep us so absorbed that we may forget how unendurable life would be without them, our case is desperate indeed. Children often come closer to reality in these matters than adults, which is the reason why when we ask them what they "did" today we

[6]This consideration has been overlooked by those who see in Isabel "affronting" her destiny an image of young Henry James. To the artist life is raw material; he observes it and familiarizes himself with it so that he may mold and recharacter and recreate it; even when he seems outwardly idle, his is therefore one of the most active enterprises in which human beings can engage. It is important, too, to differentiate clearly between those who create characters in fiction and those who try to manipulate real people for selfish ends; if there were not a difference here, Iago might well be as great an artist as Shakespeare. Some critics see Isabel, Ralph, and Osmond as a kind of grand mishmash of character, all egotists reaching out to control others' lives. But both Ralph and Isabel give, while Osmond only takes. It is true that the Touchett bequest to Isabel attracts Osmond to her and thus contributes to her misfortune, but this was not the intention. The Touchetts could not control what came of their gift; had they tried to do so, they *would* have been guilty of what their critics accuse them of. Instead, they widened Isabel's range of choice and set her free to make what she could of it; it was not their fault that she chose unwisely.

are generally told only that they "just played." And the little girl who, upon being told that she must live for others, inquired who, then, the others were supposed to live for gave richer promise of developing a philosophical mind than her teachers did.

Isabel's first suitor is the American industrialist Caspar Goodwood. She has refused him in America; she refuses him again in England; in fact, she goes on refusing him to the end of the book. Though Caspar is a very good and respectworthy man, no reader has ever had any difficulty in understanding her decision. Once her aunt has opened up a suddenly enlarged way of life to Isabel, Caspar does not "fit in"; instead he represents everything she is trying to get away from. Isabel is still naïve enough to believe that if he had lived a little earlier Caspar might have been a great figure in the Civil War and to allow her imagination to be stimulated by him in this hypothetical aspect, but she has no more taste for the American businessman than was possessed by her creator. Caspar, we are told, has "a kind of hardness of presence" with "a disagreeably strong push." His jaw is "too square and set and his figure too straight and stiff."

Her rejection of Lord Warburton, an English nobleman of wealth, sound character, excellent disposition, and liberal principles, is a more complicated matter, and Ralph Touchett and his mother are not the only ones who have found it difficult to understand it. Isabel's first reaction to Warburton is very favorable; she sees him, "though quite without luridity," as a romantic hero. His person emits a "radiance of good-feeling and good fare," surrounding him "like a zone of fine June weather," and she admits frankly that she likes him very much. Nevertheless he always has much less chance with her even than Caspar, and the reasons are clear enough, though they are not all spelled out. To begin with, of course, she is not in love with him; had she been, nothing else would have counted for much. As Mr. Touchett tells her, girls are not required to give reasons for rejecting their lovers, and she herself writes Warburton that "these things cannot be reasoned about." When he first approaches her, she is not yet ready to be married, which is not an unbelievable situation for a girl in her position, and if it be objected that she changes pretty quickly when she is captivated by Osmond, it may be replied that this is not unusual with girls either.

Her essential objection to Lord Warburton is that, despite all his radicalism, he is part of a system that she does not wish to be drawn into. "She couldn't marry Lord Warburton; the idea failed to support any enlightened prejudice in favour of the free exploration of life that she had hitherto entertained or was now capable of entertaining." Much as Europe attracts her, Isabel has no idea of being swallowed up by it; she desires more to subsume than to be subsumed. She tells Mrs. Touchett that she wishes to know what girls must not do in Europe not so that she may do it but simply so as to choose; she wishes also to remain an American girl who has possessed herself of whatever Europe possesses that has meaning for her. Moreover, though she thinks it vulgar for a girl to think about marriage very much, her ideal is very high; if she takes a husband, she must surrender to him completely, and she cannot see Warburton in this light.

Later, when Osmond wins her, his lack of all nonspiritual "advantages" is a tremendously important asset. The "advantages" are all hers—to give away—and she values her acquired wealth as an extension of her love. Half mystically, half crazily, she feels that she would, in a sense, be evading life or escaping her fate by marrying Warburton, and even Ralph sees a certain validity in this. But it is more important that, even from the beginning, Isabel has sensed a certain inadequacy in Warburton; though he has no real faults, he is something of a lightweight. Later, when he is courting her stepdaughter Pansy, she feels that he is limited, as Pansy herself is limited, and also, not quite consistently, "that it was strange a man of his mettle should take an interest in a little maid." So, I think, it is, under the circumstances posited, and when this courtship too comes to naught, partly because Pansy does not respond to Warburton even as much as Isabel did, he becomes engaged to a young lady of the aristocracy whose name Mrs. Touchett does not even remember.

With Caspar it was different. In her early days in America, Isabel had admired and respected him beyond any other "splendid young man" she had ever seen, and even at the end she is still wondering whether she might not have married him if she had never come to Europe. She turns pale when his partisan, Henrietta Stackpole, mentions him, and admits that she had once encouraged him. Rejecting him again in England, in Chapter XVI, she not only refrains from closing the door absolutely but, once he has gone, falls on her knees beside the bed and buries her face. Later, in Chapter XXXII, she bursts into tears after sending him away from her in Florence, and as late as Chapter XLVII she feels that he alone holds an unsatisfied claim upon her. Even at the end she does not dismiss him until she has "listened to him as she had never listened before." She tells him frankly that she is returning to her husband to get away from him and begs him to leave her if he loves and pities her. But in her heart she knows that "to let him take her in his arms would be the next best thing to her dying," and when he kisses her passionately (it is the only passionate kiss she receives in the novel), the effect is like white lightning. No, poor Lord Warburton never had anything like this.[7]

Isabel's marriage to Gilbert Osmond is the result of a conspiracy between that fine gentleman and his discarded mistress, Madame Merle, the mother of his illegitimate daughter, but it is engineered so that Isabel, who is ignorant of all this background, imagines herself to be choosing freely,

[7] See Sister Lucy Schneider, "Osculation and Integration: Isabel Archer in the One-Kiss Novel," *CLA Journal*, X (1966–67), 149–61: "Viewing Isabel in relation to the twenty-some kisses of the novel necessarily excludes much interesting and valuable matter, but it does satisfactorily demonstrate her apparent growth in womanly wisdom and love."

and there can be no doubt that she is deeply in love, not indeed with Osmond, for she does not know him, but rather with what she believes him to be. She has "invented a fine theory about him," and, as Mrs. Touchett says, there is nothing to prevent her marrying him if she looks at him in a certain way. Not all readers have found her choice completely convincing, for, while nobody could seriously question that such tragic mismatings do occur in life, we do not perhaps feel the inevitability of the doom by which Isabel is drawn quite as strongly as it is satisfying to feel such things in a work of art.

James has helped us and himself to a degree by omitting most of the courtship and the beginning of their married life; improbabilities are never strengthened by elaborating their details or arguing about them. So we pass abruptly from the happy, deceived engaged girl to the tortured wife of a man who has "deliberately, almost malignantly, . . . put the lights out one by one," making everything he touches wither, spoiling everything he looks at, "as if his presence were a blight and his favour a misfortune." For *The Portrait of a Lady* is not a love story, and our whole interest in Isabel's disastrous marriage is to be centered upon how Isabel reacts to her changed situation and how her "portrait" is to be altered by it.

He married her, of course, for her money. But did this completely cover the case? Did he ever, in any sense, love her? Was he, to any degree, disappointed in her, as she was in him? Such questions hardly seem worth asking about a man whom Graham Greene has described as a "precious vulgarian, cold as a fishmonger's slab,"[8] and they might be safely dismissed if James himself had not told us that Isabel's first year of married life had been happy, and if Ralph Touchett, who loathed Osmond and was not likely to give him unearned credit for anything, had not reminded her, during

[8] *"The Portrait of a Lady,"* in *The Lost Childhood and Other Essays* (Eyre & Spottiswoode, n. d.).

their last interchange, that "He was greatly in love with you," to which she replied, "Yes, he was in love with me. But he wouldn't have married me if I had been poor." This, then, must have been part of James's idea, though I do not think he makes the reader feel it. This much *is* true, however, that Isabel's beauty and social charm were not unappreciated by Osmond. He relished them as he relished the innocence of his daughter Pansy, whom he brought up "in the old way," and whom he sent back to her convent school at twenty, after he failed in his plan to marry her off to Lord Warburton!

Osmond has no morals whatever, and the only reason he is not a libertine is that he lacks the requisite passion; he is not even a good enough man to be dissipated. "He always had an eye to effect," as Ralph perceives, "and his effects were deeply calculated. They were produced by no vulgar means, but the motive was as vulgar as the art was great." He is incapable of regarding wife, daughter, or anybody else except in abject subservience to himself; he is a connoisseur who must possess his collection like the Duke in Browning's "My Last Duchess." What he wanted with Isabel was to "tap her imagination with his knuckle and make it ring," and even when they are hopelessly estranged, he tries to cover up by telling Caspar that they are "as united . . . as the candlestick and the snuffers." The horrible simile he has chosen is the right one for him, and it is part of his damnation that he could never understand why every sensitive reader of *The Portrait of a Lady* has shuddered over it.[9]

What attracts Isabel to Osmond is his freedom from all the soiled attachments and involvements of this world: he

[9] The difficulty of understanding Osmond is complicated by the elements of melodrama which James employs. In "Ironic Melodrama in *The Portrait of a Lady*," *MFS*, XII (1966), 7–23, Manfred Mackenzie, who sees Isabel as enacting the role of "Heroine," advances the idea that Osmond is a "villain" only in her imagination. This finds no support in the text, but Dorothea Krook also gives Osmond more charity than he deserves. Note the sinister quality of the scenes between him and Madame Merle. as at the end of Chapter XXVI. where they appear as a pair of con-

does nothing; he has nothing; thus he seems to her "a speci-
men apart," a surpassingly beautiful, perfectly pure individual, who has achieved a completely symmetrical development of all the highest human powers without ulterior motive. On the other hand, "he knows everything, he understands everything, he has the kindest, gentlest, highest spirit."
Unless we are intended to regard Isabel as a complete fool,
we must therefore be intended to think of him as possessing
extraordinary personal charm when he chooses to exercise
it, though nobody in the book besides Isabel seems to feel
it. It was a fine touch to have his sister, the Countess Gemini,
who, though an immoral woman, is not without heart, warn
Isabel against him. Mrs. Touchett sums him up quite fairly
when she says, "There's nothing *of* him," and Caspar Goodwood is hardly more harsh than this when he calls him "the
deadliest of fiends," for what is this but to be nothing in the
Elizabethan sense? ("O Regan, thy sister's nought!")[10]

In Osmond, then, James has offered as devastating a
study of the emptiness of a life stripped of all save aesthetic

---

spiratorial fiends, and the picture-poster kind of interview between them in Chapter XLIX, where she calls herself vile and accuses him of having made her as bad
as himself. Isabel is not present at these scenes. See also Leo B. Levy, *Versions
of Melodrama, A Study of the Fiction and Drama of Henry James, 1865–1897*
(University of California Press, 1957). Incidentally, the "Henry James Number" of
MFS in which Mackenzie's article appears also contains a number of other articles
bearing upon the works considered in this book. Stephen Reid writes of *Lady* and
The Spoils of Poynton, Walter Dubler of *The Princess Casamassima*, Lotus Snow
of *Roderick Hudson* and *The Tragic Muse*, Ernest H. Lockridge of the *Muse*,
Stephen Koch of *The Wings of the Dove*, and Alan Rose of *The Golden Bowl*.
There is also a very valuable checklist of James criticism by Maurice Beebe and
William T. Stafford.

[10] It has sometimes been suggested that Osmond's real appeal to Isabel was
sexual and that James did not make this plain because the novelistic mores of the
time did not permit him to discuss such matters. This is altogether wrong; even
though Isabel bears Osmond a child, who dies, James makes it unmistakably clear
in the final chapter that her sexuality, though always potentially normal, was never
really roused before her final interview with Caspar. Perhaps the most ill-advised
article ever written about *Lady* was H. G. Flinn and Howard C. Key, "Henry James
and Gestation," *CE*, XXI (1959–60), 173–75, in which it was argued, on the basis
of a misunderstanding of the novel's chronology, that Isabel's child was conceived

values as Walter de la Mare achieved in his wonderful story, "The Connoisseur." Whether he ever loved Isabel or not, we may well believe that, at some point in his now hopelessly corrupted life, he did love beauty for its own sake. At some point, there may even have been an element of honest moral revulsion in his turning away from the prizes which a corrupt world can give. All this, however, was long ago, and Osmond as we know him rejects only what he knows he cannot have and wraps himself in scorn as a garment. Dread of vulgarity,

---

three months before her marriage! The replies by Jack E. Wallace and John C. Broderick (pp. 497–99) are decisive, and Wallace's concluding sentence has a wider application than to one particular article: "As long as certain critics are blindly preoccupied with ironies that 'reach out in all directions,' someone must look, now and then, at the text."

Joseph P. O'Neill, *Workable Design: Action and Situation in the Fiction of Henry James* (Kennikat Press, 1973), has a very full discussion of how and why Isabel decides to accept Osmond and an account of the changes in her state of mind after her marriage. John A. Clair, *The Ironic Dimension in the Fiction of Henry James* (Duquesne University Press, 1965) also considers her acceptance and rejections at length.

Tony Tanner, "The Fearful Self: Henry James's *The Portrait of a Lady*," *Critical Quarterly*, VII (1965), 205–19, sees Isabel as well as Osmond an egotist at the outset, "cold and dry," and paying "excessive attention to appearances," "preferring art to life," with "more theories than feelings, more ideals than instincts." Osmond is "a collector of things, and she offers herself up to him as a fine finished object. . . . Her later shock and revulsion is the uncertain self discovering the true worthlessness of what it might have become." By the end she achieves internal freedom, can see through false appearances, and will never again be taken in. "If nothing else, *The Portrait of a Lady* shows us the birth of a conscience out of the spoiling of a life." Unconvincing considerations of these matters include Juliet McMaster's notion that Isabel rejects Warburton and accepts Osmond because alongside her desire for happiness she has a perverse desire for suffering ("The Portrait of Isabel Archer," *AL*, XLV [1973–74], 50–66) and J. M. Newton's view that she marries Osmond because of her own shortcomings but that, since James shared them, he fails "to give an honest account of the matter," and hence the novel fails ("Isabel Archer's Disease and Henry James's," *Cambridge Quarterly*, II [1966–67], 3–23). R. W. Stallman, "The Houses That James Built— *The Portrait of a Lady*," *Texas Quarterly*, Vol. I, No. 4 (Winter, 1958), 176–96, finds that "the scene at the opera house which opens Book II . . . initiates a decline in the heroine's subsequent destiny, a falling away from the romantic ardor of her soaring aspirations culminating in the final scene of Book II at St. Peter's Cathedral." Like Diana, Isabel has kinship with the moon. "She is a creature of darkness, and the light she needs— the insight—is proffered in vain by her friends and lovers." Her "plight is staged by the alternation of scenes of dark houses and sunlit gardens."

as Ralph says rightly, is his special line, and no one could be so afraid of vulgarity as he is without being in bondage to it. He is "a prince who has abdicated in a fit of fastidiousness and has been in a state of disgust ever since," and Dorothy Van Ghent has noted how suitable it is that when Isabel comes to tell him of Ralph's impending death he should be engaged in *copying* (demons cannot *create*) an ancient coin. For him even art is dead, as it must always be for those for whom it is cut off from any vital relationship with life. Since there are no values left for him but aesthetic values, he can "live only by taste and by appreciation of form, form of the visual and of the social and traditional." Even his own child he must approach from this angle, feeling an "aesthetic relish" of Pansy's innocence. It has been said of Osmond that he hates his wife because he cannot dominate her as he dominates his daughter. This is true, but it is not the whole truth. Osmond fails even with Pansy, though he is too stupid to find it out. Unlike Isabel, Pansy is no heroine, but she is a strangely incorruptible phenomenon for Osmond and Madame Merle to have produced. She submits to her father's authority without complaint—and turns for comfort to the wife he loathes. Her spirit he cannot touch. In the last analysis, there is nothing left for him but form, even as a father, and he has nothing to live for save the figure he cuts in the eyes of the world he pretends to scorn and which has always ignored him.[11]

As for Isabel, he nearly kills her. At one time, there is even danger of corruption, for, in the first agony of her disillusionment, she learns to live, like a fine lady, on the surface of life, but this does not last long. Yet at the end, having defied his wishes by going to Ralph in England when he is dying, she returns to him. Or does she? Yes, she returns, but I do

---

[11]Mrs. M. Mukherji, "Role of Pansy in *The Portrait of a Lady*," *Calcutta Review*, n. s. I (1969–70), 585–94, is probably the most detailed study of Pansy and a very good one. See, further, Shine, *The Fictional Children of Henry James*, 102ff.

not see how critics can say the book has an "open" ending and still be sure she returns to stay. If this is surely known, then the issue is closed; they cannot have it both ways. *The Portrait of a Lady* originally ended, in 1881, with Henrietta's advice to Caspar—"just you wait!"—"on which," James added, "he looked up at her." In the New York Edition, James weakened the element of hope here by adding that Caspar could see she only meant that he was young. "She stood shining at him with that cheap comfort, and it added, on the spot, thirty years to his life. She walked him away with her, however, as if she had given him the key to patience." Yet if James was merely laughing at Henrietta, he would seem to have committed an error in emphasis by giving her the last word. She has been painted in primary colors throughout, but she has been clear-sighted enough about Isabel's marriage. And Isabel herself had told Ralph, just before his death, that she did not know whether she was going back.

If Isabel were a Catholic, it would be easier to be happy with her return to Osmond, but she is not. Religion has very little to do with *The Portrait of a Lady,* in which respect it differs markedly from some of the later and greater novels. The only clergyman we ever hear of Isabel being brought in touch with is the athletic Vicar of Lockleigh, whom she likes but whom she can hardly think of as a spiritual guide. There is no positive evidence that religion motivates her actions at any point, but we are told specifically that though there was (from the Catholic point of view) no gentler nor less consistent heretic than she, "the old Protestant tradition had never faded" from her imagination. For Osmond, the Church, like everything else, is a form. He would have liked to be pope, but it is the power of the papacy which attracts him; for him the pope is a prince of this world, and one cannot imagine him experiencing any of the Christian humility which a good man must feel confronting such an office. When his daughter is brought back to him from the convent, he asks one of the sisters what they have made of her. The answer is, "A good

Christian, monsieur," but this does not interest him. "Yes," he asks, "and what else?" Both he and the sister drop their eyes for a moment, but, says James, "it was probable that the movement in each case had a different spring." Nevertheless, he believes that the convent has a very important place in society: "it corresponds to an essential need. . . . It's a school of good manners; it's a school of repose." But Isabel sees it, as Osmond employs it, as "a well-appointed prison" for Pansy, requiring "the surrender of a personality." Yet she retains "all the traditional decencies and sanctions of marriage" and comes close to preserving all the inflexibility of the sacramental conception with none of its advantages.

Two different motives have been alleged for Isabel's returning to a husband who hates her. The first is that she has promised Pansy not to desert her. (Mrs. Touchett has long been aware that Isabel thinks a great deal of her promises). But this hardly seems her main motive. If Pansy is as remarkable as her warmest admirers believe, she hardly needs Isabel, and if she is not, it is difficult to see what Isabel can do for her besides making her aware of her sympathy. That, no doubt, is something. But Osmond's attitude toward Isabel being what it now is, she is about the last person he could be expected to allow to come between his daughter and himself; indeed, Pansy might well have to suffer more for Isabel's championship of her.

It is interesting that James should have allowed Osmond of all people to state the case for the continuance of the marriage:

"I take our marriage seriously. . . . I'm not aware that we're divorced or separated; for me we're indissolubly united. You are nearer to me than any human creature, and I'm nearer to you. . . . I think we should accept the consequences of our actions, and what I value most in life is the honour of a thing!"

The devil can cite Scripture for his purpose, and all this is about as convincing as Hitler's (or any warmaker's) boasted devotion to peace. In a spiritual sense, the marriage to which Osmond boasts of his allegiance, if it ever existed, has already been destroyed, yet in a way he means exactly what he says, for the form remains, and form is the only thing that has ever meant anything to this hollow man anyway.

This does not mean, of course, that Isabel's final decision, if it is that, cannot be rationally defended. It is no accident that some of the most convincing defenses have been entered by Catholic writers like Graham Greene, Courtney Johnson, and Vincent F. Blehl.[12] Says the last:

James is trying to convey the paradox that Isabel Archer comes to self-fulfillment and integrity but in a situation which on one level of perception seems to militate against the development of her personality. Commitment always involves risks and Isabel long since recognized that one does not achieve happiness by escaping from the suffering which responsibility for one's actions may entail.

But such writers do not stand alone. Sheldon W. Liebman, for example, seems quite in agreement with Father Blehl that her spiritual achievement is worth all the suffering it costs. In his view, she

passes through three distinct phases of moral awareness, at last graduating to a final stage of moral, aesthetic, and psychological superiority, having acquired through experience, knowledge, and through knowledge, virtue. Isabel comes to light only by immersing herself in the destructive element, darkness, like Conrad's Lord Jim. And she manages to survive and conquer in the end by rising on the steppingstones of her "dead" selves.

And with this John Rodenbeck is quite in accord. It is Isabel's

[12]Courtney Johnson, "Adam and Eve and Isabel Archer," *Renascence*, XXI (1968–69), 134–44, 167; Vincent F. Biehl, S. J., "Freedom and Commitment in James's *The Portrait of a Lady.*" *Personalist.* XLII (1961), 368–81.

wretched marriage, he thinks, that saves her from becoming like her aunt, Mrs. Touchett.[13]

Of course, such reasoning will not satisfy everybody, nor can it be expected to do so. When Graham Greene sums up Isabel's choice as a choice between betraying and being betrayed, these persons reply angrily that to apply such a word as betrayal to anything Isabel might do to end her marriage is merely silly. It is true that she married Osmond because she thought she wanted to, but it is equally true that he and Madame Merle tricked her into marriage for interested motives. She was no match for their scheming because, with her character and at her time of life, she could not possibly have been that, and of this they were quite aware; in any proper sense of the term, therefore, her choice was not made freely.

The dissenters take up their stand with the dying Ralph Touchett when he tells Isabel, "I don't believe that such a generous mistake as yours can hurt for more than a little." Without masochism, quixotism, monstrous pride, or an inhuman sense of duty, sane people do not, they argue, voluntarily condemn themselves to lifelong penance for having made an honest mistake. So Victor H. Strandberg points out that the marriage to whose sanctity Osmond proposes to commit himself means "the rather pleasant fact of being married to a woman of great wealth" for him, while to her it spells spiritual and emotional starvation, and Marion Montgomery finds Isabel committing spiritual suicide as Emma Bovary committed physical suicide in "a romantically conceived unhappy ending, an almost heroic renunciation, but a renunciation that appears unjustified."[14]

In the last analysis, what one believes about the ending of *The Portrait of a Lady* will be determined by what one

[13] Sheldon W. Liebman, "The Light and the Dark: Character Design in *The Portrait of a Lady*," *Papers on Language and Literature*, VI (1970), 163–79; John Rodenbeck, "The Bolted Door in James's *The Portrait of a Lady*," *MFS*, X (1964–65), 330–40.

believes about many other things. One can, however, justify James's ending without going into any of these deep moral and religious considerations. This is what Viola Hopkins Winner does when she declares that Isabel accepts "actuality and necessity" in what was meant to be a "tragically affirmative conclusion." Being what she was, she could not have acted in any other way.[15] Thus it becomes true of *The Portrait of a Lady* as of every other considerable work of art that every man has the work that he deserves.

[14] Victor H. Strandberg, "Isabel Archer's Identity Crisis: The Two Portraits of a Lady," *University Review*, XXXIV (1968), 283–90; Marion Montgomery, "The Flaw in the Portrait: Henry James vs. Isabel Archer," *UKCR*, XXVI (1959–60), 215–20. See also Dominic J. Bazzanella, "The Conclusion to *The Portrait of a Lady* Re-Examined," *AL*, XLI (1969–70), 55–63; Lyall H. Powers, "*The Portrait of a Lady*: The Eternal Mystery of Things," *NCF*, XIV (1959–60), 143–55. F. O. Matthiessen's study of the text in *Henry James: The Major Phase* (OUP, 1944) is valuable. Annette Niemtzow, "Marriage and the New Woman in *The Portrait of a Lady*," *AL*, XLVII (1975), 377–95, who finds more sexuality in Isabel than other critics have discerned, studies her return in the light of the views about marriage and divorce entertained by Henry James, Sr. William Veeder also considers the ending in his *Henry James— The Lessons of the Master: Popular Fiction and Personal Style in the Nineteenth Century* (UCP, 1975), especially 84–86. Among much other valuable material, this book has also the fullest and most penetrating analysis of both Osmond and Madame Merle that has been made; consult especially 119ff. and 178–83.

[15] *Henry James and the Visual Arts* (University Press of Virginia, 1960); cf. Thomas F. Smith, "Balance in Henry James's *The Portrait of a Lady*," *Four Quarters*, Vol. XIII, No. 4 (May, 1964), 11–16. A. R. Mills, "*The Portrait of a Lady* and Dr. Leavis," *EIC*, XIV (1964), 280–87, probably stands alone in entertaining the incredible notion that, though Isabel may "arouse some tender feeling in us," we "cannot respect her," since not even at the end does she recognize her share of the responsibility for the failure of her marriage.

It is amusing that, though Maisie Farange is the James character most generally compared to Huckleberry Finn, at least two writers have compared Huck to Isabel Archer. The first was Henry Seidel Canby, *Turn West, Turn East: Mark Twain and Henry James* (HM, 1951), 161–62. See also Ray K. Kohli, "Isabel Archer and Huck Finn: Two Responses to the Fruit of Knowledge," in Sujit Mukhergee and D. V. K. Raghavacharyulu, eds., *Indian Essays in American Literature* (Bombay, Popular Prakashan, 1969). This volume also contains O. P. Sharma's "The Albany Cousin and Two Heroines of Henry James," which concerns both *Lady* and *The Wings of the Dove*, and N. Krishna Rao's "The Idea of Refinement in James's *Roderick Hudson*."

IV. JAMESIAN FEMME FATALE

CHRISTINA LIGHT

LEON EDEL REMARKS of Christina Light, later the Princess Casamassima, that James loved her "as he loved few of his heroines." I cannot quite believe this, for, though Christina was incomparably the most beautiful girl he ever created, he has others who bury her fifty fathoms deep so far as character is concerned, and I am sure that he was aware of this. There can be no question, however, that he was deeply interested in her and even fascinated by her. She was about the only thing in *Roderick Hudson* (1876), where her "presence and action" were "all firm ground," with which he seems to have been satisfied, and he suffered "a real pang" at parting from her at its close. "Wound-up" as she had been "with the right silver key," he had achieved in her "even more life than the subject required" and thus equipped her to "go on." To use up her unrealized potential, he welcomed the opportunity to reintroduce her, now "world-weary," consumed by "restless vanity" and the need "to feel freshly about something or other—it might scarcely matter what" (it turns out to be revolution) in *The Princess Casamassima* (1886). But she is not really the principal character in either of the books in which she appears, and she is almost as much a puzzle at the end of the *Princess* as she was before. Strictly speaking, it was no more inevitable to drop her after the death of Hyacinth Robinson than after that of Roderick Hudson, though we may doubt that we should ever have completely fathomed her mystery, nor that she should really have done so herself, no matter how many the novels in which this inexhaustible lady might have figured.[1]

Oscar Cargill thought her dual nature suggested by her name, "in which charity is set off against frivolity or light-

[1] Critics have found Balzac, Dickens, Zola, George Sand, George Eliot, Hawthorne, Cherbuliez, and others as literary influences upon the two novels in which Christina Light figures, but Viola Dunbar, "A Source for *Roderick Hudson*," *MLN*, LXIII (1948), 303–10, has shown that the direct source was *L'Affaire Clemençeau* by Alexandre Dumas, *fils*. The pioneering study of Turgenev's *Virgin Soil* as the source of *The Princess Casamassima* was in Daniel Lerner, "The Influence of Turgenev on Henry James," *Slavonic and East European Review*, XX (1941), 28–54; for later discussion see R. J. Kane, "*Virgin Soil* and *The Princess Casamassima*," *Gifthorse*, (Ohio State University, 1949), 25–29; Eunice C. Hamilton, "Henry James's *The Princess Casamassima* and Ivan Turgenev's *Virgin Soil*," *South Atlantic Quarterly*, LXI (1962), 354–64; Jeanne Delbaere-Garant, "Henry James's Divergences from his Russian Model in *The Princess Casamassima*," *Revue des Langues Vivantes*, XXXVII (1971), 525–46; Anthony D. Briggs, "Someone Else's Sledge: Further Notes on Turgenev's *Virgin Soil* and Henry James's *The Princess Casamassima*," *Oxford Slavonic Studies*, V (1972), 52–60; also Cargill's chapter on *The Princess* in *The Novels of Henry James*. Charlotte Goodman suggests an additional possible source for the earlier novel in "Henry James's *Roderick Hudson* and Nathaniel Parker Willis's *Paul Fane*," *AL*, XLIII (1971–72), 642–45.

The popular idea that before World War I James had no interest in social or political questions simply shows unfamiliarity with his letters and nonfiction writings; in 1896 he wrote A. C. Benson that he had "the imagination of disaster." Lionel Trilling's introduction to the 1948 Macmillan edition of *The Princess*, reprinted in his *The Liberal Imagination* (Viking Press, 1950), did much to establish his knowledge of contemporary radicalism; see further W. H. Tilley's admirable study, *The Background of* The Princess Casamassima, University of Florida Monographs, Humanities, No. 5 (University of Florida Press, 1960). Other discussions include George Woodcock, "Henry James and the Conspirators," *SR*, LX (1952), 219–29, and Taylor Stoehr, "Words and Deeds in *The Princess Casamassima*," *ELH*, XXXVII (1970), 95–134. Woodcock argues that James misinterpreted contemporary anarchism and credited it with more organization than it possessed.

Leon Edel (*Henry James: The Conquest of London, 1870–1881* [Li, 1962], 111–13) suggested Elena Lowe, whom James knew, as a possible original for Christina. Other suggestions are Violet Paget (Burdett Gardner, "An Apology for Henry James's 'Tiger Cat,'" *PMLA*, LXVIII [1953], 688–95); Princess Oblensky, an associate of Michael Bakunin (M. S. Wilkins, "A Note on the Princess Casamassima," *NCF*, XII [1957–58], 88); Princess Christina Belgiojoso (Bebe Spanos, "The Real Princess Casamassima," *PQ*, XXXVIII [1959], 488–96) and her daughter, Princess Maria Belgiojoso (George Monteiro, "Another Princess," *PQ*, XLI [1962], 517–18). Adeline R. Tintner, "Keats and James and *The Princess Casamassima*," *NCF*, XXVIII (1973), 179–73, traces Keatsian influences in *The Princess*, including those suggesting Christina's *femme fatale* aspects. Gardner's perception in Christina of "incipient Lesbianism which James shows operating at the highest potential for destruction" has validity only as a testimonial to the critic's powerful imagination.

ness," but Christina is not "a light woman" in the usual sense of that term, and surely the suggestion of light, as opposed to darkness, is not sinister (Joseph J. Firebaugh believes, to the contrary, that "her maiden name suggests the perfection of some neo-Platonic goddess"). Nobody seems ever to have asked whether her Christian name was derived from that no less enigmatic lady Queen Christina of Sweden, but the question, I think, has point.

I have called her James's *femme fatale,* but though she is involved in the death of two men (Hyacinth Robinson certainly a suicide and Roderick Hudson very likely one), nobody is in any danger of thinking of her as Theda Bara in *A Fool There Was.* Neither death can be laid wholly at her door. So far as Roderick is concerned, James ranges himself on both sides of the question when he speaks of the "determinant function" assigned to "this unfortunate young woman," making her the "well-nigh sole agent of [Roderick's] catastrophe" yet at the same time finds this role "forced upon her" and thus failing to achieve full conviction. Yet the immediate occasion of Roderick's wandering off on the mountain ramble from which he never returns is his good angel Rowland Mallet's at last forcing him to face up to the truth about himself, while the straw that breaks the camel's back for Hyacinth is his vision of Millicent Henning having at last betrayed him for Captain Sholto. Roderick Hudson essentially dies of being Roderick Hudson, and his collapse has been carefully prepared for almost from the beginning of the book, while the roots of Hyacinth's conflict go clear back to his being the bastard son of a passionate Frenchwoman who finally murdered the English nobleman by whom she had been seduced. Admittedly Christina's patronage of him contributes to his being impossibly poised at last between his revolutionary principles and his attachment to a "civilization" encrusted, as he sees it, with guilt, but so does the experience of Paris which he acquires when the small legacy he inherits from his loving foster mother, Miss Pynsent, enables him to visit there.[2]

Edel raises another interesting point when he finds that the "moral" of *Roderick Hudson* "seems to be that a great physical passion can be fatal to art." Roderick is indeed, as he himself observes, "damnably susceptible" to women, but there is no reason to suppose that Christina's appeal to him was primarily voluptuous; it would have been a shame to waste a creation of her complexity on a situation in which something like the antiheroine of Somerset Maugham's *Of Human Bondage* would have served just as well. Roderick may well have encountered a Mildred in his occasional plunges into vulgar dissipation, but, as he himself says, it is "the grace and the beauty and the mystery of women" and "their power to turn themselves 'on' as creatures of subtlety and perversity" that especially enthrall him, and for that he needs a Christina.

[2] This book is concerned with Christina's character rather than with that of persons connected with her, but some attention must be given to both Roderick and Hyacinth in order to comprehend her. The young sculptor has talent but not the character required for the development of a talent, and his "fizzling out" is no surprise to those who read attentively. Rowland writes Cousin Cecilia that "the poor fellow isn't *made* right, and it's really not his fault; Nature has given him his faculty out of hand and bidden him be hanged with it." Certainly he stands passive "in the clutch of his temperament," and he alienates the reader's sympathy by never making any effort to transcend it. Completely self-centered and never seeing himself as part of a larger whole, he demands the right to any experience that will feed his imagination as an artist. Toward both his mother and his fiancée he is quite heartless; his engagement becomes a "funny, poor dear little fact" as early as when he begins modeling Christina, and his mother means nothing to him except when he sees her as a model for a work of art. Even after Rowland tells him the truth about himself, the only thing that concerns him is that he has been rendered shabby in his own eyes; about what he has done to others he cares not at all. I may add that, though James believes in the freedom of the will, a good case can be made for determinism in both the Christina Light novels; in this connection, Joseph J. Firebaugh, "A Schopenhauerian Novel: James's *The Princess Casamassima*," *NCF*, XIII (1958–59), 177–97, has interest, though it goes too far and tries to prove too much. Robert L. Gale, "*Roderick Hudson* and Thomas Crawford," *AQ*, XIII (1961), 495–504, suggests that James had that famous sculptor in mind in creating Roderick, but Viola Hopkins Winner, whose *Henry James and the Visual Arts* is the best study of the novel's artistic background, thinks Crawford might have been a better model for Gloriani and suggests William Morris Hunt for Roderick. For further consideration of Roderick's character, see Viola R. Dunbar, "The Problem in *Roderick Hudson*," *MLN*, LXVII (1952), 109–13, and John A. Cook, "The Fool Show in

   This brings us to the whole question of Christina's own sexuality. Nineteenth-century novelists in general were reticent about sex, and James had a tendency toward reticence concerning everything else besides, in the sense that he preferred to leave to implication what the ordinary novelist spells out.

   It is clear to begin with that Christina's beauty is of the radiant rather than the voluptuous variety. Lady Aurora thinks she looks "as if she had known nothing bad since she was born," and Madame Grandoni, who knew her and her shortcomings much better,[3] feels that her appearance suggests "an angel who came down from heaven yesterday and

Roderick Hudson," Canadian Review of American Studies, IV (1973), 74–86.

   Hyacinth Robinson has a French revolutionary in his background and has been reared in poverty. Far more sympathetic than Roderick, he appeals through his sensitiveness and capacity for devotion, but it is remarkable how often he is called "poor" and "little." When he falls in with the revolutionaries, he offers to bind himself to carry out any mission that the "Führer" of the group may see fit to entrust to him, and it is understood, though not specifically stated, that this will probably be an act of assassination which will in all likelihood cost him his life. His subsequent contacts with the Princess and his visit to Paris do nothing to lessen his sympathies with the underprivileged (romantic that he is, he still feels himself bound by his "sacred vow"), but he can no longer bring himself to have a hand in bringing down a civilization which, for the first time, he is beginning to understand. In the last chapter, the bullet which had been intended for the Duke finds lodgment in his own heart. It is nonsense to speak of this ending, as some critics have done, as a "solution" of Hyacinth's problem or, worse still, as "representative of the artist's triumph." Even Louis Auchincloss's statement that "his final vote is for the china shop and not the bull" (*Reading Henry James*, [University of Minnesota Press, 1975]) is more clever than perceptive. As Elizabeth Stevenson perceived, "there are two insoluble points here, the wrongs of the poor and the rights of a high civilization" (*The Crooked Corridor* [Macmillan, 1949]), and Hyacinth never brings them into harmony. His death solves nothing; it is merely an evasion of his problem and a gesture of despair. See Sister Jane Marie Luecke, "*The Princess Casamassima*: Hyacinth's Fallible Consciousness," *Modern Philology*, LX (1962–63), 274–80; and John L. Kimmey, "*The Princess Casamassima* and the Quality of Bewilderment," *NCF*, XXII (1967–68), 47–62, which is the best detailed study of Hyacinth's character. In another article, "*The Bostonians* and *The Princess Casamassima*," *TSLL*, IX (1967–68), 537–46, Kimmey sees James trying to avoid in *The Princess* the mistakes he had made in the earlier novel.

   [3] For a particularly good discussion of Madame Grandoni's function as interpreter of Christina, see Ellen Douglas Leyburn, *Strange Alloy: The Relation of Comedy to Tragedy in the Fiction of Henry James* (UCP, 1968), 99–103.

has been rather disappointed in her first day on earth." At Rosy Muniment's bedside, Hyacinth sees her as "full of the imagination of sympathy and pity," her "high mildness . . . deepened to a rapture of active ministering charity. She had put off her splendour, but her beauty was unquestionably bright." And even at the end, he sees that beauty shining

like a trimmed lamp, clearer and further, so that—if what was already supremely fine could be capable of greater refinement— it might have worked itself free of all earthly grossness and been purified and consecrated by her new life. Her gentleness, when she turned it on, was quite divine—it had always the irresistible charm that was the humility of a high spirit.

Appearances can be deceitful, of course, but there can be no question that, to the end of *Roderick Hudson* at least, Christina is completely chaste.[4] Roderick's appeal to her is not basically physical; at one point she even wishes he were her brother. She had dreamed of a man she could respect and admire, and it was not her fault that Roderick did not turn out to be that man. She sounds very much like Beatrix Esmond (whom Thackeray also reintroduced in a later novel) when she cries:

"I'm a poor weak woman; I've no strength in myself, and I can give no strength. I'm a miserable medley of vanity and folly. I'm silly, I'm ignorant, I'm affected, I'm false. I'm the fruit of a horrible education sown on a worthless soil. I'm all that, and yet I believe I have one merit. I should know a great character when I saw it, and I should delight in it with a generosity that would do something toward the remission of my sins."

What Christina may be in *The Princess Casamassima* is a more complicated matter. Still beautiful, she is now no longer young, and she has not been improved as a spiritual

---

[4]Joseph P. O'Neill, *Workable Design*, is, to my knowledge, the only critic who stresses sexual frustration as an important element in Christina's problem, and he not only does not establish this but makes no effort to do so.

being by her contacts with the good, enormously wealthy, but very dull Prince Casamassima, whom her mother tricked her into marrying by threatening to reveal the illegitimacy the girl has until now never suspected (this is hardly the most effective of the various melodramatic devices in which James sometimes indulged). Christina, who now lives apart from the Prince, hates him because he was forced upon her, and she hates herself even more for having been weak enough to give in.

It is to her credit, though I have nowhere seen her receive credit for it, that she does not seem to hate anybody else, not even her mother, who had wronged her far more deeply all her life, first by neglecting her and then, when it became obvious that she would be a great beauty, by spoiling and exploiting her outrageously and training her toward nothing but the exploitation of others. It is interesting that there is no indication in *The Princess Casamassima* that Christina ever experienced any remorse over Roderick Hudson's fate. Did James intend this to indicate hardness of heart, or is it simply a part of his consistent avoidance in the later novel of all reference to the earlier one? On this point Cargill says cruelly that "presumptively . . . there have been other infatuated men to displace his memory," but we know nothing about that one way or the other.

James is himself, I think, misleading when in one passage he has Hyacinth feeling almost as if he were married to Christina and in another remarks that "it is forbidden us to try the question of what Hyacinth, face to face with an aggrieved husband, may have had on his conscience." Nevertheless, if we can be sure of anything in fiction, we can be sure that there is (in the narrower sense) no sex between Christina and Hyacinth. Paul Muniment is another matter however; though we cannot be sure that he becomes Christina's lover, various circumstances seem to suggest it, and when the Prince accuses her to Madame Grandoni, that lady replies that she has ceased to be able to tell him. James apparently intended us to believe that Muniment has considerable charm or a coarse, ruthless masculinity which sometimes appeals strongly to women, or so at least men profess to believe. He is rude to Christina from his first contact with her, but even Lady Aurora is represented as having fallen in love with him.[5]

At Christina's first appearance in Chapter V of *Roderick Hudson* she passes across the scene in silence, like Ilyena, upon her first appearance in *Uncle Vanya,* leading her wonderful poodle, Stenterello, whom she considers a perfect gentleman and a great Florentine personage, "decked like

[5] It is important to see Christina, of course, in relation not only to the men she knows but also to the women. Of Mary Garland, who loves Roderick Hudson and whom Rowland Mallet loves, enough is said elsewhere in connection with Christina's attitude toward her. She is completely New England, the daughter, granddaughter, and sister of clergymen, and there has been some difference of critical opinion concerning her, but she gains in contrast with the smaller, less intelligent, and less generous nature of Roderick's mother. Paul Muniment's interesting invalid sister, Rosy, in whom Lionel Trilling found suggestions of Alice James, and whom he ingeniously compared and contrasted to Dickens' Jenny Wren, awakens sympathy by her courage and alienates it by what James himself calls her capacity for "serene transitions from pure enthusiasm to the imaginative calculation of benefits." Lady Aurora stands over against Christina as the nonrevolutionary rebel against her class. Though she has no ideas, she lives a life of self-denial, using her means to alleviate the lot of as many unfortunates as she can reach. Too intelligent not to be aware of Lady Aurora's absurdities, Christina feels and gladly acknowledges her moral superiority; in her presence she feels like a French milliner.

More interesting than any of these is Millicent Henning, whom Hyacinth retains as a friend from the slum neighborhood in which he grew up. Millicent is "vulgar, clumsy and grotesquely ignorant," but she is also "bold and generous and incalculable" and "neither false nor cruel." Superbly realized and presented with complete sympathy, she is all the more one of James's triumphs because she is so utterly unlike what anybody might expect from him. Like Miriam Rooth, she prides herself on being a "good girl" and won't give up church for a lark with Hyacinth. It is a bitter piece of irony that she should share with Christina the disillusionment which triggers his suicide. Actually he had no right to resent her turning from him to Captain Sholto (if that is what she did), though he might still be disgusted by her choice, for she had given him abundant opportunities to which he had remained blind, and it was only at the end that he began asking himself "if at bottom he hadn't liked her better than almost any one." If he had married her, she would have bossed and babied him no end, but it may be that this was just what he needed, and she might have been his salvation. About her affection for him there is no question whatever, and one would very much like to know how she reacted to his death.

a ram for sacrifice." She is accompanied by her mother and her mother's hanger-on, the Cavalière Giacosa, who is also her natural father, though she does not yet know it. The Chekhov play was of course later than *Roderick Hudson,* but James may very well have been thinking of Faust's vision of Marguerite in the first act of Gounod's opera and of her quick passage across the stage in the Kermesse scene of Act II. Indeed, Roderick, who is so smitten by the sudden vision of beauty she brings him that he can hardly believe her alive ("she's a phantasm, a vapour, an illusion"), says that Stenterello too "may be a grotesque phantom, like the black dog in *Faust.*"

From the beginning James gives us a kind of prismatic view of Christina by permitting us to see her through the eyes of those with whom she comes in contact. Mary Garland detests her on sight, which is natural enough. The minor artist Miss Blanchard thinks she looks like a cross between a Madonna and a ballerina. Roderick himself, though he is her slave from the beginning, admits that he does not know where to have her. She is not one woman but fifty, like the legionary spirits who possessed the demoniac in the Bible. "She's never the same, and you never know how she'll be." Roderick does not draw the Biblical comparison, but she reminds the sculptor Gloriani of a more important New Testament figure, Salome, daughter of Herodias. Rowland Mallet, Roderick's patron and the reflecting consciousness of the novel, senses at once that she is as inordinately deep as her half-English, half-American mother is inordinately shallow and warns Roderick that she will bring him trouble. When she poses to the young sculptor for her bust and Rowland has a chance to observe her more closely, he judges her unsafe, complex, willful, passionate, and dangerous, quite capable of drawing "a too confiding spirit into some strange underworld of unworthy sacrifice." Yet, for all his mistrust of her, "he felt it a rare and expensive privilege to watch her, and he found her presence in every way important and momentous. The background of her nature had a sort of landscape largeness and was mysterious withal, emitting strange, fantastic gleams and flashes." Later he tried to sum her up in a letter to his cousin in America:

"She is corrupt, perverse, as proud as a potentate, and a coquette of the first magnitude; but she's intelligent and bold and free, and so awfully on the lookout for sensations that if you set rightly to work you may enlist her imagination in a good cause as well as in a bad. . . . I've come to the conclusion that she's more dangerous in her virtuous moods than in her vicious, and that she probably has a way of turning her back which is the most maddening thing in the world."

The truth of this last observation both Roderick and Hyacinth Robinson were to have the opportunity to verify to their sorrow.

But it is Madame Grandoni, the kind old German woman with an Italian name, who knows Christina better than anybody else, and having known her mother before her, she understands too that the evil conditioning to which the girl has been subjected might have ruined a saint. All her life she has been "a better 'draw' than the two-headed calf or the learned pig" in a booth managed by her mother at the fair.

"She said she was weary of life [Madame Grandoni tells Rowland] and that she knew no one but me she could speak frankly to. She must speak or she should go mad. . . . She said in so many words that her mother was an infamous woman. . . . She said the life they led was horrible; that it was monstrous a poor girl should be dragged about the world to be sold to the highest bidder. She was meant for better things; she could be perfectly happy without those dreadfulnesses. It was not money she wanted. I might not believe her, but she really cared for serious things—for the good, the beautiful and the true. Sometimes she thought of taking poison."

Allow all you like for female emotionalism and Christina's incorrigible tendency toward histrionics, yet every word she says about the conditions that have been imposed upon her is true.

At Roderick's studio, Rowland felt that Christina's look was not bold; rather, "it expressed but the reserve of systematic indifference." Later, however, we learn that "violent frankness" had impressed this observer as "the keynote of her system" and that she had also given him the suggestion of "an unfathomable power of calculation." In *Roderick Hudson* she almost systematically avails herself of a very beautiful girl's privilege to say things that would not be accepted from anybody else, but this, like almost any statement one may make about her, must be subjected to endless qualification. Her "impartial frigidity" at her mother's ostentatious party is explicable by reference to her humiliation at being forced to assist at what she considers a disgraceful exhibition. Later she audaciously crashes a Grandoni party because she wishes to see Roderick's fiancée, Mary Garland, yet as late as *The Princess Casamassima* she is always nervous about fresh encounters. She is rude to the Prince from the beginning and probably would have been even without her mother's trying to force him upon her, for there is something in his personality which rouses her contempt. When Roderick asks to do her bust, she tells him frankly that she dislikes modern sculpture, and when her mother hesitates to answer him, she says that this is because Mrs. Light is wondering whether he expects to be paid or to pay her for the sitting. "You can always get something for it," she tells her mother. "You always get something for everything. I dare say that with patience you'll still get something even for me."

Her relations with Rowland Mallet are more interesting, revealing both her intense self-consciousness and self-centeredness and her dissatisfaction with herself and her way of life. In the beginning she analyzes his character by looking at his things, says she does not think she likes him, and asks him to give her an honest opinion of her own character in six months. But she does like him and trusts him and senses his quality, and it is not long before she is talking to him quite as frankly as she had talked to Madame Grandoni herself ("I'm not young; I've never been young! My mother took care of that. I was a little wrinkled old woman at ten") and asking him to prove her a better person than she thinks she is.

She has insight, then, into the characters of other people as well as her own. She senses the weaknesses of Roderick Hudson's character and even the limitations of his talent almost from the beginning, fearing that as he has gone up like a rocket he may well come down like a stick, and she is well aware of her own moral inferiority to both Mary Garland, of whose dislike of herself she is instantly and unresentfully aware, and Lady Aurora, who uncritically admires her. Certainly she is more perceptive about both these women than either is about her, but she knows too that Mary has no imagination and that she is too good a woman to interest Roderick very long.

In *The Princess Casamassima* she is still frank but less youthfully willful and less rude in the ordinary sense of the term, though perhaps she is also more ruthless. For all the emancipation she has now achieved from merely personal interests by identifying herself with a revolutionary movement, she seems less sensitive here in her relations with individuals; perhaps this is the price she has paid for widening her horizon. Hyacinth was not wrong when he discerned "a high insolence . . . lurking somewhere in the side-scenes of her nature," and indeed her own attempt to bolster his diffidence when she summons him from his obscurity and makes a friend of him is monstrous: "you cease to be insignificant," she says, "from the moment I've anything to do with you."

Yet she is never the conventional *femme fatale* in either book. Had she been "a rag and a bone and a hank of hair," she would have delighted to see Roderick risk his neck to get the flower for her in the Colosseum scene of Chapter XIII; instead, when he insanely undertakes this project on his own initiative, she is genuinely alarmed. But perhaps the most remarkable thing she does in either novel is when, after meeting Mary Garland, she breaks off her engagement with the Prince. Mary, she is sure, would not wed for interested motives, and she would like to take a lesson from her book. "I've done it. Begin to respect me!" Such is the message she sends Rowland Mallet, with whom she had talked about the matter beforehand. Eager as she is to stand well in his account, as well as in her own, she has no base motive for desiring this.

She backslides, as we know, when the knowledge of her illegitimacy forces her hand, and the results of her marriage are disastrous—for the Prince, for Roderick, and for herself. When Rowland sees her again after her marriage, her eyes are "almost tragic." "You've seen me at my best," she says. "I wish to tell you solemnly, I *was* sincere." From now on she means to "cultivate delight" and pass the time. "You remember I told you that I was in part the world's and the devil's. Now they've taken me all. It was their choice; may they never repent!" Though this statement is probably the extreme example of her characteristic self-dramatizing, it is true that she is never the same again. Certainly Roderick believes she intends to continue to trifle with him after her marriage, and certainly there is no excuse for her inviting him to follow her and the Prince to Interlaken. It is this invitation which leads directly to his final encounter with Rowland and to his death.

There can hardly be a character in American fiction concerning whose motives there has been more critical speculation than Christina Light. D. G. Halliburton, perhaps her most determined enemy, calls her "not a visionary but a destroyer," with "a selfish quality to her dedication," but Pelham Edgar too sees her as fundamentally insincere and speaks of her "tainted idealism" and "theatrical enthusiasms," and Miss Grenander describes her life in *The Princess Casa-massima* as "one long seeking after sensation." To Lionel Trilling she is similarly "a perfect drunkard of reality" who is "ever drawn to look for stronger and stronger drams." Mildred Hartsock stresses her contradictions; she is "never quite genuine and never quite *not* genuine," while Bruce McElderry finds in her "a convincing combination of whim and principle; she is too shrewd to be wholly naïve, but too undisciplined to be an effective revolutionary." Louis Auchincloss in effect throws up the sponge by thinking that James never quite made up his mind about her, and W. J. Harvey sees him caught between the impulse to dignify her and the impulse to degrade her. Quentin Anderson and Richard Poirier are more psychological. Christina is trying, says Anderson, "to destroy the image for which she has sold her soul—and ultimately to destroy herself," and Poirier finds that "in her search for some ideal of a noble self-realization" she "assumes different moral and dramatic postures in the way an actress might assume a given role."[6]

The doubts of the critics are shared—and were antic-ipated—by other characters in the novel. Even Lady Aurora, though captivated by Christina, asks Hyacinth, "Does she really care for the poor?" and Hyacinth himself has a sense of tour de force in the sacrifices she makes for the revolu-tionary cause, granting that "if her attempt to combine plain living with high thinking were all a burlesque it was at least

[6] See D. G. Halliburton, "Self and Secularization in *The Princess Casamassima*," *MFS*, XI (1965–66), 116–28; Pelham Edgar, *Henry James, Man and Author* (HM, 1927); M. E. Grenander, "Henry James's *Cappricciosa*: Christina Light in *Roderick Hudson* and *The Princess Casamassima*," *PMLA*, LXXXV (1960), 309–19; Mildred E. Hartsock, "*The Princess Casamassima*: The Politics of Power," *Studies in the Novel*, I (1969), 297–309; Bruce R. McElderry, Jr., *Henry James* (Twayne, 1965); W. J. Harvey, *Character and the Novel* (Chatto and Windus, 1965), 81–89; Quentin Anderson, *The American Henry James* (RUP, 1957); Richard Poirier, *The Comic Sense of Henry James* (OUP, 1960). George Monteiro, "The Campaign of Henry James's Disinherited Princess," *English Studies*, XLV (1964), 442–54, defends Chris-tina against her severer critics.

the most finished entertainment she had yet offered him," yet obviously thinking of her as something like Marie Antoinette at the Petit Trianon. Paul Muniment shares this impression, feeling that, for one who claims to have sold everything to give it to the poor, she appears to have a good deal left. Her husband is still supporting her, and she gets a grim pleasure out of using his money to finance the revolution, but a number of critics, and Muniment too, feel sure that after he cuts off her funds she will cave in and go back to him, throwing in her hand here as she did when her mother played her trump card before her marriage. This is not certain, of course, and if she does, one must feel sincerely sorry for both parties. We do learn, however, that Christina has kept some things in reserve, and Madame Grandoni tells the Prince that she will never be able to hold the revolutionary line or any other indefinitely but must surely bore herself to death before the situation comes to a head.

The doubts and questions about Christina's sincerity in *The Princess Casamassima* center about her relationship to the revolutionary cause and to Hyacinth Robinson. I believe that in the usual sense of the term she is completely sincere in both aspects, though her sincerity, like everything else about her, must be interpreted in terms of the extraordinary complexity and volatility of her nature. What James wrote of her in *Roderick Hudson* is quite as applicable to the Princess: "It was Christina's constant practice to remind you of the complexity of her character, of the subtlety of her mind, by her troubled faculty of seeing everything in a dozen different lights."

There can be no question of the commitment she has made to the revolution or the closeness of her contacts with unquestioned revolutionaries. She says she wants to be in a place of danger, and Paul Muniment, who ought to know, tells her she is in up to her neck and may succeed in getting herself hanged. Upon first approaching Hyacinth, in her attempt to learn to know "the people" through him, she begs him to trust her and not to believe that she is amusing herself by "peeping and running away." She believes the ground is heaving under a fool's paradise and stands ready to give up her own advantages for the cause. Her vision of the human predicament shows grasp and competence, and her presentation of it is, upon its own terms, unanswerable. "There is less and less work in the world, and there are more and more people to do the little there is. The old ferocious selfishness *must* come down. They won't come down gracefully, so they must just be assisted."[7] In the end she even turns against art as savagely as fanatical religionists have sometimes turned against it. One cannot serve both God and mammon. Hungry people need bread before beauty; when justice has been achieved, beauty will follow. When her husband calls Christina a devil for her revolutionary activities, Madame Grandoni, who has no sympathy whatever with her views, replies that she is not a devil because she is trying to do good.

Her relations with Hyacinth are as capricious as everything else about her. When she first receives him at Medley, she seems like an actress performing for him alone. In a sense she turns from him to Muniment before the end, and though she has never been, in the proper sense of the term, Hyacinth's lover, her condescension toward the little bastard bookbinder, as we are so often reminded that he is, has been sufficiently great so that he may well be excused for feeling that he has suffered a betrayal. But once she knows he has received his "call" to kill the Duke, she pulls every string at her command to save him, and the book ends, after those tremendous closing chapters of mounting menace and

---

[7] James shared Christina's convictions concerning the rottenness of contemporary society and politics, though not of course her willingness to encourage revolution. It is interesting that in Chapter XXXIV of *The Princess* Christina tells Lady Aurora that "a great new deal is destined to take place." This was three years before Mark Twain's famous use of "new deal" in *A Connecticut Yankee*, which is supposed to have supplied Franklin D. Roosevelt with the phrase.

tension, with her bending in anguish over his bleeding body. Hyacinth himself had done her justice in this aspect at a comparatively early stage; she was earnest for herself, he thought, but not for him, and therefore she wished to "frustrate the redemption of his vow." Like a true woman, she thinks of him, in other words, as himself and not merely as a cog in the revolutionary machine. She tells Paul Muniment, that perfect careerist revolutionary, that she loves Hyacinth very much and wonders why, if his job needs to be done, somebody else could not do it just as well! If necessary, she would even do it herself. And if this is feminine logic, it must be admitted that she puts her finger on the chink in Muniment's armor when she asks him why he does not do it himself and that when she asks, "And can you see a dear friend whirled away like that?" she marks the difference between Heart and No-Heart or between Muniment and herself.[8]

It is true, as many critics have insisted, that in fostering the revolution, Christina is, in a sense, still working at her own problem. Actually we did not need to wait for any critic to point this out. She herself tells Hyacinth that everything in her life has disappointed her and that everything in her world is "corrupt and dreary." It is not quite clear whether it is Hyacinth or James who tells us that "her behaviour . . . was more addressed to relieving herself than to relieving others" and that she felt that "to do something for others was not only so much more human—it was so much more amusing!" For all that, it is to her credit that she is amused by social amelioration rather than by social exploitation, as so many others have been, though I think it is also to her discredit that she seems willing to embrace violent and immoral means to bring about desirable changes. It is emphatically not to her discredit, however, that her own personal needs and interests are enlisted in her work. This is

[8] On Muniment's character see P. K. Grover, "Two Modes of Possessing— Conquest and Appreciation: *The Princess Casamassima* and *L'Education Sentimentale*," *Modern Language Review*, LXVI (1971), 760–61.

true of everybody who works at anything in a vital way, even of the saints, for the simple reason that this is the only way in which anything vital can be done. Even Lady Aurora finds in her own work for the poor an escape from a way of life which bores her, and Morris Bishop has written of Saint Francis of Assisi that "the lepers revolted him; he served them out of spiritual bravado, to discipline his own repulsion. Kissing the leper's sores, he kissed his own." Nevertheless, the anarchist leaders are, from their own point of view, quite correct in mistrusting Christina at the end, not only, or even mainly, because she is, as Madame Grandoni calls her, a *capricciosa* but also, and much more, because, as her attempt to save Hyacinth shows, she is a human being, an individual, and a woman, and she cannot completely submerge or destroy herself in a "movement." Paul Muniment can and does, but the price he pays is that he becomes something of a monster in the process ("if I were on the top," he says, "I'd stick"), and a woman who could achieve anything comparable would be even more of a monster.

The basic truth about Christina Light, then, is that at heart she is not a cynical adventuress but a romantic idealist, and for this very reason she is far more dangerous, both to herself and to others, than any mere adventuress could be. This is the quality which, despite her immensely greater sophistication, she shares with Hyacinth (whose own romanticism achieves at times an almost mystical quality), and this is the bond that unites them. Madame Grandoni senses all this in *Roderick Hudson* days:

"She's certain to do every now and then something disinterested and sincere. . . . She needs to think well of herself; she knows a fine character easily when she meets one; she hates to suffer by comparison, even though the comparison be made by herself alone. . . . But of course she must always do that at somebody's expense—not one of her friends but must sooner or later pay. . . . Her attitudes and pretences may sometimes worry one, but I think we have most to pray to be guarded from her sincerities."

With this her natural father, the Cavalière Giacosa, substantially agrees when he tells Rowland Mallet that Christina is a *drôle de fille:*

"She has many romantic ideas. She would be quite capable of interesting herself seriously in a remarkable young man like your friend and doing her utmost to discourage a splendid suitor like the Prince. She would act sincerely and she would go very far. But it would be unfortunate for the remarkable young man, for at the last she'd go back!"

But she always does suffer by the comparisons she herself makes, and she always does "go back." This is her tragedy and the misfortune of everyone who comes near her. As a girl she was fascinated by Roderick Hudson and hoped vainly to find greatness in him. As a frustrated revolutionary, she recognized a kind of inhuman greatness in Paul Muniment even while, in Hyacinth's interest, she was doing her utmost to batter it down. When she reproached Roderick for lacking the courage to choose and being willing to bear the penalty for his choice, she was castigating herself; he was no good to her, nobody could be any good to her who was not greatly better than she was. If she had been able to junk her ideals and accept herself for what she was (as her mother did), she would have been a much worse woman than she was, and there must have been much less hope for her as a spiritual being. But she would probably also have put much less pain into the world. Henry James was as subtle about his *femme fatale* as he was about everything else.[9]

[9] William Veeder, who develops a comparison and contrast between Christina and Emmeline de Mirveil in Victor Cherbuliez's *Le Roman d'une honnête femme* (*Henry James–The Lessons of the Master*, 113–17), remarks: "The connections between Christina and Emmeline not only increase our awareness of James's debt to Cherbuliez; they also help us understand how James first transforms a conventional type into a great character." Veeder's is one of the most sympathetic studies we have of Christina.

V. BRIGHT PARTICULAR STAR

MIRIAM ROOTH

THE THEME OF *The Tragic Muse* (1890) is the conflict or opposition of values between art and "the world," but only the actress Miriam Rooth carries the artist's banner triumphantly. She is not the only person in the novel who is aesthetically sensitive. Nick Dormer's calling is painting, and there can be no real question about his talent. Miriam herself tells him that "you're the sincere artist so much more than I" and prophesies that "you'll do things that will hand on your name after my screeching is happily over." The problem he faces is more difficult than Miriam's, and he is required to make a more difficult choice than is ever presented to her. Certainly his sincerity would seem to be sufficiently attested by his resigning his seat in Parliament to devote himself to his art, even though this involves giving up both Julia Dallow and the settlement which the wealthy Mr. Carteret, who cannot see the pencil and the brush as the weapons of a gentleman, would otherwise have made upon him. Yet he fails to make a real commitment and never achieves genuine faith in himself as an artist, politician, or lover. Mr. Carteret is not wholly obtuse when he calls Nick flighty, and Nick's own insight is true when he sees himself as two different human beings. He allows his family and Julia to steer him into politics without being sure that he wants either it or her, and having given it up, he fails to devote himself to art with anything like the single-minded devotion that jealous mistress imperatively demands. And if it is early in the novel that he tells his sister Biddy that he is a duffer and a "wretched broken reed," he is not sure even at the end that he has anything more than facility. It is precisely this kind of wavering that is impossible for Miriam, and her freedom from it redeems all her faults. When she cries, "The world be hanged! The stage, or anything of that sort—I mean one's artistic conscience, one's true faith—comes first," she is not boasting but merely stating the principle of her being. James himself felt that he had failed with Nick. He seems to me, on the contrary, a successful characterization on his own terms, but he will not do for a hero, and he might have imperiled the unity of the book if he had.

Nick's sister, Biddy, is also an artist of some talent, but she does not play a very important part in the novel. The other two persons who understand art are Gabriel Nash and Peter Sherringham. Nash is a critic, a connoisseur, and a trifler, a man of excellent taste but without creative faculty. He seems to have been influenced in some aspects by Oscar Wilde, whom James called "repulsive and fatuous" and "an unclean beast." (Wilde *was* creative, of course, but James apparently granted him only a cheap facility.) The particular qualities which repelled James in Wilde do not appear in Nash, however, and James lends him a touch of poetry at the end when, like Miss M. in Walter de la Mare's *Memoirs of a Midget,* he simply disappears; he had already called himself indestructible and immortal and had prophesied that he would never grow old.[1]

Peter Sherringham is quite another story. Miriam's guide and mentor in her earlier stages, he ends as a kind of aesthetic abortionist when, having aided notably in the development

[1] Gabriel Nash has inspired a surprising amount of comment: see Oscar Cargill, "Mr. James's Aesthetic Mr. Nash," *NCF*, XII (1957), 177–87, and "Gabriel Nash—Somewhat Less Than Angel?" *NCF*, XIV (1959–60), 231–39; Lyall H. Powers, "James's *The Tragic Muse*—Ave Atque Vale," *PMLA*, LXXXIII (1958), 270–74, and "Mr. James's Mr. Nash Again," *NCF*, XIII (1959), 341–49; William F. Hall, "Gabriel Nash: 'Famous Centre' of *The Tragic Muse*," *NCF*, XXI (1966–67), 167–84; Ronald Wallace, "Gabriel Nash: Henry James's Comic Spirit," *NCF*, XXVIII (1973),

of her genius, he tries to kill it by fatuously proposing that she give up her career and subordinate herself to him as the wife of an ambassador. That he should rather attach himself to her, though she is already an established actress while he has just secured his first foothold in the diplomatic world, he regards as preposterous, describing it contemptuously as a matter of holding her shawl and her smelling bottle. They debate the matter at length in Chapter XLVI, but Miriam learns little that she had not known before, and she never shows more penetration than when she tells Nick that Peter is "trying to serve God and Mammon, and I don't know how God will come off" and again that he "wants to enjoy every comfort and to save every appearance, and all without making a scrap of sacrifice. He expects others—me, for instance —to make all the sacrifices."

Though Miriam Rooth is the center of *The Tragic Muse* and the book focuses on her, James has chosen to portray her objectively. "I never 'go behind' Miriam; only poor Sherringham goes, a great deal, and Nick Dormer goes a little, and the author, while they so waste wonderment, *goes behind them.*" Surely Edmund Wilson was wrong in his feeling that "James does not show us the inside of Miriam Rooth . . . because he does not know . . . what the insides of such people are like," and Oscar Cargill was right when he declared that "the novelist was thoroughly acquainted with his heroine, inside and out. He knew her as he knew an artist, as he knew himself."

He may nevertheless have found it difficult to give her his entire sympathy because of his own ambivalent attitude

---

220–24; Robert S. Baker, "Gabriel Nash's 'House of Strange Idols': Aestheticism in *The Tragic Muse*," *TSLL*, XV (1973), 149–66. Baker sees Nash as symbolizing the aestheticism of the 1880's. "Gabriel stands not only as an indictment of Walter Pater, but as an indictment of the aesthete, who despite his intelligent social criticism would abandon society and life itself, devoting his mind and soul to a peculiarly Jamesian version of narcissism." The most surprising suggestion is that of Powers that there was much of James himself in Nash. See also Dorothea Krook, *The Ordeal of Consciousness in Henry James*, 83–87. Her comments on James's possible use of Wilde and others, including John La Farge, are particularly interesting.

toward the theater. Robert Louis Stevenson wrote James of *The Tragic Muse* that "he was at a loss to conceive how one could find an interest in anything so vulgar or pretend to gather fruit in so scrubby an orchard." We may be thankful that James himself was less obtuse, but it remains odd that the author of one of the greatest novels we have about the theater should have thought he needed to explain why it was necessary for him to present that institution "in another light than the satiric" or to assure Thomas Bailey Aldrich, when he was planning to serialize it in *The Atlantic Monthly*, that it would not be improper despite the elements of which it was composed. *The Tragic Muse* had as long roots in James's own life as anything he ever did. He had been stage-struck ever since, as he tells us in *A Small Boy and Others*, he had pored over the theatrical billboards in his youth, but he hemmed and hawed about the theater in his most distinguished and tentative fashion, and after the failure of his own attempt as a playwright, he was more and more inclined to be repelled by what his friend Mary Anderson[2] called the grease-paint side of her profession and to decide that though he still loved the drama, he hated the theater. He also agreed with another actress friend, Fanny Kemble, that the histrionic gift was a thing apart from other endowments, implying no

---

[2] Cargill, *The Novels of Henry James*, 184–86, makes a strong case for the influence upon *The Tragic Muse* of Mrs. Humphry Ward's first novel, *Miss Bretherton* (1884), which took its point of departure from Mary Anderson. Cargill further conjectures "cautious touches from the Goncourts' Manette Salomon, a Jewish model, and from Edmond de Goncourt's creation of an actress in *Le Faustin*." Edward Stone, *The Battle of the Books*, suggests the possible influence upon *The Tragic Muse* of William Black's *Macleod of Dare*, which James reviewed in *The Nation* in 1878. Though the two books are entirely different, both have a virtuous actress as heroine, and Stone has an interesting analysis of the resemblances and differences between the two characters. Though there are no resemblances between Miriam Rooth's personality and that of Mary Anderson, D. J. Gordon and John Stokes discuss the *Miss Bretherton* matter at some length in "The Reference of *The Tragic Muse*," in John A. Goode, ed., *The Air of Reality: New Essays on Henry James* (Methuen, 1972). This valuable book also contains discussions of *What Maisie Knew* (by Juliet Nitchell), *The Awkward Age* (by Margaret Walters), *The Wings of the Dove* (by John Goode), and *The Golden Bowl* (by Gabriel Pearson).

general superiority of either mind or character, and he seems to have been unpleasantly impressed by the self-centeredness of theater people, though it is at least a question whether writers are not quite as self-centered.

One cannot but ask why James chose to make Miriam Jewish, or rather, since her English mother is gentile, half-Jewish (her late father was a stockbroker named Roth, with an interest in aesthetic matters). James may have seen Miriam's ancestry as one means of accounting for her artistic bias, or he may have thought of her Jewishness as one more means of distinguishing her from the other characters in developing the art-versus-the-world antithesis of his novel.[3] At one point she herself jumps at Peter's emphasis upon her Jewishness "as he was destined to see later she would ever jump at anything that might make her more interesting or striking," but this was not because of any Jewish loyalty as such but rather because Rachel, a Jew, had been the kind of great actress that Miriam wishes to be. Though James came too late to see Rachel, there are a number of significant references to her both in the novel and in his critical writing,[4] and it is clear that he was interested in her. He did of course see, and often commented upon, her great successor, Sarah Bernhardt, who, like Miriam, was Jewish in part. Some of James's references to Madame Sarah are slighting. She could be "painfully shrill and modern," and there was "something sceptical and cynical" about her. As "the muse of the newspaper," she is clearly inferior to both Rachel and Desclée. She profits by the idiosyncrasies of her time and succeeds even more as a celebrity than as an artist. But he also called her "a very interesting actress" who had "perennial freshness" and "extraordinary intelligence and versatility." She

[3]Leo B. Levy, "Henry James and the Jews: A Critical Study," *Commentary*, XXVI (1958), 243–49, not only deals with Miriam but also collects material on James's other references to Jews. Mr. Levy's conclusions are reasonable and temperate.

[4]See Allan Wade, ed., *Henry James, The Scenic Art: Notes on Acting and the Drama, 1872–1890* (RUP, 1948).

was "charming, strange, eccentric, imaginative" and "one of the great figures of the day. . . . She understands the art of motion and attitude as no one else does, and her extraordinary personal grace never fails her" (it was never to do so, even when she was nearly eighty and had lost a leg). There are only oblique references to her in *The Tragic Muse*, but she seems clearly in the author's mind when he speaks of the unfortunate effect upon an actress of playing before undiscriminating foreigners who do not understand her language and in what he writes about Miriam's success in managing the press, for Bernhardt, like Mary Garden, was one of the greatest public-relations women the theater has known. Surely the least that can be said is that Madame Sarah's fame and that of Rachel before her did not make the Jewish element in Miriam Rooth seem less appropriate and convincing. Nevertheless, more than one commentator has suggested that she might simply have taken both her given name and her Jewishness from Hawthorne's Miriam in *The Marble Faun.*

Like Marie Bashkirtseff (and unlike Sarah and Rachel), Miriam is fond of insisting that she is "a good girl," in which, it seems hardly necessary to state, she differs notably from the protagonists in many novels of the stage. To be sure, there may be a touch here of the vulgarity with which she is sometimes reproached in other connections, since to feel the necessity to proclaim one's virtue is, by implication, to admit the possibility that it might be called in question. It is amusing that William James, who was nothing if not critical of his brother's work, thought *The Tragic Muse* "original, wonderful, delightful and admirable," the best thing Henry had ever done, because everyone in it was so "human and good." The appearance of this novel, Howells' *Hazard of New Fortunes*, and "last, *but by no means least*," his own *Psychology* must, he thought, make 1890 "the great epochal year in American literature"!

Miriam's virtue is another example of James's disdain of easy contrasts: he carefully avoids bringing a moral differ-

ence (in the narrower sense of the term) into his consideration of the basic conflict which is his theme and thereby confusing the issue. To be sure, Peter Sherringham once reflects
of Miriam that she "was neither fish nor flesh; one had with
her neither the guarantees of one's own class nor the immun-
ities of hers," but Peter does not turn out to be a high authority on the subject. The same avoidance of easy contrast may
be seen in James's treatment of Julia Dallow. Julia not only
fails utterly to understand art but actually hates it, her notion
of a painter being that he is a man who enjoys having half-
dressed women "lolling" about his studio. For that matter,
she has no deep understanding of politics either, which she
values mainly as a means of power and the proper occupa-
tion for an English gentleman. Yet, for all her obtuseness
and material-mindedness, Julia is not "bad." Though she puts
a degraded interpretation upon everything that has to do
with art (never really distinguishing between creativity and
mere connoisseurship), she still has the wit to perceive the
irreconcilability between it and the world, and though she is
repellent in her opening scenes, we cannot but sympathize
with her suffering and recognize the sincerity of her love for
Nick when she bravely recognizes the necessity of their parting.

Miriam's harping on her virtue is, moreover, a little misleading, for though she is at no point even tempted to surrender it, she is not obsessed by it, or by morality as such, as her
mother is. For Mrs. Rooth there are no virtues except the
"moral" virtues, for she understands nothing else, yet, in the
larger sense, her daughter is a far more deeply moral, more
committed person. Mrs. Rooth enters the book as almost the
stock "stage mother" of an aspiring actress daughter. There
is nothing she will not do for her girl, and it is not the least of
that young lady's virtues that, though she fully understands
her mother's embarrassing gaucherie, she serenely pursues
her own course of development and never ceases to be grateful to Mrs. Rooth or dreams of reproaching her for her limi-

tations. The mother, proclaiming her respectability "with a misguided intensity," would not like to see her daughter enact a really bad woman, but Miriam perceives that everything in life is grist to the actor's mill; for her the world "bristles" with suggestions for what she wishes to do, and she can admire the "hard polish" and "inimitable surface" of an actress like Mlle Voisin, even though she knows it covers depths she has never plumbed. "To be too respectable to go where things are done best is in my opinion to be very vicious indeed; and to do them badly in order to preserve your virtue is to fall into a grossness more shocking than any other." As far as the book is concerned, the development of Miriam's gift is all Mrs. Rooth has lived for, yet she understands and values it so little that at the end she would have her give it all up to marry Peter Sherringham. For the girl, on the other hand, "the honours, the orders, the stars and garters" are meaningless. Though she recognizes all the limitations of the theatrical profession, her commitment to the way of art is, for herself, absolute and unwavering.

"Good girl" though she is, Miriam has, as I have already indicated, often been accused of vulgarity—"immense egotistical vitality," "shallow, coarse manner," "ruthless professional ability and competence." She can be pert and brusque. Her conversation with Biddy about Nick in Chapter VIII causes Peter to fear that she is "something of a brute," yet she is touching again in her frank admission and discussion of her limitations with him immediately afterwards. Even her mother says that she is very direct and considers her rude to her colleagues after she has established herself. She is almost irresistible in following her star and going after what she wants, which is shown not only in the use she makes of Peter himself but in the way she woos Madame Carré, who at the outset had been quite unimpressed by her, and induces that hard-grained old actress to accept her as a pupil. Yet her lack of petty vanity is even more striking than her nerve. A lesser person would have been so piqued by Carré's judgment as to refuse to accept anything from her, to say nothing of seeking a favor. Miriam knows that Carré has what she needs, and to get at it she is even willing to be abused.

"She has been back to see me twice," Madame Carré tells Peter; "she doesn't go the longest way round. She charges me like a grenadier. . . . If she doesn't succeed it won't be for want of knowing how to thump at doors." Miriam makes the great actress recite for her: "I don't know how—and she sits there gaping at me with her big eyes. They look like open pockets!" At first she is only able to give a coarse imitation of her instructress, but she shows her mettle when, upon Madame Carré's showing her how she has done it, "making this imitation of an imitation the drollest thing conceivable," Miriam drops exhausted on a sofa, stares "flushed and wild," then, grasping the point, gives way "to pleasure, to interest and large laughter." In her own mind the battle is won at an early stage, and if she seems brash when she tells Peter that Madame Carré will want to keep her for the French stage and not let her go back to England, she is justified by the event, for this is just what, in the final outcome, the old actress wants to do. Once having grasped "a fine understanding . . . of how bad she was," Miriam develops rapidly, and it is only some thirty pages after her rash prophecy that we find Madame Carré telling Peter that, for the first time in her life, she was wrong in her initial impression. To Miriam herself she says, "You've learned all I've taught you, but where the devil have you learned what I haven't?" Fortunately the girl is proof against flattery as well as discouragement: "I'm not so very good yet. I'm only in the right direction." And she retains too her saving independence: "I shall have to work it out, what I shall be."

After fortune has begun to smile upon her, Miriam does develop a certain swagger and a liking for "superlatives and tremendously strong objections," so that Peter thinks being married to her would be like being "hooked to a Catherine-wheel and whiz round in flame and smoke." She is quite willing to be looked at ("if you're going to be an actress you must get used to being looked at"); she also becomes something of a name dropper. "I don't read the papers," she says frankly, "unless there's something in them about myself." Not only does she expect to dominate her colleagues; she soon finds herself the central figure in any assembly of which she is a part.

Some taint of vulgarity Miriam inevitably acquires from her surroundings. During her early years this was the kind of vulgarity inseparable from the Rooths' kind of poverty, living from hand to mouth and meeting people in cafés because they had no place to receive them. It is an immense testimonial to the girl's having been made for her art that she was drawn so irresistibly to the theater even before she had money enough to see many plays; later she revels in the photographs that are showered upon her as a celebrity because "in all my life I never had but one poor little *carte-de-visite*, when I was sixteen, in a plaid frock, with the banks of a river, at three francs a dozen." And if it is destiny and devotion to art and to her star that draws her to the theater, who can blame her if she also welcomes this means of escape so that she and her mother can "stop living like pigs"?

It has been pointed out that her career brings her into more, not less, bohemian surroundings. Her mother is distressed by her toleration of some of her professional associates, especially the *cabotine*, "that dreadful Miss Rover." But under the circumstances presented, Miriam would have needed to be a brute to repel the advances of this actress, and there is no evidence that she was corrupted by her. "What did she care who came and who didn't, and what was to be gained by receiving half the snobs in London?" And she tells her mother, no doubt justly, that all her improprieties are of the mind.[5]

---

[5] There is an odd passage in Chapter XXXI: "They all smoked cigarettes in the garden." Since both Miriam and Mrs. Rooth were present on this occasion, the "all" would seem to embrace them, but since neither one is ever spoken of as smoking elsewhere, the author's intent seems doubtful.

Miriam's self-centeredness and the way she brings everything in her world to focus upon her particular interests is undeniable, however, and testifies to James's understanding of the artist's nature. It was part of his idea to give "a picture of some of the personal consequences of the art-appetite swollen to voracity." But she is no more unconscious of her weaknesses along this line than she is of either the limitations or the rackety side of her profession. Some, no doubt, must find her apologies and protestations as vulgar as her proclamation of her virtue, and I think a good case could be made for James having included too much of this, but at least it is clear that she has not been swallowed up by an unconscious egotism. She knows she gives a bad impression "perpetually chattering about my vulgar shop. What will you have when one's a vulgar shop-girl?" Perhaps her taste is bad when she continues:

"I'm not so taken up with myself, in the low vulgar sense, as you think. I'm not such a base creature. I'm capable of gratitude, I'm capable of affection. One may live in paint and tinsel, but one isn't absolutely without a soul. Yes, I've got one, . . . though I do smear my face and grin at myself in the glass and practise my intonations."

Nevertheless, what she says is true, and I am sure James knew it was; if not, why did he allow Nick's mother, the aristocratic Lady Agnes, to emerge as the true vulgarian of the novel in her disappointment over the relinquishment of her son's political career and the cash bonuses that would have come with it, her worldliness, her conniving in her own interest and that of her family? Indeed the only relative of Nick's who shows any delicacy in this crisis is his sister, Biddy, and she is herself an artist.

Miriam is introduced to the reader of *The Tragic Muse* under heavy handicaps. We see her first in the art gallery in Chapter II without knowing who she is. She has "a pale face, a low forehead, and thick dark hair," is badly, even eccentrically, dressed, and gives such an impression of intensity that Biddy is almost frightened by her. And this is all we learn of her in Book I except that she is eager to go on the stage but cannot act and that she is Jewish and "splendidly stupid" (though she knows several languages).

The accusation of stupidity is itself stupid, though, like everything else about her, Miriam's intelligence is of a highly specialized sort. Despite her language proficiency (which is more like what one might expect of a singer than a dramatic actress), she is no scholar. It is to her credit that she takes no interest in the trashy novels which her mother devours, but she reads nothing else either, being indeed "on almost irreconcilable terms with the printed page." In the art galleries, she has remarkable, though quite undisciplined, "flashes of perception," always responding to things she thinks she can use. But she is remarkably shrewd and intuitive always, with an instinctive awareness of people's reactions to her, even before she has anything objective to base it on.

Our first real meeting with her is in Chapter VII, where she recites for Madame Carré. This time Peter finds "a strange strong tragic beauty" in her and tells Nick he must paint her as the Tragic Muse. But her voice is colorless and her reading monotonous. She makes mush of de Musset in a bad imitation of a celebrated actress whom she had heard declaim his verses, and all four of her recitations are "funereal," "artlessly rough," droning and dragging in the manner of a bad pulpit exhortation. Though Madame Carré concedes that she has "rude force," privately she thinks her loud, coarse, and stupid and sees no future for her. Yet we are made to sympathize with her because of her heroic determination and the terrible strain she is under. "The girl was very white; she huddled there, silent and rigid, frightened to death, staring, expressionless," and she has all she can do to hold back her tears. On top of all else, she has the handicap of her mother, who is never more gauche than on this occasion. All in all, she is probably more touching in this chapter than any James heroine since Daisy Miller.

She seems less sympathetic at first in Chapter VIII, where she reads for Peter's friends, shaking her hair down and "flowing" so "copiously" that Peter wonders how he can shut her off and we are embarrassed for her. Julia Dallow, who does not care for tragedy, thinks she is "like a cow who has kicked over the milking pail," but Julia has so little judgment in aesthetic matters that she also thinks that what she heard was probably "extremely fine." Yet, in an odd sort of way, even Miriam's blunders are made to redound to her advantage and raise her in our esteem, for the difference between her behavior here and at Madame Carré's shows what she respects and testifies to the soundness of her values. "She has been deadly afraid of the old actress, but was not a bit afraid of a cluster of *femmes du monde,*" who are rather afraid of her. Two worlds, therefore, skillfully confront each other in this scene. Miriam's performance, "with its badness, the absence of criticism," may be "indecent," but it is alive. What is opposed to her is dead.

A novelist who writes a novel about the development of a novelist can give the reader specimens of his genius (provided he himself has the power to create them), but obviously a novelist who writes about a composer cannot enable us to hear his music, nor can the novelist who writes about an actress take us to witness her performances. If he can indicate the steps in her progress, he cannot show in any detail how she achieves them. When Miriam reenters *The Tragic Muse* after an absence in Chapter XIX, "she had found the lock to her box of treasures"; hearing her do Shakespeare's Constance, Peter now realizes for the first time how stupid he himself had been when he thought her stupid. By Chapter XXIV she is famous and Nash tells Nick about her, and when immediately thereafter she comes to Nick's studio to be painted, she is a "brave free rather grand creature" who, having "shaken off her clumsiness, the rudeness and crudeness that had made him pity her," now fills the room with "unexampled presence." There is another great gap before her first appearance as Juliet toward the end, and this is as far as we take her in her development.

If James cannot describe her acting, he can and does indicate its nature by describing the effect it had upon her audiences. We hear more especially about her voice—"the richest then to be heard on earth"—than about any other particular endowment, and it is tempting here to discern another reference to Sarah Bernhardt, in whose throat was carried the most glorious actress voice within human memory. "Its richness was quite independent of the words she might pronounce or the poor fable they might subserve." No wonder her Juliet was "an exquisite image of young passion and young despair, expressed in the truest divinest music that had ever poured from tragic lips. The great childish audience, gaping at her points, expanded before her like a lap to catch flowers."

It is difficult not to see Bernhardt again in Miriam's poetic style, which was at once passionate and otherworldly, as Sarah's always was. "Miriam's performance was a thing alive, with a power to change, to grow, to develop, to beget new forms of the same life." She was "beauty, melody, truth; she was passion and persuasion and tenderness. She caught up the obstreperous play in soothing entwining arms and, seeming to tread the air in the flutter of her robe, carried it into the high places of poetry, of art, of style." Thus she transports her auditor out of the world of "ugly fact" and into the realm of universal values. And this, surely, is a characteristically Jamesian as well as Bernhardtian note.

The plays in which her first great successes are won are trash, but since Miriam knows it, she is not corrupted by them. She knows well that she has been "pitchforked into the *mêlée* and into the most improbable fame" at the very time when what she needs is "five quiet years of hard all-round work in a perfect company, with a manager more perfect still, playing five hundred things and never being heard of at all." With London at her feet, she never forgets "that my glories are still to come, that I may fizzle out and that my little success of to-day is perhaps a mere flash in the pan," yet she goes on, "indifferent to the noise one's going to make" and clinging to "my idea, even if it's destined to betray me and sink me." While as for "the poor old 'person,' " which those who disparage acting as the most personal of the arts talk so much about, "it's only the envelope of the idea, it's only our machinery, . . . and in proportion as the idea takes hold of us do we become unconscious of the clumsy body."

The critic who thought Miriam's interest in the theater "governed by cynical ambition" certainly managed one of the most curious judgments on record; the truth is rather, as Elizabeth Stevenson expressed it, that her career was "a continual sacrifice of one personal and human advantage after another." She relishes her own performances and those of others, and one must be pretty hard-hearted not to share the innocent and overwhelming joy she experiences once she has achieved her emancipation not only from the cruelly constricting social and financial limitations of her early life but, more importantly, from all that had hitherto limited her full development. Once she has learned how, she acts off stage as well as on, receives her admirers like a gracious queen, and makes virtually the same kind of "entrances" into drawing rooms as into her "scenes" on the stage.

She has the same protean quality as an actress which, in a much more magnificent way, has always troubled such dogmatists as Shaw and Tolstoy in Shakespeare; coming closer to Miriam's own world, she recalls Mary Garden's illuminating statement that she put so much into her life on the stage that her private life was empty. Peter Sherringham, who of all the other characters in the novel understands Miriam best and least, is sometimes troubled by the uncomfortable feeling that she has no nature of her own and that her most genuine emotions are those she feigns, her trouble being not that she has no character but rather that she has a hundred. "It struck him abruptly that a woman whose only being was to . . . make believe she had any and every variety of being you might like . . . and whose identity resided in the continuity of her personations . . . was a kind of monster in whom of necessity there would be nothing to 'be fond' of, because there would be nothing to take hold of." Basically, he feels, her sincerity is "the sincerity of execution," her genuineness "the genuineness of doing it well. . . . She uttered the things she felt as if they were snatches of old playbooks, and really felt them the more because they sounded so well." But he concludes significantly that this "didn't prevent their really being as good feelings as those of anybody else," and, for all his obtuseness in some aspects, he still grants her "the truth of gentleness and generosity." Miriam's domination hurts nobody. On the contrary, it is through expressing herself to the utmost that she expresses others also and brings beauty and enrichment into others' lives. And this, much more than the fact that she does not go to bed with men, is the final justification for her claim that she is a "good girl."

Though love plays a very minor role in James's account of Miriam Rooth's life, her complete dedication of herself to her art is as well illustrated in this connection as anywhere else. The actor Basil Dashwood, to whom her marriage toward the end is reported rather than described, is hardly characterized at all, and we do not know him well enough to be able to judge whether she has chosen wisely. It is obvious that he is not her equal as an artist, but the marriage may have a better chance for survival on that account, for certainly their careers will not come into conflict. Gabriel Nash had remarked that "she ought to marry the prompter or the box-keeper. Then it would be all right. I think they generally do, don't they?" Dashwood is not that, but he may well fulfill the same function in her life, not merely holding her shawl and her smelling bottle, as Peter Sherringham contemptuously describes what she might expect from a husband, but giving her rather what she herself speaks of as "the whole precious service, the protection and encouragement, for which a woman in my position might be indebted" to a man who truly understands and cherishes her work.

In his Preface to the New York Edition, James indicates not only that Miriam might have married Nick if he had made any effort to win her but even that, because he practiced an art which she respected in some aspects more than her own, she might even have been capable of giving up the stage to do it, though this last, I, at least, find it difficult to believe. In any case, this is exactly what she will not do when Peter Sherringham proposes to make her an ambassador's wife; if art can be sacrificed for art, it cannot be sacrificed for the world, and Peter's offense is all the more heinous in her eyes because he, having made such large and important contributions to her development, might have been expected to understand and value her art beyond any other man she knows. "How you hate us!" she cries—"us" being the whole artist tribe (he had just called her type "bad, perverse, dangerous"). "Yes, at bottom, below your little cold taste, you *hate* us!"

Perhaps she has not always been quite so clear-sighted as this. Peter, indeed, has been under the impression that she preferred "men of the world—men of action" to artists of any kind, and it is true that she had "talked after the manner of a lovely Philistine" in expressing her disappointment when Nick gave up his parliamentary seat. Later she says she was not serious in such utterances, and this may well be true, since even here she was theater-centered: she had wanted him to win a cordon and a star so that he could then "come to see her in her *loge*: it would look so particularly well"! But there is no reason to assume that she may not have grown in insight as well as in her art, and the final choice she makes is surely decisive enough.

All in all, then, it seems fair to say that many critics have made much too much of Miriam Rooth's faults and paid insufficient tribute to her superb courage, perseverance, insight, and devotion. There are, to be sure, people who simply do not like actresses; such had better let her alone.[6] But she is one of the best, not the worst, of her breed, and though James himself seems a little hesitant about her at times, he does make it clear that he saw her as something very different from the "vivid monsters" in kind of Anatole France. We shall not overpraise her if we apply to her the immortal words of the Mount Auburn gravedigger at the grave of Charlotte Cushman: "She was considerable of a woman, for a playactress."

[6] Alan W. Bellringer, "*The Tragic Muse*: The Objective Center," *Journal of American Studies*, IV (1970–71), 73–89, for example, advances the odd thesis that "Throughout *The Tragic Muse* James is involved in questioning the value of success on the stage. This doubt adds everything to the poignancy of the sacrifices which Miriam Rooth both makes and extorts." Ernest H. Lockridge, "A Vision of Art: Henry James's *The Tragic Muse*," *MFS*, XII (1966), 83–92, also takes a dim view of her: "Miriam pays attention to things, it seems, only because she has an idea she can use them." At the end, "Art is all that is left. . . . It seems even to cancel out love." Lotus Snow has, however, some interesting commentary on Miriam in " 'The Prose and the Modesty of the Matter': James's Imagery for the Artist in *Roderick Hudson* and *The Tragic Muse*," *MFS*, XII (1966), 61–82, and John L. Kimmey, "*The Tragic Muse* and its Forerunners," *AL*, XLI (1969–70), 518–31, gives a good general critical study of the novel, arguing its superiority to both *The Bostonians* and *The Princess Casamassima*.

VI.   THE CONFLICT BETWEEN
LOVE AND HONOR
FLEDA VETCH

WHEN SARAH BERNHARDT was too much annoyed
by some of the more trying kinds of admirers with whom
a great actress is beset, she remarked that all the crazy
people in the world seemed to be attracted to her. She was
wrong. Some of them have always devoted themselves to
the elucidation of literature. The Bible (especially the apoc-
alyptic books) and Shakespeare (especially *Hamlet* and the
sonnets) have consistently drawn their share, and now that
James is "in" as a kind of modern scripture, he too has
manifested considerable magnetic power. Not many years
ago, this type of mind seemed irresistibly drawn to "The
Turn of the Screw," and if the worst is now over here, we
pay for it by the emergence of *The Spoils of Poynton* as a
strong runner-up.

Bernhardt's "crazy" would be a harsh and ill-mannered
as well as an inaccurate word to apply to such critics, whose
fault is not so much lack of intelligence as a wantonly perverse application of it. The impressionistic critics of the
nineteenth and early twentieth centuries, whom the modern
sophisticates hold in such contempt, were, to be sure, often
arbitrary enough, and we find Sir Arthur Quiller-Couch declaring frankly that few of us doubt that Shakespeare (and,
by implication, all other literature) is "what we can read
into it," which is an excellent statement of what scholarship
does not stand for. But what these people did casually and

arbitrarily, and comparatively tentatively and modestly, their successors do ponderously, deliberately, and arrogantly, setting up exorbitant claims of infallibility and developing elaborate (and oh! so tiresome) methods of "explication" and analysis. In practice, however, these "methods" turn out to be quite as untrustworthy as was ever the personal essayist's "taste." To begin with, the author's intention, even if specifically declared, is thrown out the window, and fidelity to the text turns out to be a highly selective thing. For if what the author intended is no safe guide anyway, why need your emphasis coincide with his? and why cannot you ignore all the obvious, evidently important things which stand in the foreground because that was where he wanted them, so that you may fasten your attention instead upon some subordinate, inconsequential detail, which you may then proceed to magnify until it swallows up the story itself, because only in that way can you present your own original, revisionary, or revolutionary interpretation of a work of art which the world never knew it possessed until you came along to unveil it?

I am of course stating the practice of one school of contemporary critics at its worst, and there is nothing peculiar to *The Spoils of Poynton* and its heroine Fleda Vetch in their vagaries. It is not their findings which will be presented in this study, and since I am not writing a history of Jamesian criticism, it is not necessary for me to list their lucubrations or proceed to specific refutation of them, but I do need to make it clear that my failure to make use of their insights has not been determined by my ignorance of them. A considerable proportion of recent studies of *The Spoils of Poynton* has been vitiated by these tendencies, and if these essays are not "crazy," they are certainly not sensible either, so that one can only think of Fleda at the railroad station on the last page of the novel, asking the stationmaster about the fire—"Poynton's *gone*?"—to which he replies, "What can you call it, miss, if it ain't really saved?" Thus:

Fleda Vetch is not a heroine but an antiheroine, with a will to failure, who can love only in fantasy (except for the writer who believes that she loved Mrs. Gereth, and that this passion ruled out any other relationship!). Owen loves only Mona; his love for Fleda is one of the elements which Fleda invents. Fleda's values are, in fact, totally unrelated to life, against which they form a defense, and her way of possessing Owen was to keep him away from herself (this would look to some of us very much like losing him, but when the Humpty Dumpty critics use a word, it means what they want it to mean). She desires the Maltese Cross because she fancies herself a saint and a martyr, but James denies it to her because she is not worthy of it. She is responsible for the fire which destroys Poynton and the spoils, and this symbolizes the destruction which her quixotism has brought into the lives of all she touched. Actually she is quite happy at the end, for now that she has nothing, she has achieved what she was working for all along without realizing or declaring it.

Thorstein Veblen's *The Theory of the Leisure Class* has been invoked to understand *The Spoils of Poynton:* Fleda is corrupted by Mrs. Gereth's standards, and the burning of Poynton is her just punishment for seeing herself as its fantasy mistress. One writer is so impressed by the humor of the story (she laboriously points out all the comic touches, evidently under the curious impression that nobody has ever noticed them before her) that she concludes by describing *Poynton* as one of the comic masterpieces of literature (Rabelais, Dickens, and Mark Twain—move over!). Because we never see Poynton's treasures for ourselves, Mrs. Gereth's good taste has been questioned along with Fleda's; if both his parents were gifted collectors, how can Owen be what he is? Perhaps Fleda's aesthetic judgment is really on a level with that of her father, who collects brandy bottles and ashtrays and fancies himself a connoisseur; one writer even throws out the astonishing idea that the one character who achieves a true evaluation of the spoils is Mona Brigstock. So far as I know, nobody has yet suggested that not Poynton but the Brigstock residence is the true home of beauty and good taste in the story, but let us be patient: this will surely come. For with this school nothing is but what is not.

One commentator is gravely troubled by James's failure to see through the "incredible self-deceptions" of Fleda and other Jamesian characters, but fails to perceive that, since James did not conceive of or present these things as self-deception, they do not so exist in his work and that therefore what he himself has to say about them has no critical value, however interesting it may be as autobiography. "My discussion of *The Portrait of a Lady* and *The Spoils of Poynton*," writes another, "is in absolute contradiction of James's declared intents." And still another: "This interpretation of the book is not one James would have endorsed," but this does not trouble him because he believes that *Poynton* is not the novel James meant to write but a different and much better one (perhaps, as Harriet Beecher Stowe said of *Uncle Tom's Cabin*, God wrote it). If James admired Fleda, this only proves that his outlook was as unbalanced as hers. Very likely it was, since he created her. And certainly the critic has a perfect right to reject James's standards along with hers if they seem to him to lack validity. But this does not justify him in twisting and torturing *The Spoils of Poynton* into the book he wishes James might have written or that he might very well write himself if he were capable of writing a novel at all.

We know more about the origin and development of *The Spoils of Poynton* than we do about most of James's works, for the novel gets much attention in his notebooks.[1] It all began at an 1893 dinner party at Lady Lindsay's, where

---

[1] F. O. Matthiessen and Kenneth B. Murdock, eds., *The Notebooks of Henry James* (OUP, 1947), 136–38, 198–200, 207–12, 214–20, 247–56. O'Neill's *Workable Design* contains a close analysis of James's purpose in creating Fleda in the light of the Notebook entries.

Mrs. Anstruther-Thompson told of a lady in the north involved in a bitter controversy with her son, who, upon his father's death, had come into exclusive legal possession of their house with its valuable contents. Though James did not produce *The Spoils of Poynton* until 1896, he seems immediately to have sensed that here was the germ of a story and to have agonized over the possibility of the narrator's inhibiting the workings of his imagination by giving the details of the real-life situation. Though Violet Hunt says he would sometimes, under such circumstances, stop an anecdote in the middle, saying he had got as much as he wanted, he did not, according to his own account, do this at Lady Lindsay's, but he did know how to choose and reject, for the woman in the anecdote, obviously much coarser than Mrs. Gereth, went to the length of trying to invalidate the will by proclaiming her son illegitimate.[2]

The actual writing began in an attempt to give Horace E. Scudder a short story for *The Atlantic Monthly,* but the narrative was destined to undergo such growth and transformation that James always thought of it as "the poor little 'long' thing." The accommodating editor agreed to allow it to expand to a three- or four-part novel of about 35,000 words, but what he finally got, beginning in the April, 1896, number, was a seven-installment narrative of 75,000 words. That was "The Old Things." It did not become *The Spoils of Poynton* until it appeared between covers, and at one time it had been in danger of being called "The House Beautiful." Let us shudder and pass on.[3]

The conflict which lies at the heart of the novel is fought

---

[2] Cargill's suggestion that James took the idea for *The Spoils* from Guy de Maupassant's "En Famille" is not, I think, convincing. Adeline R. Tintner, " 'The Old Things': Balzac's *Le Curé de Tours* and James's *The Spoils of Poynton*," *NCF*, XXVI (1971–72), 436–55, has recently argued the influence of the story indicated.

[3] Nina Baym's comparative study of the Notebook entries, the novel, and the Preface, in "Fleda Vetch and the Plot of *The Spoils of Poynton*," *PMLA*, LXXXIV (1969), 102–11, has some value for understanding the development of the story,

around the "things" or "spoils," the rich, rare, beautiful furnishings which Mrs. Gereth and her late husband gathered through a lifetime of devoted collecting and which she arranged with such consummate skill. James has been blamed for not telling us more about them, but he was writing a novel, not a sales catalogue, and he was well aware that he was not Balzac, or Theodore Dreiser or Arnold Bennett either. Whatever else James may have disagreed with Trollope about, they were surely at one in seeing the novelist concerned with men, as Trollope puts it, outside their businesses. There is not much point, therefore, to Oscar Cargill's objection that Mrs. Gereth is not convincing as a connoisseur because she does not talk like a professional collector.[4]

James knew surely what Emerson meant when he saw things in the saddle and riding mankind. Mrs. Gereth does at times see her possessions as almost if not quite sentient: "They're living things to me; they know me, they return the touch of my hand." For James, on the other hand, they were inarticulate; "magnificently passive"; contended for, not contending; and what becomes of them remains in itself "a comparatively vulgar issue." It is interesting that he should, in his Preface, speak of Helen of Troy in connection with them ("the passions, the faculties, the forces their beauty would . . . set in motion, was what, as a painter, one had really wanted of them"), and his instinct in not describing them directly was quite as sound as Homer's had been when

---

but I can accept almost nothing she writes about Fleda, whom she sees introduced as a plotting device and later invested with various complexities and contradictions in an attempt to resolve the narrative problems which arise. On "The Composition of *The Spoils of Poynton*," see also Emily K. Izsak, *TSLL*, VI (1964–65), 460–71, who reads the text instead of reading into it.

[4] See, besides James's Preface, M. A. Goldberg, " 'Things' and Values in Henry James's Universe," *WHR*, XI (1957), 377–85; A. W. Bellringer, "*The Spoils of Poynton*: James's Unintended Involvement," *EIC*, XVI (1966), 185–200; Lotus Snow, " 'A Story of Cabinets and Chairs and Tables': Images of Morality in *The Spoils of Poynton* and *The Golden Bowl*," *ELH*, XXX (1963), 413–35.

he showed us Helen's beauty only through its effect upon others. Throughout the story they act as a catalyst, and we understand the characters by reference to their attitude toward them.

To Owen Gereth they are "furniture," and the way he speaks the word makes Fleda think of washstands and bedding. To Mona Brigstock, the handsome, stubborn, vigorous young barbarian he wishes to marry, they are definitely spoils.[5] She cares nothing about them because she is incapable of understanding or appreciating them ("She thinks they're all right" is the extent of her tribute, as Owen passes it on to his mother), but "they go with the house," and she must take a stand for them even though she risks losing Owen in the process. For Mrs. Gereth they are Beauty, not merely beautiful objects, but the purity of her appreciation is flawed with the zest of possession; when she surreptitiously moves them to Ricks, in defiance of the will, her enjoyment of them there is obviously quite unimpaired by either the illegality of her action or her knowledge that placing them in this new cramped setting had destroyed "the spacious unity which made Poynton so matchless." Only Fleda appreciates them perfectly, like an unspoiled spirit's morning apprehension of the world, without ulterior consideration or lust of possession, and it was not until James had created her as a "free," truly sentient, understanding spirit, to apprehend the true significance of the action, that *The Spoils of Poynton* could be written. In one notebook entry he makes the point that only her capacity for doing something really fine makes the story worth telling, and even in Chapter I he describes her as "that member of the party in whose intenser consciousness we shall most profitably seek a reflexion of the little drama with which we are concerned."

Stephen Spender glances at some of this in *The De-*

---

[5] Alan H. Roper, "The Moral and Metaphorical Meaning of *The Spoils of Poynton*," *AL*, XXXII (1960–61), 182–96, studies James's imagery of battle, storm, and flight.

structive Element,[6] but he is quite wrong when he declares that "it is the things themselves, the Spoils, which are evil, which destroy the happiness of the people who are interested in them." This is animistic superstition, revealing much the same confusion as that shown by those who imagine that the New Testament calls money rather than (as it does) the love of money, the root of all evil. The spoils, like money, are morally neutral, taking on moral significance only as they are used or misused; James is quite as clear on that point as Tennyson was in "The Palace of Art."

Some of these matters come up again at the end, when Fleda goes down to Poynton to get the Maltese Cross which Owen has asked her to accept from him, only to find the place in flames and the contents totally destroyed. This has been called melodramatic, and if everything in art which involves accident and is not firmly and completely and quite adequately grounded in character is to be so labeled, then this is fair enough.[7] Nevertheless there is something about it that is very satisfying on that deeper, subrational level which is perhaps quite as important for art as the forces and considerations we can weigh and measure, for it leaves Fleda "in possession of the past in the only way finally it can be known and redeemed: in memory and in art." The

---

[6] Jonathan Cape, 1935.

[7] If the fire is melodramatic in the sense of being contrived, it is not the only such effect in the book. The bringing "on" of Mrs. Brigstock in the scene at Fleda's father's is very theatrical, more like what one might expect in a play which can present only a limited number of scenes than in a novel which can shift at will. J. A. Ward, *The Imagination of Disaster: Evil in the Fiction of Henry James* (UNP, 1961) has even suggested that the first meeting of Fleda and Mrs. Gereth is incredible since it leaves us wondering how Fleda could possibly have been invited to Waterbath; and Arthur Hobson Quinn, *American Fiction* (Appleton-Century-Crofts, 1936) was so offended by two ladies of allegedly good taste founding their friendship on shared confidences concerning the appalling bad taste of their hosts that he seems to have been incapacitated from finding anything of value in the novel. An article by Winthrop Tilley, "Fleda Vetch and Ellen Brown, or Henry James and the Soap Opera," *WHR*, X (1956), 175–80, undertakes a detailed comparison between *The Spoils of Poynton* and a radio serial called *Young Widder Brown!*

physical spoils are gone now for everybody, but she can still hold the spiritual or archetype spoils, visualizing them "as immortal, outside of human concerns, existing only in her mind which no desire for possession can violate."[8] As a matter of fact, however, the calamity is *not* completely unrelated to character. I have already reported that some of Fleda's enemies hold her responsible for the fire; one commentator even got it figured out that Owen was "the strongest and most humane figure in the story" and that the fire proved to Fleda that he had never loved her! Had Fleda got Owen away from Mona and married him and lived with him at Poynton, the fire might very well not have occurred, but if we are to blame her for this, then we must also hold the mother of every murderer responsible for his crime because she bore him. The stationmaster does suggest, however, that the fire was caused by incompetent service at Poynton while Mona was dragging her husband about foreign parts, for though the wretched woman had to possess the spoils, she obviously felt no desire to live with them. The Mona Brigstocks of the world can always win on the mere issue of possession, but as soon as any higher values enter, their victory becomes Pyrrhic; spiritually they possess nothing because they have nothing to possess it with. When inexplicable things occur, simple people are fond of saying that "it was—or was not—to be." Perhaps the stationmaster and others like him might even see the spoils as tired of being contended for and shifted about from pillar to post; the time has come when it is more in keeping with their dignity to submit to the purification of fire.

Fleda Vetch was "slim, pale and black-haired." At the outset at least Mrs. Gereth thought she "had no beauty" and "was dressed with an idea, though perhaps not with much else." The editors of James's notebooks call her "one

[8] The quotations are from Walter Isle, *Experiments in Form: Henry James's Novels, 1896–1901* (HUP, 1968), and Holland, *The Expense of Vision.*

of James's most extreme embodiments of imagination, taste, and renouncing sensibility," and he himself avers that no one in the world was less superficial than she and that even in a tight place she was able to think ten thoughts together. Though there had been nothing in her family background to account for it, her capacity for appreciation was tremendous, and her sensibilities, which were almost as great as her capacity for developing them had been small, had been cultivated partly through the museums but even more by reference to her own innate powers. Her freedom is shown in her isolation, even from her family, as well as in her intelligence. Both Owen and his mother tell her, in the course of the story, that they understand neither her language nor her motives, and it is fitting that, as Walter Isle has remarked, she should be introduced to the reader in "deep and lonely meditation." Inevitably, therefore, James surrounded her with what he calls "fools," who are supposed to interest us by contrast and as they "minister, at a particular crisis, to the intensity of the free spirit engaged with them."[9]

It may be helpful to view Fleda, as it were centripetally, in her relation with these "fools," and this means beginning with the one with whom the contrast is sharpest, "the awful Mona Brigstock." Where Fleda is all sensibility, Mona is all stubborn will and mulishness, a handsome, athletic girl, with big feet, from whose composition "the principle of taste had been extravagantly omitted," and who presents a completely impenetrable surface even when she has been "romp-

---

[9] In both his Preface and his Notebooks, James compares Fleda to the heroines of "A London Life" and "The Chaperon," both of whom share her "high lucidity" as well as her "acuteness and intensity, reflexion and passion." In *The Complete Plays of Henry James* (Li, 1949), 521, the editor, Leon Edel, suggests a resemblance between *Poynton* and *Summersoft*, a one-act play, written for Ellen Terry but not produced by her. James rewrote *Summersoft* as the story "Covering End," which was published with "The Turn of the Screw" in *The Two Magics*, and then turned "Covering End" into a full-length play for Forbes-Robertson and his wife, Gertrude Elliott, *The High Bid*, acted in 1907. But none of these works have the same theme as *Poynton*.

ing." Mona finds challenge, not charm, at Poynton, and how much she cares for Owen may be inferred from her fury after Mrs. Gereth removes the spoils. She now feels that he has obtained her under false pretences; it has become less a matter of getting the spoils with the man than the man with the spoils. James mercilessly dehumanizes both Mona and her stupid, meddling mother, of whom we are told that "she was really somehow no sort of person at all" and that, since her face was not green or blue or yellow, it was impossible to describe. Except for their restless wanderings to and fro upon the earth after their marriage, we are given no actual information about how Mona and Owen are getting on, but surely Fleda's idea that Owen offered her the Maltese Cross as a keepsake because he wished to testify to his gratitude for her share in bringing him and a beloved wife together is too generous. The offer *must* have been made behind Mona's back; she would have made the welkin ring had she had any idea her husband had offered to relinquish such a treasure to a girl she hated, and it is perhaps the final commentary on her ignorance and insensibility and lack of interest in Poynton that, even if the place had not burned down, she would never have become aware of the absence from it of the richest and rarest of all the spoils.[10]

Fleda's behavior toward Mona is irreproachable; not even in thought does she ever take an advantage of her. Fleda has been called a female Quixote. In the larger aspects the accusation is unjust, but it does have a limited application to her treatment of Mona. In the light of the controversy over the spoils, Owen's eyes are opened; he now sees Mona as "so different, so ugly and vulgar" that a word from Fleda would cause him to break his engagement and come to her. Though Fleda finally admits her love for him, she will not speak that word—or, more accurately, she will

[10] Arnold Goldsmith, "The Maltese Cross as Sign in *The Spoils of Poynton*," *Renascence*, XVI (1963–64), 73–77, is an excellent interpretation of the military and religious symbolism of the artifact.

not speak it until too late—because she does not wish to hurt Mona or see her humiliated, and cannot lift a finger against her because she would be ashamed forever to think that she owed her happiness "to an interference." She sees Mona's point of view and expresses no resentment even when Owen quotes the vulgar things Mona has said about her, and she will not inflict upon her rival the suffering she knows she would experience if their positions were reversed, and this even though she is intelligent enough to realize that Mona is not capable of suffering as she herself understands it. If there is to be a break between Owen and Mona, it must come from the girl, and Fleda can have no part in it. She will not say yes when he asks her, "Do you mean to tell me that I marry a woman I hate?" ("Anything's better than that"), but she does think it all important that Owen should keep faith. "Where's a man if he doesn't? If he doesn't he may be so cruel." So, in effect, though not in intent, Fleda sacrifices herself and Owen and Mrs. Gereth (all three) to the impervious Mona. That Mona herself is sacrificed also I hesitate to add, even on the assumption that the marriage is as unhappy as some readers believe, for James has told us nothing to indicate that she is capable of deep feeling of any kind.

Some readers of *The Spoils of Poynton* have seen Owen as such a barbarian that they find it difficult to believe that Fleda could have loved him. In the country, "Owen shooting was Owen lost"; his town sophistication quite amazes Fleda when she encounters him accidentally in London. It is difficult to see how such a view could survive much knowledge of actual marriages in this world, but it is not fair to Owen, who is a far kinder person than his mother (we may be sure he would never have gone to law against her). When Mrs. Gereth first suggests she would like Fleda to marry him, Fleda replies that he is too stupid, but James adds that she came closer thus to betraying her love for him than she was ever to come again until she admitted all. In the very first chapter she sees him as "absolutely beautiful and delightfully dense." His eyes attract her because they look like those of a child, and as early as Chapter IV, when she has no hopes and no reasonable expectation of any, her creator briefly reports her dreaming of him, for, as he later tells us, she had an imagination "that easily embraced all the heights and depths and extremities of things." Owen asks Fleda for advice from the moment he tells her he is engaged to Mona, and there is no denying that his behavior after his mother has moved the spoils to Ricks and Fleda, much to her own discomfort, has become the only liaison man between him and Mrs. Gereth, is boyish in the extreme: "*Am* I to tell my solicitor?" But if Owen is weak at times, he is also quite consistently good, and because it is now necessary to do so in order to protect Fleda, he behaves admirably and manifests a strength few readers can previously have given him credit for when Mrs. Brigstock comes upon him and the girl together in London.

There can be no question then about Fleda's passionate love for him; her language to Mrs. Gereth, when she finally makes her confession, is quite conclusive. "I love him so that I'd die for him—I love him so that it's horrible." But her love is not all passion: "I'd trust him to the last breath." Even what she had formerly considered his stupidity is now transformed and glorified by her love. "He's ever so much cleverer than he makes any show of; he's remarkable in his own shy way." Shocked to find "no fundamental tenderness" between him and his mother, out of which a solution of their difficulties might be expected to spring, she is sure Mrs. Gereth has never appreciated him, and she is probably right about this, though there is one solitary passage in which the elder lady calls her son a dear with no harm in him and implores Fleda to save him. But it is when his mother finds it difficult to understand how she can excuse his disgusting weakness that Fleda makes one of her most revealing observations: "Because I love him. It's because he's weak that he needs me." Perhaps we are intended to remember that James had told us at the very beginning that Fleda "was prepared, if she should ever marry, to contribute all the cleverness" and to serve as the directing spirit of her grateful husband. "She was in her small way a spirit of the same family as Mrs. Gereth." Less than a hundred pages later Owen speaks "with the stupidity she didn't object to" when he tells Fleda that if he were as clever as she is, he might be able to get around Mona.

Yet the comparison to Mrs. Gereth, taken by itself, is misleading. We really do not know much about that lady's twenty-six years of married life; she looks back upon it in terms of "perfect accord," but she also tells Fleda that her husband was like Owen and that he needed her as Owen will need Fleda. What is important to remember is that though there is a maternal element in Fleda's love, she is never the mother who does not want her son to grow up. Owen does his best to get her to make his decision for him, but she resolutely refuses to do so, and if she plays the "nice old Mummy" that Mona, in one of her more refined moments, calls her, she is always the mother who is training her son so that, when her guiding hand is removed, he may be prepared to be "superior" and "sublime" without her. After the interview with Mrs. Brigstock, in which he is seen at his best, her tenderness increases with her admiration for him. For the moment she even believes that he has shown himself a stronger person than she is, and she rejoices in this belief. Nor does she ever force her standards upon him. She merely refuses to abet him in any attempt to lower what she assumes to be his own.

Walter Isle has called Mrs. Gereth "creatively sterile," with a "purely materialistic" passion for possessions. Edwin Bowden, on the other hand, acquits her of material selfishness and credits her with desiring the good of others as well as her own. The truth lies somewhere between these views. Bowden is certainly right when he dissociates her from such monsters as Gilbert Osmond;[11] that he is also correct in granting her a measure of redemption in the course of the narrative may well be more doubtful: "Yet Mrs. Gereth and Fleda, too sensitive for the crude and predatory world in which they must live, have at last found their strength; after their moment of recognition they know finally where true happiness lies." Since we are never told how she received the news of the fire, I suppose this refers to her achievement at Ricks, but Bowden seems to me to bring her and Fleda too close together. She has a great sensitiveness to beauty, and bad taste sets her teeth on edge, but her moral sensitiveness has not kept pace with her aestheticism. In the Preface, James calls her, *contra* Fleda, the "very reverse of a free spirit" and a false character, "floundering . . . in the dusk of a disproportionate passion," not intelligent but only clever and therefore unable to serve as a center for his story. Certainly she is not wholly sterile. Poynton *does* reveal a species of creative power, and this comes out again, less brilliantly but even more remarkably, in the near miracle she creates, out of much less impressive materials, at Ricks. It is not mere love of possession which governs her attitude toward the spoils but "the need to be faithful to a trust and loyal to an idea." Under the cruel English law which gives Poynton to the son and banishes his mother, its creator, to the dower house, she would be prepared to relinquish her home to Fleda or, presumably, to anybody qualified to appreciate and care for her treasures, but she cannot bear the thought of turning them over to the likes of Mona Brigstock. At one time, Fleda is so much impressed by this that she applies

[11]On the other hand, John C. Broderick, "Nature, Art, and Imagination in *The Spoils of Poynton*," *NCF*, XIII (1958–59), 295–312, compares Mrs. Gereth not only to Osmond but also to Madame Merle and to John Marcher in "The Beast in the Jungle." Broderick quotes suggestively from the *Daniel Deronda* conversation in James's *Partial Portraits*: "In life without art you can find your account; but art without life is a poor affair." For Bowden see *The Themes of Henry James* (YUP, 1956).

to her companion such words as "grandeur," "purity," "august," and "sublime."

Mrs. Gereth's position is cruel and her opponents unspeakable; at the outset, therefore, all our prejudices are enlisted in her favor. But James begins to undercut our sympathy for her at least as early as the brilliantly narrated magazine incident in Chapter IV. Mrs. Brigstock, visiting Poynton, had thoughtfully paid her tribute to Mrs. Gereth as a collector by bringing with her a copy of a new ladies' magazine featuring antimacassars, which she had picked up from a newsstand and which she had intended to leave behind her as a souvenir. But, as the party prepares to take its departure, Mrs. Gereth catches it up: "For heaven's sake, don't let your mother forget her precious publication, the female magazine with the what-do-you-call-'em? the grease-catchers," with which she tosses it from the doorstep toward the carriage, "higher in air than was absolutely needful," and the athletic Mona catches it on a reflex action as if it had been a tennis ball while Owen cries, "Good catch!" This has been compared to Becky Sharp's casting the dictionary out the window in *Vanity Fair,* and the comparison has point, but Becky's action is completely in character, while Mrs. Gereth's seems contrived to give Fleda a chance for her "How *could* you? Great God, how *could* you?" In his notebooks James spoke of Mrs. Gereth's indecency, "unconscious brutality and immorality." Legally at least, her removal of the spoils from Poynton to Ricks is theft, and the impression of "age and cunning" which she gives Fleda in her self-admiring account of her coup is faintly sickening. "I'm quite coarse, thank God!" she says; later she admits that she understands neither the fine-spun Fleda nor her son: "You make me feel very old-fashioned and simple and bad." Later still, when displeased by Fleda's scruples, which now seem to have wrecked all her plans and lost her the spoils besides, she grows almost bawdy, like a female Justice Shallow remembering her youth. "You're not quite a saint in heaven yet. Lord, what a creature you'd have thought me in my good time!" And when she is angry enough, she slashes into the situation, as Fleda tells her, "with a great pair of shears," as if she were one of the fates: "What are you, after all, my dear, I should like to know, that a gentleman who offers you what Owen offers should have to meet such wonderful exactions, to take such extraordinary precautions about your sweet little scruples?"

Mrs. Gereth, we have seen, can be happy with stolen goods while Fleda cannot, but this is not merely because, as I have already observed, Fleda has moral as well as aesthetic sensibilities but also because the younger woman has not allowed her aestheticism to rob her of her humanity. Mrs. Gereth is certainly not, compared to some of James's harpies, a "bad" woman, but I know of no more striking manifestation of his always severe morality than his attitude toward her, and I can think of no more impressive presentation anywhere of the spiritual perils that lie in wait for the aesthete than James achieves in her portrait. As we have seen, he thought her clever but not intelligent, and the reason for this was that "she had no imagination about anybody's life save on the side she bumped against." It will be remembered that Emerson took pains to be not a writer but a "man writing," but Mrs. Gereth is at least in grave danger of being swallowed up by her specialty to such an extent that she is merely a collector. This, presumably, is why Fleda, who has had some training as a painter, cannot create at Poynton, and even more why she finds it difficult to imagine Mrs. Gereth except in the "thick, colored air" that her treasures have created around her; "it took all the light of her treasures to make her concrete or distinct." The process has not been completed, however, for there is more than a touch of disinterestedness in Mrs. Gereth's attitude toward her young friend and even some unselfish affection, and so we may have some hope for her at the end.

The difficulty of Fleda's position is caused not only by

the conflict within herself between her love for Owen and her scruples about accepting it but, if possible even more, by the fact that she stands in the position of confidante to both him and his mother (neither relationship is of her own seeking; both have been thrust upon her). It is quite true, as some of her supermoral critics have pointed out, that she does not give either one a full account of what the other had said, but her reserves are not dictated by self-interest; she merely respects the confidences that have been reposed in her. Her "lies," if you wish to call them that, are all made to protect the interests of others, even, or especially, those of her rival. Actually, neither Owen nor his mother is ever seriously deceived by her, and James carefully absolves her from responsibility for the ill-advised action of Mrs. Gereth's which finally resolves the situation, through having this brought about by the clumsy intervention of Mrs. Brigstock, when she comes to "plead" with Mrs. Gereth ("If a cow should try to calculate, that's the kind of happy thought she'd have"). She had already, of course, been to plead with Fleda, an enterprise which had drawn from that young lady only the sarcastic inquiry whether she was being treated like "one of those bad women in a play."

This is quite the sharpest thing Fleda ever says, and I have never been wholly convinced that she would say it, nor yet that Mrs. Gereth would risk all as she does on so desperate a throw of the dice as sending the spoils back to Poynton, but neither of these matters needs be considered *in extenso* here. Mrs. Brigstock had left Mrs. Gereth with the impression that Mona's patience was nearing its end; in the exultation of approaching victory, the mistress of Poynton attempted to force Fleda's hand. From her point of view, the relinquishment of her treasures was virtually equivalent to offering Fleda her life, for what other life had she ever had? With everything back at Poynton, how then could the girl, in common decency, do other than sacrifice any silly scruples she might still be entertaining and tell Owen she would have him?

So far as Fleda is concerned, the scheme works. She has never actually refused Owen. On the contrary, she has frankly confessed her love, both to him and to his mother. She has only consistently maintained that she cannot build her happiness on the misery of another woman. If Owen can come to her free, and honorably free, there has never been any question that she will accept him.

She has fought a good fight. But, as both James and Mrs. Gereth have informed us, she is not quite a saint or a martyr either, especially when this would involve martyrizing Mrs. Gereth with her. Like Joan of Arc at Saint-Ouen, she knows her moment of recantation. She telegraphs Owen: "I send this to Waterbath on the possibility of your being there, to ask you to come to me." But apparently only Mrs. Brigstock ever saw the telegram. For as soon as the spoils were returned to Poynton, Owen and Mona had been married.

Under the existent circumstances there can be no talk of "treachery" or "deceit" on Fleda's part toward either Owen or Mrs. Gereth that is anything more than merely hysterical. The character is consistently developed throughout, and if her heroism fails at last, few of James's readers are in a position to judge her. There is not the slightest evidence to support Walter Isle's idea that she "sees herself for much of the novel as the noble heroine of a high-minded romance, a figure much like Conrad's Lord Jim." She is simply a girl who fell in love under extremely difficult conditions and who, because of scruples which most human beings would have overriden, struggled so hard against accepting her lover that when at last she gave in to her desires, it was too late.[12]

James sympathized with and admired her throughout, and he expected the understanding reader to do the same.

[12] C. B. Cox, *The Free Spirit* . . . (OUP, 1963), 52–55, argues that the change involved in Fleda's sending the telegram illustrates what William James called "radical empiricism." James W. Gargano, *"The Spoils of Poynton*: Action and Responsibility," *SR*, LXIX (1969), 650–60, defends Fleda against her extreme critics. Other sympathetic interpretations of Fleda are offered by Charles Thomas

It is neither his fault nor hers if we set up an inhuman or unreasonable standard for her and then abuse her for not achieving what she was never meant to achieve. When James called her a free spirit, he did not say she was a superwoman. No more with her than with Isabel Archer are we to assume that because he admired her he must portray her unrealistically, and the converse of this proposition is that when we learn that she was not superhumanly perfect, we need not feel called upon to suppose that either he or ourselves must reject her. Mrs. Gereth sizes her up quite accurately when she tells her that, though she comfortably understands, she is no good at all for action. For that matter, James says the same thing in his Preface; she was "only intelligent" is the way he puts it, "not distinctively able." There is a touch of Mr. Micawber about her: she does not refuse love but simply makes conditions and retreats and withdraws and waits. "If the rupture should come from Waterbath they might all be happy yet." In the end she loses because her lover (it is the only way in which he really resembles her) is also weak in initiating action and because her rival is "*all* will, without the smallest leak of force into taste or temperament or vision, into any sense of shades or relations or proportions." Not everybody can admire such a temperament, but it is respectworthy for all that, and it puts very little pain into the world. Broderick discusses the matter in philosophical terms, finding suggestive comparisons in "The Liar" and in Hawthorne's

---

Samuels, *The Ambiguity of Henry James* (University of Illinois Press, 1971), and by Akio Namekata, "Some Notes on *The Spoils of Poynton*," a very sensitive study in *Studies in English Literature*, XL, English Number (1970), 17–35. Says Samuels: "A reader who fails to respond to this authentic note of heroism [Fleda's willingness to lose her chance for marriage so that Owen may be left free to make his own decision] fails to respond to the moral center of James's universe. Good, in James, is no more than this act of Fleda's; the ability to restrain egoism in our relations with others so that they may fulfill their own souls, just as evil is the exploitation of others for personal ends." For further commentary, especially in connection with the telegram, see Edmund L. Volpe, "The Spoils of Art," *MLN*, LXXIV (1959), 601–608; also Philip L. Greene, "Point of View in *The Spoils of Poynton*," *NCF*, XXI (1966–67), 359–68.

"The Prophetic Pictures" and "The Artist of the Beautiful," and quoting Thoreau's

> My Life has been the poem I would have writ
> But I could not both live and utter it,

though I doubt that James was saying "that disembodied artistic perceptiveness is more admirable than if it had lost its freedom and been committed to form." Fleda's problem has nothing to do with committing artistic perceptiveness to form; it is merely a question of whether or not she should marry the man she loves. When at last she learns that he has married Mona, she says, "That he has done it, that he couldn't not do it, shows how right I was." This may show a will to failure, but to me it sounds much more like common sense.

VII. LILY AMONG THORNS

MAISIE FARANGE

MARIUS BEWLEY, who thinks *What Maisie Knew* "by far the greatest novel of the later James—and second only . . . to *The Portrait of a Lady* in the entire canon of James's work," calls Maisie Farange herself "the most magnificent portrayal in the language of the unfolding discretionary powers of a human being."[1] This may be an overstatement, but certainly there is nothing elsewhere of a comparable subtlety. Most of the great books about little lambs—*David Copperfield, Tom Sawyer,* and *Huckleberry Finn,* to say nothing of such junior officers in the company as *Little Women* and *Rebecca of Sunnybrook Farm*—make some concessions to the little lambs among their readers.[2] James makes, in this instance, none whatever; if *The Spoils of Poynton* is to be taken as his first extended essay in the famous "later manner," he must be said to have continued and elaborated and complicated his method here. Though

[1] Marius Bewley, *The Complex Fate: Hawthorne, Henry James and Some Other American Writers*, with an Introduction and Two Interpolations by F. R. Leavis (Grove Press, 1954).

[2] Tony Tanner, *The Reign of Wonder: Naïvety and Reality in American Literature* (CUP, 1965), has much to say about Huck and Maisie; see especially pp. 279–80. See also William Walsh, *The Use of Imagination: Educational Thought and the Literary Mind* (Barnes & Noble, 1960). In *The Fictional Children of Henry James*, Muriel G. Shine beautifully establishes James's knowledge of, interest in, and deep concern for, the child. Dorothea Krook's interesting footnote in *The Ordeal of Consciousness in Henry James*, 114, is also relevant in this connection.

What Maisie Knew may not be quite as difficult as *The Awkward Age* or *The Golden Bowl,* it is still sufficiently implicational so that one may read it almost any number of times and still find something fresh to ponder and puzzle over at each reading. And to many it must seem almost perversely anomalous that this should be true of a book with a small girl at the heart of it.[3]

Even James, who delighted in fictional problems, never set himself a harder task than when he went to work to portray a corrupt society as seen through the eyes of a child. It is hardly an exaggeration to say that both Ida and Beale Farange are presented as moral monsters. When they are divorced, under disgraceful circumstances, the court decides that their child must live six-month terms with each of them, and she enters accordingly upon a career as a helpless shuttlecock, battered to and fro between people who have no use for her save as "a ready vessel for bitterness, a deep little porcelain cup in which biting acids could be mixed. They had wanted her not for any good they could do her, but for the harm they could, with her unconscious aid, do each other."

Both parents are grossly immoral; in her father's rackety establishment Maisie is required to sit on the knees of gentlemen who have her light their cigarettes and who blow smoke in her face and pinch her skinny legs. Miss Overman enters the picture as a governess employed by Mrs. Farange. She is beautiful, and Maisie loves her. So does her father, as

---

[3] Though Maisie's exact age is not spelled out, hardly anybody seems to agree with Leon Edel, *Henry James: The Treacherous Years, 1895–1901* (Li, 1969), 291, who would have her introduced to the reader at five and withdrawn at seven or eight "or perhaps a bit older." McElderry gives us a range of six to ten or twelve, and Cargill would have her thirteen when, at the end, she, as he quite wrongheadedly believes, offers herself to Sir Claude. John C. McCloskey considers the matter in some detail in "What Maisie Knows: A Study of Childhood and Adolescence," *AL*, XXXVI (1964–65), 485–512. The writer who makes the most determined effort to work out a time scheme for the novel is Joseph Wiesenfarth in his valuable study of *Maisie* in *Henry James and the Dramatic Analogy: A Study of the Major Novels of the Middle Period* (Fordham University Press, 1963).

he is capable of loving, and before long she leaves Ida's establishment to become first Beale's mistress and then his wife, after which she is always called Mrs. Beale. Meanwhile Mrs. Farange has become "her ladyship" by marrying one Sir Claude (we never learn his last name or Mrs. Beale's first), who functions, until at the end she outgrows him, as Maisie's white knight in shining armor. But neither of the second marriages endures, and a liaison develops between Mrs. Beale and Sir Claude. Now Maisie has one set of parents after the flesh who care nothing for her (and indeed ultimately quite give her up) and a second unmarried pair who love her and would have her live with them. The fifth important character in her world is another governess, the decidedly Dickensian Mrs. Wix, who loves her deeply but is obsessed with "the moral sense" and distressed over what seems to her Maisie's failure to develop it.

Like *The Spoils of Poynton,* as James explains in his Preface, *What Maisie Knew* originated in a dinner-table anecdote.[4] That was in 1892, but he did not begin to write until 1896. Not uncharacteristically, he first projected a story of some 10,000 words. In September 1896 he recorded in a notebook that he had written the first four sections; in December he thought another 10,000 words would see him through. By the time the story had been completed, seven or eight months later, it had run to about 90,000. It was serialized in America in *The Chap Book* between January 1 and August 1, 1897, and in England in *The New Review* between February and September. Book publication followed in both countries in the fall.[5]

James's first thought was to confine himself to what the child could understand, but he was soon convinced not only

[4] J. D. McFarlane, "A Literary Friendship—Henry James and Paul Bourget," *Cambridge Journal*, IV (1950–51), 144–61, compares *Maisie* with Bourget's *Odile* (1896), which began with a similar situation but developed quite differently and more simply. In any case, James would seem to have had the idea for *Maisie* before he could have read *Odile*.

that this must be expanded to what she *saw*, even if she was not able to understand it, but that, since "small children have many more perceptions than they have terms to translate them," her own vision must, if the situation were to be fully explored, be supplemented by a commentary which should extend and amplify. His "point of view," his "*line*," remained "the consciousness, the sweet, scared, wondering, clinging perception of the child," who, from her "ironic centre," was to shed a light "far beyond any reach of her comprehension." She was too young, however, for her light to shine brightly enough to illuminate the whole picture; hence the need for the guidance, the interpretation, the humor, the stylistic enrichment which commentary could supply. It would, no doubt, be too much to claim that this commentary is always successful. "Oh decidedly I shall never get you to believe the number of things she saw and the number of secrets she discovered!" This comes as late as Chapter XX, but whoever can accept it without wincing ought never to complain when Thackeray or Trollope or any other creator of the "loose baggy monsters" that James found in Victorian fiction pokes his head through the curtains to tell the reader what he is supposed to think or believe. Generally, however, James *is* successful, often splendidly successful, and Tony Tanner has some suggestive comments on the differences between Mark Twain's confining himself to Huckleberry Finn and James's "going behind" Maisie, but not to make "final moral judgments," as Tanner rightly insists: "James intends to fill out

---

[5] The editor of *The New Review*, William Ernest Henley, hated *Maisie*, and the later installments were drastically cut, possibly to bring English serialization more in line with the American and/or to prevent serial publication from running too far past the date of book publication. See Ward S. Worden, "A Cut Version of *What Maisie Knew*," *AL*, XXIV (1952–53), 493–504. For the American publication, see also Sidney Kramer, *A History of Stone & Kimball and Herbert S. Stone & Co. with a Bibliography of Their Publications* (UCP, 1940). Another article by Worden, "Henry James's *What Maisie Knew*: A Comparison with the Plans in the *Notebooks*," *PMLA*, LXVIII (1953), 371–83, is important for understanding the development of the story.

the picture, not to introduce judicial pronouncements and verdicts."

F. R. Leavis, I think, overstates the case when he interprets *What Maisie Knew* as essentially comedy; the book is very serious, ending in spiritual triumph for Maisie and an ignominious self-defeat for Sir Claude, which is all the sadder because of his clear perception yet acceptance of it. Nevertheless, there is a great deal of comic material in it, and even the evil characters are often presented in terms of comic exaggeration. Both Beale and Ida might be described as mechanized fantasies if there were such a thing; they look and act more like robots than human beings. Ida has big eyes, many bracelets, and an exceptionally long arm which has contributed notably to her skill at billiards! On one of the rare occasions she embraces her daughter, the girl felt "amid a wilderness of trinkets, . . . as if she had suddenly been thrust, with a smash of glass, into a jeweller's shop-front"; the hard, sharp, metallic sensations suggested are ideally calculated to communicate the lady's sweet maternal tenderness.[6] Ida is supposed to be beautiful in her way, and she certainly attracts an endless succession of lovers, but though she is said to have charm, it is hard to believe that she could ever have interested so sensitive a man as Sir Claude or so decent a one as the Captain. Some critics have debated the respective shortcomings of Ida and Beale, but this is a little like weighing the qualities of the demons in *Paradise Lost*. Perhaps she is more cold-hearted and he more coarsely and blatantly lecherous ("if she infuses the novel with an atmosphere of hate," writes Mrs. Shine, "he imbues it with an atmosphere of irresponsibility"), but each has so much of the other quality also

---

[6] Like *The Spoils of Poynton, Maisie* contains a good deal of war imagery; for these and other images, see pp. 82–84 in the excellent study of the novel in Philip M. Weinstein, *Henry James and the Requirements of the Imagination* (HUP, 1971); also Robert L. Gale, *The Caught Image: Figurative Language in the Fiction of Henry James* (UNCP, 1964). Tanner sees teeth and hands and arms as snatching and holding dangers in Maisie's world.

that one tends at last to give up differentiation in despair. What can one do with a man who had

natural decorations, a kind of costume in his vast fair beard, burnished like a gold breast plate, and . . . the eternal glitter of the teeth that his long moustache had been trained not to hide and that gave him, in every possible situation, the look of the joy of life.

And what can he do, even at his best, for his daughter, even when he holds her

on his knee, stroking her hair, playfully holding her off while he showed his shining fangs and let her, with a vague affectionate helpless pointless "Dear old girl, dear little daughter," inhale the fragrance of his cherished beard?

The last dying spasm of his conscience manifests when, after he has descended to being kept by the rich "American Countess," he offers to take the child but makes the offer in such a way that even she

understood as well as if he had spoken it that what he wanted, hang it, was that she should let him off with all the honours—with all the appearance of virtue and sacrifice on his side. It was exactly as if he had broken out to her: "I say, you little booby, help me to be irreproachable, to be noble, and yet to have none of the beastly bore of it. There's only impropriety enough for one of us; so *you* must take it all."

When the countess invites Maisie to go with her and Beale to Spa, we learn that he had been lying when he asked her to go to America with him, and we learn that Ida lied about going to South Africa for her health when Mrs. Wix sees her in London with her latest acquisition, Mr. Tischbein.

It is never made quite clear whether the countess belonged to one of the dark-skinned races or whether she was merely extremely dark-complexioned, but James presents her in terms of even broader caricature than Ida and Beale.

He hit upon the brilliant idea of letting us see her first emerging from the "Flowers of the Forest" sideshow—"a large presentment of bright brown ladies . . . in a medium suggestive of tropical luxuriance"—but she is even more hideous when Maisie encounters her in her own rich quarters:

She literally struck the child more as an animal than as a "real" lady; she might have been a clever frizzled poodle in a frill or a dreadful human monkey in a spangled petticoat. She had a nose that was far too big and eyes that were far too small and a moustache that was, well, not so happy a feature as Sir Claude's.

James uses burlesque methods also in his presentation of Maisie's grubby but loving old governess (she is incapable of teaching anything, but she is cheap), who looks like a beetle and is determined never to desert Miss Farange. He never succeeds in making her talk like a woman of her class, as Dickens would have done; Walter de la Mare, who had much of the Shakespeare-Scott-Dickens gift of creating a character in terms of distinctive speech and allowing him to talk himself alive, did much better in this aspect with the "somewhat Dickensian" landlady Mrs. Bowater in *Memoirs of a Midget*. On her own terms, however, Mrs. Wix is one of James's most brilliant eccentrics, and he walks a very narrow line here, introducing much more shading than generally appears with this type of character. I do not accept the most serious charge which some critics[7] bring against Mrs. Wix, and I believe her to be a true motherly figure whose love for

[7]Bewley, *op. cit.*; J. A. Ward, *The Imagination of Disaster: Evil in the Fiction of Henry James*; Sister M. Corona Sharp, O. S. U., *The Confidante in Henry James: Evolution and Moral Value of a Fictive Character* (University of Notre Dame Press, 1963); and Judith Fryer, *The Faces of Eve: Women in the Nineteenth Century American Novel* (OUP, 1976). This last writer is much more convincing in her studies of Daisy, Isabel, Milly, and Maggie in the same volume. The foundation for the notion that Mrs. Wix's confessed adoration for Sir Claude is sexual and that she is making a play for him for herself (Mrs. Wix being what she is, such a passion would be almost as distasteful, though not so reprehensible morally, as Beale's entanglement with the "Countess") stems from the "upward grimace" and

Maisie, though not very enlightened, is both deep and sincere, but she certainly has more than merely intellectual limitations. "Mrs. Wix took her," James writes as early as Chapter IV, "and, Maisie felt the next day, would never let her go." It must not be forgotten that Maisie is Mrs. Wix's meal ticket as well as the object of her devotion; I do not say that she would be incapable of making a sacrifice for her, but she is never called upon to do so. Her eyeglasses, appropriately called her "straighteners," typify her way of looking at life, and James dares to let us see the comic side of even the "moral sense" upon which she harps and, very delicately, in passing, also of her love for her dead daughter, who had been killed in traffic; "it was quite comfortably established" between Maisie and her governess, we are told, "that Mrs. Wix's heart had been broken." In Boulogne we learn that even her "moral sense" has striking limitations. She is easily won over by Mrs. Beale, whose immorality has until now greatly repelled her, just as soon as that lady begins to flatter her and make her seem important. She can live and feed in luxury

---

"great giggling insinuating naughty slap" which she gives him in Chapter XXIV, and I admit that this is a difficult passage. But four pages over we read that Mrs. Wix had long ago "obtained a 'hold' " on Sir Claude, "as she called it, different in kind from that obtained by Mrs. Beale and originally by her ladyship." I do not think her tears on p. 261 of the New York Edition necessarily indicate sexual disappointment, nor do I believe that her eloquent plea beginning on p. 262 ("I beseech you not to take a step so miserable and so fatal") can reasonably be interpreted as an offer of herself sexually, made before Maisie (cf. also her "Have I lost all delicacy," etc. in Chapter XXVI). Leavis thinks that "Mrs. Wix's and Maisie's 'adorations' are of the same order," and so does Maisie herself; see Chapter XXX, pp. 331–32, where Sir Claude, who by this time seems to be afraid of everybody, is apparently afraid of Mrs. Wix. On such a matter Maisie cannot be cited as a final authority, but it is not reasonable to believe either that if there were any guilt connected with Mrs. Wix's adoration she would confess it so openly to a child or that she could be so shameless as to entertain it without thought of guilt. The most complete and thoroughgoing consideration of Mrs. Wix's character is that of Lee Ann Johnson, in "James's Mrs. Wix: The 'Dim, Crooked Reflector,' " *NCF*, XXIX (1974), 164–72, who rejects her as either "a malevolent figure" or "a standard of serious respectability," to see her instead as a comic character "whose self-interested, misguided attempts to educate her charge serve as a source of humor and irony within the novel."

with perfect satisfaction on Sir Claude's money, and she shows much less conscientiousness than Sir Claude's own when he proposes to take Susan Ash back to England after having dismissed her as a maid. Mrs. Wix cannot understand why he should think it necessary to return the girl to the place from which he had taken her. "She has had an experience that she never dreamed of and that will be an advantage to her through life. If she goes wrong on the way it will be simply because she wants to. . . ." And she is so pleased by Ida's final desertion of Maisie because it brings the girl closer to her that she quite forgets to be shocked by the act itself.

There is no grotesquerie, on the other hand, about the other pair of Maisie's "parents," and nothing monstrous either. Because Sir Claude is much the better of the two, his fall at the end, where he finally makes the wrong choice, is greater; it is he who dislikes the idea of bringing Maisie into such a household as he and Mrs. Beale could set up, for the lady can see no harm in it. But if Mrs. Beale is quite immoral in her way of life, she is more frivolous than evil, and she is never positively nor intentionally cruel. Neither has her conduct yet destroyed her capacity for honest, normal affection. Tanner sees her at the end "hysterically clutching at Maisie, trying to detain her, presumably because of some money which has now been settled on her," and this factor may well appear, yet I do not doubt the sincerity of her affection for the child, which has survived unaltered since her first sight of her, though I must add I do not think she would give up any self-gratification for her, for that is not in her nature. Clear to the end, Maisie's "beautiful friend" was as charming as a woman can be without virtue, but James never permits her to pass beyond that delicate line.

Of Sir Claude we shall see more in another connection; here let me record Maisie's initial impression that he was "by far the most shining presence that had ever made her gape." "It was as if he had told her on the spot that he belonged to her." So he did, or the best part of him, but the rest of him belonged at last to Mrs. Beale, from whom he could not break away, even though already they did nothing but quarrel. "Through Sir Claude," writes Mrs. Shine finely, "James is saying that feeling and perception are, in the final analysis, not enough to make a complete human being; true virtue must include self-discipline and the strength to reject momentary satisfaction."

This is the cast with which Maisie plays out her drama and in contact with whom she develops her perceptions. The others are judged almost wholly by reference to their attitude toward and relations with her, and for this reason it is necessary to have them in mind in order to understand her and the development of her knowing. James says that her part in the novel was that of "keeping the torch of virtue alive in air tending infinitely to smother it . . . drawing some stray fragrance of an ideal across the scene of selfishness." Was it for that reason that he did not think it necessary to tell anything about her appearance? When Sir Claude speaks playfully of her "fatal gift of beauty," Mrs. Beale explains that he is not talking about the "vulgar beauty" of "personal loveliness," which she lacks, but only of "plain dull charm of character." It is perhaps unfortunate that James should have given so serious a piece of literature a title suggestive of a *feuilleton* or the kind of paperback novel that we used to think of snobbishly as having been addressed particularly to shopgirls and the servants' hall. In such works what somebody knows is always some hideous secret, preferably with black sexual overtones, and this has so much upset many readers of *What Maisie Knew* that some of the critics have not recovered from it to this day. In James's novel, however, nothing of this kind appears. There is sexual corruption and to spare, but this stands in the foreground from the beginning and is well understood by everybody. What Maisie knows —or learns—is something much more important.

Everybody understands, that is to say, except Maisie.

The child oscillates between thinking she knows "most" or "everything" or "all' and nothing whatever (James plays with the idea of her knowing almost as remorselessly as his great contemporary Henry Adams was to play with the idea of education). "There's nothing she hasn't heard. But it doesn't matter—it hasn't spoiled her." "It isn't as if you didn't already know everything, is it, love?" Yet it is clear that one large and, for this novel, key area of human knowledge lies beyond her horizon altogether. This, of course, is sex. Despite the appalling corruption mid which she is being reared, Maisie is sexually innocent—and unawakened; though familiar with all the counters in the game that is being played around her, she has no idea of the values they represent.

Her innocence, however, is not merely sexual. Physically, as well as mentally and spiritually, James limits her to the vantage point of the small child who must look up to the adults around her and who neither sees nor understands more than her eyes and her interest can take in. In many passages indeed he uses language much as D. W. Griffith learned to use the motion-picture camera, focusing on the particular significant or illuminating detail of the moment and blotting out everything else. For Maisie her mother's revolting lover Mr. Perriam is not a banker in the city but "a heathen Turk" with eyes like billiard balls.

When Mrs. Wix reports of Sir Claude that "he leans on me," Maisie takes the statement literally, and when that same lady regrets that she had not become a Catholic before it was too late, she wonders "what degree of lateness it was that shut the door against mistakes from such an error." She does not wish "to be bad" to Mrs. Beale, and though she is repelled by the countess, she rejoices, childlike, at the sovereigns that person presses into her hand. When Sir Claude takes her to Boulogne, she wonders whether they are not going on to Paris (was that not the "real thing" to do when one went abroad?), and when he tells her he has come to France to save money and plans to stay in Boulogne three or four days, she is astonished at the thought that money can be saved in so little time.

Up to the very time of her last terrible encounters with them, Maisie's innocence is shown too in her pathetic eagerness to love her worthless parents and to believe that they love her, in spite of all her bitter experience to the contrary, to accept them and to believe them "good." "Mamma doesn't care for me," she tells Sir Claude calmly as early as Chapter X, and later, when he apologizes for discussing that lady under her daughter's sharp little nose ("the fact is I forget half the time that Ida's your sainted mother"), she replies simply, "So do I!" Yet even at the end they might have won her had they gone about it rightly, but that would be like asking Satan to repent. "It must be either one thing or the other," Ida tells her; "if he takes you, you know, he takes you." And again: "Your father wishes you were dead—that, my dear, is what your father wishes. You'll have to get used to it as I've done —I mean his wishing that *I'm* dead." And I know not which is the more remarkable or the greater triumph—Maisie's capacity for forgiving past injuries or the superb courage with which, her eyes open at last, she simply, and without rancor, dismisses her parents as a factor in her concerns.[8]

But as to sexual awareness specifically, there can be no question concerning James's intentions. Maisie, he tells us, is growing up among things she is not to ask questions about.

[8] Mrs. Shine has an interesting passage (pp. 122ff.) in which she sees the absence of anger and resentment in Maisie as placing a limitation on the complete believability of the characterization. "Essentially a typical Jamesian heroine" and "an ideal child" through whom his readers can share James's "dream of emancipation from our baser feelings," she exists only "in the world of James's rich and creative imagination." In general I think this is right, but I believe Maisie *is* angry in Chapter XXI, when her mother challenges and outrages her moral perceptions by calling the Captain a cad, and I believe she also feels and rejoices in a sense of growing power as she moves toward independent judgment in the final chapters. On the other hand, I dissent altogether from Naomi Lebowitz' judgment, in *The Image of Loving: Henry James's Legacy to the Novel* (Wayne State University Press, 1965), that "the corruption in terms of her own desire for manipulation at the end of the novel is a regular part of the growth process in the Jamesian heroine, though it is not always so explicitly sketched."

"Everything had something behind it; life was like a long, long corridor with rows of closed doors." It was her fate "to see much more than she at first understood, but also even at first to understand much more than any little girl, however patient, had perhaps ever understood before." She keeps "images and echoes to which meanings were attachable . . . in the childish dusk, the dim closet, the high drawers, like games she wasn't yet big enough to play."

In her world everything is as distorted as the scenery in *The Cabinet of Dr. Caligari.* Parents, for example, are experienced not simultaneously, as by other children, but consecutively, like mutton and pudding or a bath and a nap, and relationships change without warning, as when Miss Overman ceases to be a governess and becomes first her father's lover and then his wife, from which she goes on to sustain the same relationships, in order, to Sir Claude, being Maisie's "mother" with both gentlemen. For Maisie, however, Mrs. Beale is Sir Claude's "lady-intimate"; she has no idea what they "do"; in fact she insists, when the subject is brought up, that "you don't do any harm—*you* don't." At an earlier stage, she had known that her own presence in Beale's house made it "proper" for Miss Overman to be there too, but she had no idea why: "Did papa like you just the same while I was gone?" she asked her. Even very late in the novel she cannot understand why she, Sir Claude, Mrs. Beale, and Mrs. Wix cannot "be four" together, nor why she should have to choose between them or sacrifice one to another, especially now that both Sir Claude and Mrs. Beale are "free," though neither one is divorced. This horrifies Mrs. Wix, who replies that nobody is "free" to commit a crime "branded in the Bible" and asks, "Haven't you really and truly *any* moral sense?" but to Maisie, to whom their being "free" means simply that they can make their own living arrangements and establish a home for her, all this is quite meaningless. When Sir Claude wonders aloud whether Ida may now have two lovers in tow, Maisie thinks he means she is traveling with two maids, and when Mrs.

Wix tells her that Sir Claude *pays* Mrs. Beale, she shows how little she understands about such things and horrifies the poor woman by asking, "Then doesn't he pay *you* too?"

Some of the critics, however, have been almost as much distressed as Mrs. Wix over the absence of Maisie's "moral sense." John C. McCloskey, for example, who was the most intelligent of Maisie's detractors and who made a very careful effort to trace the development of her knowing, makes the astonishing statement that the terms "purity" and "innocence" are "difficult to apply" to her, "for they imply a moral system which seems to be peculiarly absent." I should say rather that only the absence of a "system" could make "innocence" possible. Knowledge of good and evil began (did it not?) with the Fall. There was no "moral sense" in Eden. But there was innocence there.[9]

It has been said that Maisie makes her choices and evaluations on an aesthetic rather than a moral basis, but this is not altogether accurate. It is true that aesthetic considerations are very important to Maisie and that this gives the beautiful Mrs. Beale an advantage with her, but when, as in Chapter XIX, she seems most indifferent to adult moral codes which she is too young to understand, her primary concern is not with aesthetics but with her own need for what every child needs—love, kindness, and security. How hard she tries to believe her terrible parents "good," and how pathetic she is in the scene with the Captain (Chapter XVI), who thinks her mother "an angel" until poor Maisie, in her very anxiety to help, frightens him away! Leavis is wrong, I think, in crediting her rejection of the countess, who tries to be kind to her, wholly to Maisie's horror over her physical ugliness. Mrs. Wix, though not so ugly as this

[9]Comparison between *What Maisie Knew* and *Huckleberry Finn* is again involved at this point; see Glauco Cambon, "What Huck and Maisie Knew," *Studi Americani*, VI (1960), 204–20; also see my article, "Huckleberry Finn as the Devil's Disciple," *Boston University Journal*, XVIII, 2 (1970), 20–24. Mark Twain's discussion of the "moral sense" in *The Mysterious Stranger* is also relevant.

woman, is surely ugly enough, and in a grotesque way, to repel a beauty-loving child, but Maisie accepts her because she knows her to be good and kind. In the presence of the countess, in her luxurious love nest, on the other hand, she scents a moral miasma in the air and shies away from it because she cannot breathe in such an atmosphere without in the least knowing why.

The same strange, intuitive moral sensitiveness may be observed operating in reverse in the most touching scene in the novel, where Maisie has her only meeting in the park with her mother's latest and most deluded flame, the otherwise unnamed Captain, while Ida and Sir Claude quarrel just out of earshot (Maisie only hears him call her "a damned old brute"). James's treatment of this character is somewhat anomalous; he is not noted for an admiration for military men. It is clear that this is a thoroughly decent man who is being badly taken in ("a candid simple soldier; very grave"), who has even been made to believe that Ida is "tremendously" fond of her daughter and is now suffering agony because she thinks Maisie does not care for her. "Fairly hushed with the sense that he spoke of her mother as she had never heard any one speak," and deeply moved by his avowal of affection for her, the little girl cries, "You *do* love her?"

> "My dear child—!" The Captain wanted words.
> "Then don't do it only for just a little."
> "A little?"
> "Like all the others."
> "All the others?"—he stood staring.
> She pulled away her hand. "Do it always!" She bounded away to meet Sir Claude, and as she left the Captain she heard him ring out with apparent gaiety:
> "Oh I'm for it!"

The mingled shame and innocence of the passage brings tears, for without herself understanding the terms of the game, the child is reaching out to try to save and protect the mother who loathes and rejects her, as at the end she tries to save Sir Claude himself, only once more to fail. She herself is so much affected by this encounter that she risks Sir Claude's anger afterwards by refusing to give him an account of it. But she does save the Captain. It is only, we may be sure, with "apparent" gaiety that he avers being "for it," for when Maisie mentions him to her mother in Chapter XXI, the spell has already been broken, and all Ida can remember about him is that he is "the biggest cad in London," to which she adds that, for having mentioned him, her daughter is a "little horror" and "a dreadful dismal deplorable little thing."[10]

Maisie's leading detractors are Harris W. Wilson, Oscar Cargill, Edward Wasiolek, John C. McCloskey, and Sister M. Corona Sharp.[11] I admit that the extreme complexity of *What Maisie Knew* and the obscurity of some passages in it make

[10] Cf. James W. Gargano's perceptive comments on Maisie's encounters with both the "Countess" and the Captain in "*What Maisie Knew*: The Evolution of a 'Moral Sense,' " *NCF*, XVI (1961–62), 33–46.

[11] Harris W. Wilson, "What *Did* Maisie Know?" *CE*, XVII (1955–56), 279–82. Cargill's book has been cited in earlier chapters, and the studies by McCloskey and Sharp have been cited in this one. Edward Wasiolek, "Maisie: Pure or Corrupt?" *CE*, XXII (1960–61), 67–72, evidently intended to present a mediating view between Wilson and the orthodox interpretation, but though he thinks that at the end Maisie still knew "only what a child's soul can know," he also says that the "first tremors of sex and self interest," now moving within her, might well turn into "selfish interests" as she grew older. McCloskey too claims to reject Wilson, but he also believes that the "self-awareness" which Maisie has achieved at the end "is essentially a selfishness and a hardness. What she knows, at the end, is what she wants." He is not commenting upon James's story when he says that "as a Farange she must pursue her own desires, must have life on her own terms, without any real moral issue being at all involved," for James sees and portrays Maisie as *not* growing up a Farange; she did *not* learn relinquishment from either Beale or Ida. Neither can one argue that "her future (love and security and the power to do good by her very presence) lay with Sir Claude and Mrs. Beale." McCloskey even manages to squeeze out a tear for Sir Claude: "As Maisie was abandoned to her fate by her parents, so she abandons Sir Claude to his." Absurdity could hardly go further than making a small child responsible for the moral welfare of a twice-married man! There is a thoughtful commentary upon various critical views on this matter by Carola Osna Kaston, "Houses of Fiction in *What Maisie Knew*," *Criticism*, XVIII (1976), 27–42, who also touches upon several other aspects, including Dickensian influence.

their misinterpretations less inexcusable than is the case with the wrong-headed approaches we have already observed in connection with some other books, but the interesting thing is that in this instance they have not taken hold; all the really sensitive and authoritative later readings of the novel are willing to grant that James knew better what he was doing than Harris Wilson. What happens at the end is that Maisie counters Sir Claude's proposition that she give up Mrs. Wix to come with him by replying that she will do this if he, in turn, will give up Mrs. Beale. To Wilson and Cargill this means that she is offering herself to him as his lover; Cargill even sees the gold Virgin on the church as symbolizing the virginity which she is ready to throw into the scales for him against the more shopworn offering of Mrs. Beale.[12]

There are individual passages in *What Maisie Knew* which, without too much wrenching, might be made to support this interpretation, and it may be that James is culpable for not having made himself clearer at these points. Nevertheless, the interpretation is certainly wrong, for it runs counter not only to everything he tells us concerning his intentions but to the whole tendency of the story itself. The truth of the matter is that it is extremely difficult to explain Maisie's motives in the end, not because the choice she makes is not, in the highest degree, inevitable but because, being, as she is, still a child, she does not completely understand her own motives and intentions. We have already observed the operations of her built-in sensitiveness (whatever we may choose

---

[12] Wilson, who grants Maisie "a perverse innocence and directness in her degeneration," admits that it is possible that James may have intended no sexual element in her offer to Sir Claude, but he adds, without explaining why, that this interpretation would reduce the novel to the dimensions of "a technical exercise"! S. Gorley Putt, *Henry James: A Reader's Guide* (CoUP, 1966) has a wise and amusing comment on the gold Virgin: "But even if the symbol is deliberate, it is surely likely that Maisie, in those pre-Lolita days, was offering her virginity in appealing *contrast* to the sexual depravity of the elders, and not inviting Sir Claude to violate it. Curiously enough, I suspect Mrs. Gereth of burning down Poynton far more than I do Maisie of juvenile delinquency."

to call it) in her encounters with the Captain and the countess, as well as in her last interviews with Beale and Ida. Her final choice is the supreme manifestation of the same quality in her. In the narrower sense it is not a "moral" judgment—not at least in the sense in which Mrs. Wix would use the term— since though the illicit nature of the tie between Sir Claude and Mrs. Beale lies at the root of the difficulty, Maisie does not, even yet, thoroughly understand that. By the time she makes her decision, Maisie has been disillusioned in Boulogne about her "beautiful friend," and though she still loves Sir Claude, as she has always loved him, she has also come to sense his weaknesses (he is different to her from what he was before, and he has lied to her); perhaps she even senses something "phony" in his offer. She knows that he and Mrs. Beale are now quarreling, and she has no desire to be the third party in that kind of household; she has seen enough of that in her time. Perhaps she knows that her counteroffer will be rejected before she makes it, but she still gives him his chance. Perhaps even she only knows that what Sir Claude is asking of her would not "do," without knowing why. This is not egotism on her part or a determination to be "difficult" or throw her weight about; she simply acts under the necessity which devolves upon every human being to live his life under conditions which will permit his soul to breathe. "What helped the child," says James, "was that she knew what she wanted." Even more, she knew what she *needed*. She has already lost both her parents and Mrs. Beale, who at this point knows no more what to make of her than some of the critics. If she must lose Sir Claude too, she can brace herself to face even that.

It is the best possible testimony to the rightness and the inevitability of Maisie's decision that Sir Claude, who alone, among those who surround her, sees and understands (though not, alas! with a saving knowledge, so far as he himself is concerned), should so thoroughly approve of what she does. The Bible says that the devils believe and tremble. Sir Claude is far from being a devil, yet he cannot make the decision he knows to be right. Both Mrs. Wix and Mrs. Beale, though for very different reasons, would possess Maisie and control her; he alone would leave her free. It may seem odd that a man so much dependent upon women as he is should be so much afraid of them, but there can be no question that this is the case. As early as Chapter XIII he had admitted to Maisie not only that he could not "wholly chuck" Ida but also that he was afraid of Mrs. Beale and even that he would be afraid of Maisie herself if she were older. He is free of Ida now, but he is clearly still afraid of Mrs. Beale, in a sense disillusioned with her, recognizing the desirability of breaking with her, yet unable to make the break. Why he should scent potential danger in Maisie, unless he does not quite trust himself, is not clear. Maisie herself is at one point cold with terror, "afraid of herself," but that is when he asks her to share a home with Mrs. Beale; by the time she makes her counterproposal, her fear has been "dashed down and broken." Perhaps her eventual power to break with him had been foreshadowed as early as the end of Chapter XVI, following his displeasure after her interview with the Captain; in any case, it had been some time since she had "embraced the implication of a kind of natural divergence between lovers and little girls," a sentence which is idiotic nonsense if Wilson is right. When she has chosen, Sir Claude tells Mrs. Beale that "it's all right" and that "it wouldn't do. . . . we *can't* work her in. It's perfectly true—she's unique. We're not good enough—oh no!" and when Maisie holds out her hand to him in parting, "he took it and held it a moment, and their eyes met as the eyes of those who have done for each other what they can," which sounds very much like J. M. Barrie. Actually, however, so far as the decision is concerned, they have done nothing for each other, though heaven knows she has tried. What she has achieved has been wrought without him, even in spite of him, for, as Gargano says, he has preferred to be lost with Mrs. Beale rather than saved with Maisie. What a man lacked the necessary courage and integrity to achieve has been achieved by a child. In a sense she has even done it for him, since, though he has suffered a moral downfall, there is still enough good in him so that he can experience a genuine sense of exhilaration in her victory.[13]

I do not regret that the revisionists have been assailed so vigorously on the subject of *What Maisie Knew*, for until their misapprehensions have been cleared away, the novel cannot be properly understood. In a larger sense, however, such questions as Wasiolek's "Maisie—Pure or Corrupt?" are somewhat Mrs. Wixish. We are not testing the purity of a drug; we are observing a human being who, at the end of the story, has made a crucial decision but still has a long way to go toward maturity. It is absurd to talk about her as if her character were already completely formed. McCloskey fastens on James's remark about "the death of her childhood" to indicate that by the end she has become an adolescent, but this is somewhat forced. She has proved to herself and to us that she is capable of making an important decision, but she is far from having experienced a full sexual and emotional awakening. James himself says that she will change after she becomes mature but makes it clear that this is no

[13] For further interesting and rewarding commentary on *What Maisie Knew*, see Peter Coveney, *Poor Monkey: The Child in Literature* (Rockliff, 1957); William Walsh, *The Use of Imagination: Educational Thought and the Literary Mind* (Chatto and Windus, 1959); John Roland Dove, "The Tragic Sense in Henry James," *TSLL*, II (1960–61), 303–14; Joseph A. Hynes, "The Middle Way of Miss Farange: A Study of James's *Maisie*," *ELH*, XXXII (1965), 528–53; Abigail Ann Hamblen, "Henry James and the Power of Eros: *What Maisie Knew*," *Midwest Quarterly*, IX (1967–68), 391–99; Martha Banta, "The Quality of Experience in *What Maisie Knew*," *NEQ*, XLII (1969), 483–510, a sensitive study which places the book "within the larger tradition of Christian comedy"; Alfred Harbegger, "Reciprocity and the Market Place in *The Wings of the Dove* and *What Maisie Knew*," *NCF*, XXV (1970–71), 455–73; Paul Fahey, "*What Maisie Knew*: Learning Not to Mind," *Critical Review* (Melbourne), No. 14 (1971), 96–108. Charles Thomas Samuels, *The Ambiguity of Henry James*, pp. 179ff., has an interesting and penetrating reading of *Maisie* which is not at all points in agreement with mine. But H. R. Wolf, "*What Maisie Knew*: The Rankian Hero," *AI*, XXIII (1966), 227–34, is totally irrelevant to both James's mind and his story.

part of his story; *What Maisie Knew* is as much the story of a little girl as *Tom Sawyer* is the story of a boy. As Mark Twain wrote at the end of his narrative:

> So endeth this chronicle. It being strictly a history of a boy, it must stop here; the story could not go much further without becoming the history of a man. When one writes a novel about grown people, he knows exactly where to stop—that is, with a marriage; but when he writes of juveniles, he must stop where he best can.
>
> Most of the characters that perform in this book still live, and are prosperous and happy. Some day it may seem worth while to take up the story of the younger ones again and see what sort of men and women they turned out to be; therefore it will be wisest not to reveal any of that part of their lives at present.

Since neither James nor Mark Twain ever did carry their stories into maturity, it is not surprising that others have tried to do it for them, but one may recognize the force of a temptation and still realize that it must be resisted. Pelham Edgar saw Sir Claude eventually breaking with Mrs. Beale and coming to join Maisie and Mrs. Wix in England, which is sentimental and unconvincing, while Tony Tanner believes that "what is in store for her is a progressive dimunition, a devivification, a contraction of her sacred wonderment," which is even worse than Edgar's suggestion since it reverses her development and undercuts the whole meaning of the book. But in the interpretation of literature all such speculations are impertinent, and those who indulge in them put themselves into a class with the nineteenth-century ladies who wrote essays on such subjects as "The Girlhood of Shakespeare's Heroines."

If anything I have written about Maisie is correct, then she lives, insofar as a child can, in obedience to a built-in standard which Quakers and nineteenth-century Transcendentalists thought of as a kind of Inner Light. Mrs. Wix gets it exactly wrong when she accuses Maisie of lacking a "moral sense." It would be more to the point to say that Mrs. Wix lacks a "moral sense," for she operates by a code which she applies mechanically to any situation by which she is confronted, but she is incapable of the "great ecstasy of a larger impression of life" possessed by the girl whose "vocation was to see the world and to thrill with enjoyment of the picture." There is nothing wrong with Mrs. Wix's Bible morality as such, but it lacks spontaneity and does not proceed from the roots of her being; consequently, as when she surrenders at last to Mrs. Beale, it is sometimes inadequate.

Mrs. Wix is not satisfied to have Maisie moral in her own behavior; she must take up moral attitudes and take a stand in behalf of abstractions and legalities of which she has no need and which she is too young to understand. The elder Henry James strongly deprecated such "attitudes," and, as Tony Tanner reminds us, his son was well aware of this. It was well that Maisie should go away with Mrs. Wix at the end, but it was also vitally important that before doing so she should have learned that Mrs. Wix was "nobody." Maisie is still young enough to need a mother, and Mrs. Wix has given her, and can be trusted to continue to give her, the only mothering she has ever known. But there is no danger now that Mrs. Wix's "straighteners" will distort the world for Maisie. Intellectually she has now passed beyond Mrs. Wix; morally she has proved that she is capable of making her own decisions. It is completely appropriate therefore that the book should end with the observation that Mrs. Wix "still had room for wonder at what Maisie knew."

VIII. "THE MODERN GIRL"
NANDA BROOKENHAM

WITH THE SINGLE exception of *The Sacred Fount,* which even many of his admirers find unreadable, *The Awkward Age* (1899) has probably been the least popular of any novel by Henry James that can possibly be accounted major. It was first serialized in *Harper's Weekly,* and after the book appeared, its publisher told the author he had never sponsored anything which had been less liked. During the autumn which followed its spring publication, James himself wrote Henrietta Reubell that it had excited little besides bewilderment and denunciation.

For reasons best known to himself, James excluded *The Sacred Fount* from the New York Edition, but he was far from accepting the popular verdict on *The Awkward Age;* instead he told Miss Reubell that he thought "Mrs. Brook" (that is, Brookenham) the best thing he had ever done, and he never changed his mind about this. As late as 1912 he wrote R. W. Chapman that so far from being "dim" on any aspect of that lady, he stood ready to face a stiff cross-examination on the subject, and if he was ever smug in expressing appreciation of any of his books in the Prefaces to the New York Edition, he achieved it with *The Awkward Age:* "Were I minded to use in this connexion a 'loud' word . . . I should speak of the composition of the chapters entitled 'Tishy Grendon,' with all the pieces of the game on the table together and each unconfusedly and contributively placed, as triumphantly scientific."

Among James's early critics William Dean Howells, who probably understood him better than anybody else in his time, was one of the few who stood in cordial agreement, and *The Awkward Age* was one of the books in the foreground of Howells' mind when he penned his most brilliant tribute to his friend:

Here you have the work of a great psychologist, who has the imagination of a poet, the wit of a keen humorist, the conscience of an impeccable moralist, the temperament of a philosopher, and the wisdom of a rarely experienced witness of the world; and yet you come back at me with the fact, or rather the pretense, that you do not like to keep puzzling things out.[1]

But many readers of James, both early and late, have found better evidence to support this judgment elsewhere in his work than they could find in *The Awkward Age*.

James's "method" was of course a large part of the difficulty. He was trying to produce a novel in the manner of "the ingenious and inexhaustible, the charming philosophic 'Gyp'" (Sibylle Gabrielle Marie Antoinette Riquetti de Mirabeau, Countess de Martel de Janville) and her disciple, Henri Lavedan,[2] and though he realized that neither the English nor the American reader would permit him to create a novel wholly in dialogue, the proportion of material standing between quotation marks is still higher in *The Awkward Age* than in any other James novel. Moreover, the usual Jamesian "observer," from whose "point of view" the action is viewed (thus providing valuable guidance in the way of interpreta-

[1]W. D. Howells, "Mr. Henry James's Later Work," *North American Review*, CLXXVI (1903), 125–37, reprinted in F. W. Dupee, ed., *The Question of Henry James* (Holt, 1945).

[2]Cargill has also plausibly suggested the possible influence of George Sand's *Valentine* and of Marcel Prévost's *Lettre de femmes* and *Les Demi-vièrges*. Hamlin L. Hill, Jr., " 'The Revolt of the Daughters': A Suggested Source for *The Awkward Age*," *NQ*, CCVI (1961), 347–49, deals with a series of magazine articles on the subject indicated in prominent English periodicals between January and June, 1894, pointing out what he justly calls "many striking points of agreement."

tion for the reader) has now disappeared, being replaced by what James calls a "lamp" in the form of various characters illuminating particular "occasions." Each of the ten "books" into which the novel is divided is named for one of these "lamps"; each book is an "act," and each chapter is a "scene" within the act. The basic idea was to eliminate all "going behind" on the part of the author, the reader being required to interpret both the action and the motives of the characters, like the spectator at a play, by observing what happens and hearing what the characters say and what others say to them and about them. Joseph Wiesenfarth judges that James achieves objectivity in *The Awkward Age* at the cost of both intensity and economy. He also finds that stress often falls upon the irrelevant and the unimportant and that "subordination of treatment fails to go hand in hand with subordination of meaning." Moreover "some conversations are so tenuous and drawn out as to contribute little to the novel and much to wearing down the reader's patience." Actually, however, the author does not adhere to his method as scrupulously as he claims, for his commentary often gives much more than could be contained in the stage directions it purports to replace. Francis Gillen counted thirty direct author's comments in the course of the novel, in addition to the "semi-comments and those which were linked to a piece of stage action."[3] There was a strange combination of innocence or naïveté with extreme sophistication in James, both as artist and as man, and even after his technique had been fully developed, he was not always capable of resisting per-

[3]Joseph Wiesenfarth, *Henry James and the Dramatic Analogy* (Fordham University Press, 1963); Francis Gillen, "The Dramatist in his Drama: Theory vs. Effect in *The Awkward Age*," *TSLL*, XII (1970–71), 663–74. In the nondialogue portion of James's novel, Gillen finds a "close resemblance at times to stage melodrama and at times to simple old-fashioned character description." James "evokes, at first appearance, an emotive response toward the characters and gives a preliminary and, at times, omniscient indication of the role they are to play in the drama." Moreover, he often veils comment by adding conjectural phrases which do not deceive the attentive reader.

sonal commentary. There is a striking example in *The Awk-ward Age,* Book X, Chapter 1: "Kindness therefore becomes for us, by a quick turn of the glass that reflects the whole scene, the high pitch of the concert."

"Method" is not the only difficulty in *The Awkward Age,* however, nor have all the difficulties lessened with time. The initial idea of the book, which, like many of James's monsters, as he called them, was originally designed as a little sketch, was the problem of what happens to the "good talk" in the fashionable drawing room when the teen-age unmarried daughter begins to "sit downstairs." "Good talk," of course, is adult, sophisticated, worldly talk, that is talk which is not good at all in the primary sense of the term. This problem did not exist in France, where the daugh-ter was kept in her convent school until she was married and thus had presumably passed at a bound from knowing nothing to knowing everything, nor yet in America, where the talk was simply scaled down to her level, thus being good but not "good," but in England, with its genius for "muddling through," the matter had long been important, as Mr. Podsnap's concern to avoid anything which might bring a blush to the cheek of the young person had made clear to all readers of Dickens. In these days of deplorable manners, when children are often obliged to adjust their conversations to the sensibilities of their parents, it is surely not necessary to labor the point that such an inquiry as the basis of a five-hundred-page novel is now more likely to awaken mirth than concern and also pretty sure to strengthen the hand of those who, quite unjustly, think of James as a Miss Nancy kind of writer. Nor is this, by any means, the only kind of thing the modern reader may find strained in *The Awkward Age.* Mr. Longdon is attracted to Nanda be-cause of her striking physical resemblance to her grand-mother, Lady Julia, whom he had loved. Because he knows she loves Vanderbank (whose mother had also, less seri-ously, enthralled him), he offers to subsidize Van handsomely if he will marry Nanda, but Van will say neither yes nor no. Mitchett marries Little Aggie, whom he does not love, to please Nanda, whom he does, and Nanda, having lost Van, intercedes for him with her mother and tries to "square" him with Mr. Longdon, so that he need not lose solid cash by his refusal to accept her along with it! Finally, Nanda, Mr. Longdon, and, to a lesser degree, Mitchy, are the only admirable characters in sight, and the world in which all these persons move is as corrupt as that of Restoration comedy.

I realize that I have kept Nanda Brookenham, who is my real subject, waiting in the wings for some time. I might plead that James himself set me the example by not permitting her to enter until Chapter II in the third book and by highlighting her mother rather than herself in the New York Preface, but it is more to the point that we cannot approach Nanda "cold," without some understanding of the character of the novel in which she figures and of her relationship to the other characters against the background she shares with them.

The most important of these is of course her mother, "Mrs. Brook," who has been compared by her admirers to the heroines of Restoration comedy and to Meredith's "rogues in porcelain." Nobody gives her a clean bill of health, but some critics are clearly as much fascinated by her as James was himself. Dorothea Krook credits her with "a fugitive likeableness and even loveableness . . . which all her displaced vanity and greed, malice and destructiveness, have no power to diminish." Dupee finds "a *kind* of conscience" in "her exacting sense of social fitness, her awareness of others, her heroic respect for delicacy, imagination, humor, composure, and candor," and Cargill thought that "without her will and her command, her group would become utterly depraved."

I regret that I cannot match the charity involved in such judgments.[4] Mrs. Brook is dainty and beautiful, though her beauty does not come across with anything like the force of Christina Light's, and, though she is forty-one years old, she affects a pathetic ingenue pose ("her voice had at moments the most touching tones of any in England") which is so well carried off as to cause even her daughter to think of her, at the end, as needing to be cherished like something young, helpless, and therefore particularly vulnerable. It is true that she gains in comparison to such depraved persons as Cashmore and Lady Fanny, and also to the Duchess, who completely lacks Mrs. Brook's finesse. The out-and-out adulterers in *The Awkward Age* stand rather on the fringes of the main action. Cashmore is having an affair with Carrie Donner, whom he drops (or so he claims) when he is attracted to Nanda, shamelessly avowing his new interest to Mrs. Brook herself, who expresses no indignation; his wife, Lady Fanny, is involved with Captain Dent-Douglas; and Lady Fanny's brother, Lord Petherton, is having an affair with the Duchess. Later Petherton switches to Little Aggie and Lady Fanny to Harold Brookenham, who is mature only in his vices.

The Duchess stands in the book for the Continental system on which she has brought up her niece and loudly objects to the freedom which Mrs. Brook allows Nanda. Because Nanda turns out well despite all her knowingness while Aggie runs wild with her aunt's lover as soon as she herself has been married to Mitchy, it has been claimed that *The Awkward Age* vindicates Mrs. Brook's system as against that of the Duchess, but this is not quite clear. Nanda's brother, Harold, who has grown up in the same family with her, is so depraved that every reader of the novel longs to take him out and step on him, and it seems likely that

---

⁴The single point at which I find Mrs. Brook sympathetic is when, having received an implied compliment from her husband, she "dimly smiled," laid "her hand on his sleeve," and said, "That's the nicest thing you ever said to me. But ever, *ever*, you know," and this, touching and genuine though it is, seems little enough tenderness for a lifetime.

James, who believed in free will, was also aware of the ethical dividing line which runs through all human experience; if it would be too much to say that there are people who cannot be corrupted by any conceivable circumstances, at least there are no circumstances which can be trusted in themselves to guarantee salvation. Nevertheless, the Duchess is clearly a worse woman than Mrs. Brook (she is also much more of a hypocrite); as Mrs. Brook observes truly, Aggie *is* her aunt's conscience, and the Duchess keeps it outside herself and feels the need of no other. Mrs. Brook is probably not herself an adulteress; if the precise nature of her emotional entanglement with Van is left undefined, it is the Duchess herself who assures Mr. Longdon that there is nothing "wrong." This does not, however, go far toward redeeming Mrs. Brook in the judicious reader's judgment; in a sense, it even lowers her; as she herself once observes, she lacks the excuse of passion. To scheme, even at your daughter's expense, to hold an admirer as the ornament of such a salon as Mrs. Brook presides over is more petty and calculating, and therefore more contemptible, than to do such a thing when mastered by lust, and surely Mrs. Brook's fundamental moral indifference could not be shown more clearly than it is when she tells Van that she asks Nanda no questions because she wants the girl's life to be as much as possible like her own.

Since the contamination which Nanda is suspected of having acquired from her mother's circle nowhere appears in her conduct,[5] and since it is never even remotely suggested that she is in any sense unchaste, it has sometimes been judged that the whole to-do over whether her freedom has disqualified her for an advantageous marriage is much ado about nothing. Actually this is a superficial view, which misses James's essential point. The Brookenhams are a family of "dead beats." Unable to live in society upon what Edward

---

[5] At one point it is suggested that she smokes, but this is not pinned down.

Brookenham[6] is paid in the post his wife obtained for him, they shamelessly "sponge" on their friends; James thrusts Harold's "sponging" into the foreground as merely the extreme example of how the family lives. Mrs. Brook admits that her first interest in people is always their means and tells Mr. Longdon, of all people, that Nanda too "has her little place with the circus—it's the way we earn our living." Gerald Levin's[7] notion that "Nanda has fallen in with her mother's plan to work Mr. Longdon, and [that] she herself worked to get Mitchy married so that Van would have one less excuse not to propose" cannot, I believe, be substantiated, but she knows very well what is going on and is humiliated by it; as she tells Van, "We seem to be all living more or less on other people, all immensely 'beholden.'" In the Brookenham world, both love and friendship are things to be exploited for one's own advantage, and caring for one's children is only a matter of securing their material advantage, generally at the expense of somebody else. People are counters in a game played for gain or pleasure, and love and marriage have been placed upon a strict cash-and-carry basis. Intrigue and clandestine maneuvering are omnipresent, and no confidences are respected. Forms are preserved after all reality has departed from them, and the residue is complete moral rot and bankruptcy. The real tragedy is not merely that these people are destroying their souls but that

[6] A moral and emotional cipher, Brookenham is hardly important enough in the novel to rate more than a footnote in this discussion. As the Duchess observes, he figures in his wife's drawing room "only as one of those queer extinguishers of fire in the corridors of hotels," and Mrs. Brook herself remarks apropos of the invitations for which the family is always fishing, "Fancy people wanting Edward!" When Nanda begs Van not to desert her mother, she tells him that her father would not mind a bit his being in love with her, and Brookenham proves the truth of this by the complete lack of emotion with which he receives the finally frank announcement of her involvement which his wife makes to him. Charles Thomas Samuels can sympathize with Mrs. Brook only because "she has been a pearl worn round the neck of a donkey."

[7] "Why Does Vanderbank Not Propose?" *UKCR*, XXVII (1960–61), 314–18.

they are destroying them for nothing and playing a dangerous game for stakes that are not worth winning.

On this basis, too, the intellectuality for which some critics give Mrs. Brook and her circle credit can hardly be maintained. Thus Percy Lubbock finds here "a charmed world" of highly sophisticated men and women "who seem so well practised in the art of living that they could never be taken by surprise," and even Dorothea Krook thinks the "sophisticated worldliness" of the group "supremely brilliant and vital" and its style of life "brave, bold and free." "The free play of mind was never freer than it is here, 'good talk' was never better, perceptions and discriminations never finer or subtler or more amusing."[8] Practically every adjective here employed is supremely ill-chosen. Nobody in the Buckingham Crescent group ever says anything that shows any concern with ideas, power to grasp an idea, or any capacity for disinterested or impersonal considerations. Concentration, frequently flavored with malice, is exclusively directed toward ferreting out the motives and relationships of a spoiled, pampered group of worthless and useless people. Thus Mrs. Brook describes Lady Fanny as "the ornament of our circle" and "the delight of our life" because she has not yet been able to make up her mind whether or not she will "bolt" from her husband with Captain Dent-Douglas, and the excitement of guessing provides never-ending entertainment for them.

The "big scene" in *The Awkward Age* comes at the end of Book VIII, where Mrs. Brook, in the presence of virtually the entire "cast" of the novel, forces an issue by compelling her daughter to admit that she has read an indecent French

---

[8]This writer even praises James's reference to Mrs. Brook's "lovely silly eyes . . . . Of course, one sees at once, the eyes *have* to be 'silly': as silly as they are lovely and as lovely as they are silly. For if they were not both, Mrs. Brook would be merely devastatingly intelligent; and that would mean the end of her unique power in Buckingham Crescent." But what are "silly" eyes, and how could eyes possibly be either silly or the opposite thereof?

novel. There has been much discussion about whether Mrs.
Brook's aim here was to disillusion Van sufficiently to make
sure he will not marry Nanda (thus ensuring that her mother
can retain him for herself) or whether she is rather trying
to make Mr. Longdon believe that the circle is so corrupt
that he will move to take Nanda out of it. The situation is
obscure enough so that both these motives may well be
present in some degree. Van does not marry Nanda (Mrs.
Brook never did really believe that he would), but Mr. Longdon does finally adopt her. Whatever she may have had in
mind, however, Mrs. Brook took a desperate chance, and,
for the time being at any rate, she seems to have overreached
herself and broken up her circle.[9] However all this may be,
the use of the novel is a perfect device for dramatizing the
concentration of the whole group upon externalities and appearances. Nanda's motive for reading the book was to de-
termine whether or not it was fit reading for Tishy Grendon,
and she decided that it was not, but nobody thinks it worth-
while to take her motive or her judgment into consideration:

That in a scene in which Harold is revealed as exploiting Lady
Fanny, the Duchess and Petherton treat Mitch's marriage with
complete cynicism, and the Brookenhams virtually disown Nanda,
the single point of corruption should be adjudged Nanda's reading
Van's book indicates the completeness of James's criticism of

[9] James W. Gargano, "The Theme of 'Salvation' in *The Awkward Age*," *TSLL*,
IX (1967–68), 273–87, thinks Mrs. Brook, having learned that Van is both "self-
serving and constitutionally incapable of forthright commitment," wishes to save
Nanda "from suffering on the rack of alternating hope and despair." As a necessary
foil to the simply good Mr. Longdon, she would be immoral "only if she helped
Vanderbrook to 'succeed' as Madame Merle aids Osmond." Though he admits
that she can be malicious and devious, I still think Gargano's an idealized interpretation of Mrs. Brook's motives. William F. Hall, "James's Concept of Society
in *The Awkward Age*," *NCF*, XXIII (1968–69), 28–48, tries a different approach
and denies that she acted deliberately and consciously; instead he sees her feeling
her way from moment to moment without predevised plan. She began by wanting
Nanda back from Mr. Longdon's, but her husband cramped her style by failing to
back her up; from this point she floundered and ended by exposing both the
Duchess's code of manners and her own.

"pure behaviour" [as detached from "moral consciousness"] as a moral criterion.[10]

Mr. Longdon is Nanda's good angel, who rescues her from Buckingham Crescent by providing a refuge for her elsewhere and, at the end, virtually adopts her. Though the old man is first attracted to her by her physical resemblance to her grandmother, he has sufficient flexibility and insight to be able finally to accept her for herself alone, in spite of the modernity which is so different from what he had loved in Lady Julia.[11] The only other men who are important to Nanda (Cashmore never gets anywhere with her) are Mitchy, who loves her, and Van, whom she vainly loves. Mitchy— clumsy, ugly, pathetic, and of humble background—has been accepted into her mother's circle because of his wealth. Van has "the sacred terror," which is what it is now fashionable to call charisma, with very little else to justify or reinforce it. Neither has escaped corruption, but Mitchy has preserved in his "general abyss," as Mrs. Brook describes it, "a little deep-down delicious niceness, a sweet sensibility," which saves him by leaving him capable of unselfish, self-forgetful love. As he himself says, he is "just rotten with goodness," by which he may mean that he can only inspire liking and not passion. This capacity for commitment is just what is lacking in the weak idealist Van, who admits the lostness of himself and his circle in his very first talk with Mr. Longdon, where he says that he feels he was meant for something

[10] Ian Gregor and Brian Nichols, "The Novel of Moral Consciousness: *The Awkward Age*," in their *The Moral and the Story* (Faber and Faber, 1962). H. K. Girling, " 'Wonder' and 'Beauty' in *The Awkward Age*," *EIC*, VIII (1958), 370–80, offers the interesting observation that the characters in this novel "often give the impression of enclosing themselves in desperate chatter because their sureties are crumbling beneath them."

[11] Mr. Longdon is one of the characters in whom critics have seen something of James himself. Though I am always suspicious of this kind of criticism, it is suggestive, as Leon Edel has pointed out, that James should have used Alvin Langdon Coburn's photograph of the entrance to his own Lamb House as "Mr. Longdon's" in the frontispiece to *The Awkward Age* in the New York Edition.

better than he has achieved. A number of possible motives may well enter into his final rejection of Nanda. Much younger than Mr. Longdon though he is, his heart (what there is of it) still belongs to the "old-fashioned girl," but his self-esteem is quite as important as his idealism in making it impossible for him to accept a wife whose immaculate and untouched ignorance-purity might possibly be open to question, while his obsession with externalities and appearances causes him to shy from Mr. Longdon's offered subsidy. Probably he also knows, though perhaps without knowing he knows it, that he would feel uncomfortable with one who had achieved the degree of independence and self-awareness which Nanda now possesses. Most critics also find him handicapped by a constitutional indecisiveness. Mrs. Shine is probably the harshest of them all when she calls him a "weak, irresponsible, hypocritical anti-hero," and Joseph P. O'Neill is his principal defender. If James had intended us to condemn Van for his hesitancy, O'Neill urges, he would not have cited him so favorably in the Preface to *The Princess Casamassima*. Others argue that the issue is not really closed until Book IX, where Van calls with the idea of seeing Nanda and, after his talk with Mrs. Brook, leaves the house without having done so. Actually the *Casamassima* reference is not really decisive (James calls Van "divided"), and if the author intended us to view Van as favorably as O'Neill believes, he was a very clumsy artist in permitting him to behave with such contemptible weakness and awkwardness as he displays in his final talk with Nanda in Book X.[12]

In some ways James seems to have made a special effort deliberately to deglamorize Nanda herself. In this respect,

[12] Shine, *The Fictional Children of Henry James*; Joseph P. O'Neill, *Workable Design*. See also Eben Bass, "Dramatic Scene and *The Awkward Age*," *PMLA*, LXXIX (1964), 148–57, and the articles by Gerald Levin and James E. Gargano already cited. Mrs. Shine devoted the climactic chapter of her book to Nanda, and though I dissent from her interpretations of certain particular points, hers is the most admirable comprehensive discussion of the girl's character we have. Bass's article is probably the best analysis of the structure of the novel.

though in no other, she resembles the early heroine of *Washington Square*. To be sure, the testimony concerning her looks is not completely consistent. According to the Duchess, neither she nor her mother have beauty, but the mother has grace, and the daughter "not a line." At the very beginning, Mr. Longdon, comparing Nanda's picture to Little Aggie's, thinks Aggie prettier, and Van agrees, saying that it is a question whether Nanda is pretty at all. Van also says that she has no features unless perhaps she has two or three too many, though her expression reveals her charming nature, and that she is sufficiently removed from the London taste to make her marriageability doubtful. Longdon, however, also says that Lady Julia was exquisite and had "everything" and that Nanda is exactly like her. Later, after Longdon has met the girl, Van gives her a Lawrence face, Longdon amends it to a Gainsborough, and they finally settle on a Raphael. What it all seems to add up to is that though Nanda is certainly not ugly, her face has more character than prettiness and requires character in the observer to be adequately appreciated.

When we first meet her, at Van's rooms, where she has come, without her mother, to make tea and to meet Mr. Longdon, as a part of her calculated "coming-out" process, she is completely self-possessed (amazingly so in the circumstances posited), but almost "unnaturally grave," and she fixes Mr. Longdon "with her mild strangeness." Elizabeth Owen, who thinks her "only a child in judgment" throughout the book, "a 'little lamb,'" finds her as "comic in her loquacity" here as Little Aggie is elsewhere "in her dumbness."[13] The solemnity, however, is habitual, though it increases toward the end, when her mother declares her, after her disappointment in Van, "as bleak as a chimney-top when the fire's out." Mitchy judges her to possess everything except humor and calls her tragic, and James himself tells us

---

[13]"*The Awkward Age* and the Contemporary English Scene," *Victorian Studies*, XI (1967–68), 63–82.

that her honesty is "almost violent." She has no wit nor variety of manner, none of the high spirits of youth, and no illusions about herself. She lacks social subtlety and is completely straightforward at all times. Her solemnity helps her to adjust herself to Mr. Longdon. "Her young gravity matches his old-fashioned formality," says Ellen Leyburn; "and the two move with the dignity of a kind of quiet saraband among the whirling figures who surround them."

Gregor and Nicholas take the epigraph for their chapter on *The Awkward Age* from Milton's great words in the *Areopagitica*: "That virtue, therefore, which is but a youngling in the contemplation of evil and knows not the utmost that vice promises to her followers, and rejects it, is but a blank virtue, not a pure," and according to Joseph J. Firebaugh, the subject of the novel is the problem "represented by the fable of the fall of man—the conflict of knowledge *vs.* innocence, good *vs.* evil, or, to use more civilized terminology, realities *vs.* conventions."[14] Van thinks Nanda takes things in through her pores, and she herself says, "I don't know only what people tell me. . . . Girls understand now. It has got to be faced." Then she asks, "Don't I know everything?" She sees herself as "a sort of little drain-pipe with everything flowing through" and frankly admits that she could love only the kind of man who wouldn't have her. All this has been the inevitable result of growing up in the Brookenham family and making a close friend of the unhappily married Tishy Grendon, whose house is frequented by her disreputable sister, Carrie Donner. Yet Nanda takes Tishy under her wing and won't let her read the French novel until she has decided whether it is proper; she doesn't think much of anyone who is not loyal to her friends. If she tells Mitchy that he is so good that nothing shocks him, the same is true of her, as is shown most convincingly in her

[14]"The Pragmatism of Henry James," *Virginia Quarterly Review*, XXVII (1951), 419–35. A sense of sin has been called many things, but so far as I know Firebaugh is the first writer to suggest that it is uncivilized! C. S. Lewis says, "When poisons become fashionable, they do not cease to kill."

attitude toward Aggie after her fall (Aggie is only trying to find out what kind of person she is, she argues, and will finally come to herself). It is at least a question, however, whether this testifies more to her charity or to her naïveté, and the latter quality appears again in her capacity to love and to idealize such a man as Vanderbank.

She wants Mitchy to marry Little Aggie to save her from becoming like her aunt the Duchess, and when he asks her what she knows about the Duchess's life, she says she knows everything. But she also tells Mitchy that Aggie will save him, and this includes saving him from Lord Petherton, who "preys" upon him.[15] True, she tries her hand at "managing" here, but her motives, unlike those of other "managers" in her circle, are benevolent, and J. A. Ward is too harsh when he blames her for the failure of the marriage ("goodness, combined with ignorance, leads directly to evil"). If human beings are to be held responsible for everything that results unhappily from well-intentioned advice, then obviously it is not going to be safe for anybody to recommend anything to anyone.

Nanda does not greatly admire either herself or her type. She would much rather be like Lady Julia or Little Aggie ("Ah say what you will—it *is* the way we ought to be!"), or, rather, like what she *supposes* Little Aggie to be. Only, she realizes that this is impossible. She is not her grandmother; neither can she "shake off" her mother, whose limitations she recognizes clearly, even though "they *were* as good friends as if Nanda had not been her daughter," and though Mrs. Brook herself is quite sincere when she remarks of her daughter that "no one in London touches her." "One is just what one *is*," says Nanda; she has not watched life for noth-

---

[15] Cargill believed this meant that the relationship between Petherton and Mitchy was that which existed between Lord Alfred Douglas and Oscar Wilde and used this idea to reinforce his impression of Nanda's extremely knowledgeable sophistication, but with Petherton the indefatigable woman chaser he is, the interpretation seems unlikely. We know that Petherton "preys" upon Mitchy financially, and surely Nanda must have known that he was incapable of being a true friend to anybody.

ing. She is blowing out the gas to see how dark it is when she calls herself a drainpipe or an "old mannered slangy hack," but she is dead-serious about respecting and accepting the integrity of her own experience. "What I am I must remain. . . . I'm about as good as I can be—and about as bad." Even toward Mr. Longdon her attitude is much like that of Arabella toward her lover at the end of the great opera by Richard Strauss and Hugo von Hofmannsthal: he must take her as she is if he wants her at all, but there is more fatalism than satisfaction in her self-acceptance.

As early as Book IV, Mrs. Brook finds something "quite maternal" in Nanda. This appears clearly at the end in her attempt to mother her mother ("she's so fearfully young"), to reconcile Mitchy to the miseries of his marriage, and even to square Van himself with Mr. Longdon. Such is "the modern daughter." Though she is older than Maisie Farange, she needs Mr. Longdon almost as much as Maisie needs Mrs. Wix, but as Maisie's moral sensitiveness had, by the end of her story, already run ahead of her guide's, so it is also clear that Nanda will mother even Mr. Longdon. Once she says that she is more likely to adopt him than he her, and once she tells her mother that the advantage of their relationship will be that she can do something for him. She educates him, too, and enlarges his understanding of life and his capacity to embrace it, though I think Mrs. Shine wrong when she says that Nanda brings Longdon "completely around to her view of life," for this is to deny him the breadth of charity. Rather, I should say, he accepts her because she has brought him to recognize in her a brand of integrity which is genuine despite its difference from his own. "I dare say," she tells him, "that I make allusions you don't like. But I keep forgetting." She tells Van that Longdon's liking her has been "a painful gradual process," and she tells her mother that, as time went on, the resemblance to her grandmother which first drew him to her was almost lost sight of. At the end they have bridged the generation and, to some extent, the cultural, gap between them and achieved complete respect, each for the other.

To see Nanda as a tragic figure, as some critics have tried to do, is both to sentimentalize her and to fail to do her justice. Yet her position at the end is not triumphant. She seems to herself to have missed the kind of love that leads to marriage, and, for the time being at any rate, she has withdrawn from a world that she cannot master. For all that, her disappointment is cushioned by both Mr. Longdon's money and his devotion, and many girls might have envied her. When Mrs. Brook calls her, "Poor little thing!" her husband, impercipient though he is, has common sense on his side when he replies, "Does she strike you as poor, with so awfully much done for her?" Neither can I go along with the critics who completely rule out the possibility of future marriage for her. It is true that she says,"I shall never marry," but many later happy wives and mothers have at some time said that. What will she do at the time of the inevitable parting from Mr. Longdon on account of his death (to which he has once referred)? The truth is that we cannot be any more sure of her future than we are of our own.

James establishes Nanda Brookenham's moral integrity clearly, but though I think Gregor and Nicholas go too far when they say that "our experience of her is much more a study of Innocence than of an innocent person," the austerity of his method makes it difficult or impossible for him to give us as clear an impression of her personality as we might otherwise have received. There is nothing in *The Awkward Age* that really takes the place, as an expository device, of the great chapter in *The Portrait of a Lady* in which Isabel broods before the fire. For that matter, I am not sure that I always see Nanda as clearly as I see Nora Lambert in James's first apprentice novel, *Watch and Ward,* defective though that is as a work of art. Here, incidentally, we have a *Daddy Long-Legs* story in which James did employ the comparatively naïve and conventional ending which a few critics[16] would foist upon him here: Roger Lawrence adopts Nora as a child and raises her and, after trying misunderstandings, finally marries her.

Maisie is, of course, the other character in James with whom Nanda is most often compared. Both grow up in the midst of corruption, though Maisie's background is both more rackety and less "stylish" than Nanda's, and both escape serious contamination. The most obvious difference between the two girls is that Maisie is a child and Nanda a teen-ager; the two make a distinguished pair of companion portraits which should be examined together.

Maisie and Nora are not, however, the only James characters whom critics have compared with Nanda: *Daisy Miller*, "A London Life," "In the Cage," "Julia Bride," "The Pupil," and "The Turn of the Screw" have all been considered in this connection. "The Turn of the Screw" victimizes a boy as well as a girl, and "The Pupil" deals entirely with a boy, Morgan Moreen. It is interesting that only the two boys suffer a completely tragic fate; Morgan kills himself, and Miles expires, presumably, from heart failure, owing to the strain of what he has gone through. I should say that James certainly exercised some influence upon Edith Wharton's novel, *The Children* (1928),[17] in which Judith Wheater grows up in an even more appalling milieu than Nanda's, and also upon Forrest Reid's *The Bracknels* (1911), rewritten in 1948 as *Denis Bracknel*; here, as in "The Pupil," the solution again is sui-

[16]At least three writers—Yvor Winters (see *In Defense of Reason* [Morrow, 1947]), Joseph P. O'Neill, and Séumas Cooney ("Awkward Ages in *The Awkward Age*," *MLN*, LXXV [1960], 218–21) have all entertained the wild possibility that Mr. Longdon might himself marry Nanda. This would indeed be a comic ending for a man who had loved both her grandmother and Van's mother, but James was not that kind of humorist.

[17]See Abigail Ann Hamblen, "The Jamesian Note in Edith Wharton's *The Children*," *University Review*, XXXI (1964–65), 209–11. For other useful studies of *The Awkward Age*, not cited elsewhere, see John Holloway, "*Tess of the D'Urbervilles* and *The Awkward Age*," in his *The Charted Mirror: Literary and Critical Essays* (Routledge and Kegan Paul, 1960); Lotus Snow, "Some Stray Fra-

cide. Mrs. Wharton was of course a less considerable novelist than James, but *The Children* is one of her best books,
and Judith herself is certainly the most charming girl this
writer ever created. I confess she moves me more than Nanda does, not only because I find her more clearly defined but
also, I believe, because Mrs. Wharton, possibly because she
was a woman, succeeds in finding much more of consequence
for her to do, and everything she does is womanly and, under
the circumstances, sometimes even heroic. A "disenchanted
maiden for whom life seemed to have no surprises," Judith
wins through to triumph over crushing odds, which is more
than can be said for another helplessly moving and unfortunate girl in a famous modern novel, Margaret Kennedy's Tessa
in *The Constant Nymph* (1925), but the problem here is altogether different, and I see no Jamesian influence; thus
The Constant Nymph is, in the Kiplingesque as well as the
literal sense, "another story."

---

grance of an Ideal: Henry James's Imagery for Youth's Discovery of Evil," *Harvard
Library Bulletin*, XIV (1960), 107–25, which deals with *What Maisie Knew* as well
as *The Awkward Age*; Mildred Hartsock. "The Exposed Mind: A View of *The
Awkward Age*," *Critical Quarterly*, IX (1967), 49–59; Walter Isle, *Experiments
in Form: Henry James's Novels, 1896–1901* (HUP, 1968); Carl Nelson, "James's
Social Criticism: The Voice of the Ringmaster in *The Awkward Age*," *Arizona
Quarterly*, XXIX (1973), 151–68.

IX. TWO KINDS OF VICTORY—
MILLY THEALE AND MAGGIE VERVER
—AND TWO WHO LOST
KATE CROY AND CHARLOTTE STANT

IN ADDITION to the three great novels which Jacobeans generally single out as representing him at the top of his bent—*The Wings of the Dove* (1902), *The Ambassadors* (1903), and *The Golden Bowl* (1904)—Henry James published between 1899 and 1904 one other important novel, *The Awkward Age*; two volumes of his maturest and most carefully wrought short stories, *The Soft Side* and *The Better Sort*; and a two-volume biography, *William Wetmore Story and His Friends*. For quantity and quality combined, I doubt that this half-decade's output can be matched by any other writer.

The Ambassadors centers around Lambert Strether, probably James's most impressive male character, and will not be considered here, but the *Dove* and the *Bowl* each contain an important "good" heroine and an important "bad" one. There is a story about an old countryman who took his son to a concert which comprised only solo work during the first half but turned to duets after the intermission, at which point the old man explained, "Y'see, son, it's gettin' late now; so they're takin' 'em two at a time." My motive for treating four women in this chapter is different: I hope thus to avoid tiresome repetition and to bring out important comparisons, contrasts, and relationships.

It must not be supposed that it has always been smooth sailing for these novels. James's famous "later manner" antagonized many readers besides his brother, William (even today noninitiates always prefer *The Portrait of a Lady* to any member of the triumvirate), and the great magazines, which, financially at least, were often more important to the fictionists of the time than book publication itself, were gradually closing to him during his later years. *The Ambassadors*, rejected by *Harper's*, was serialized in *The North American Review*, but the other two novels did not achieve magazine publication at all, nor did what many consider James's greatest short story, "The Altar of the Dead." Yet when *The Golden Bowl* was published in America by Scribners, in a handsome two-volume edition, during James's last sojourn here, it astonished its author, its publishers, and everybody else by running through four printings within a year.

Judged by the standards of evaluation generally applied to novels, *The Ambassadors* is the most "successful" of these three books, *The Wings of the Dove* is the richest in charm and spiritual suggestiveness, and *The Golden Bowl* is, as James himself realized, the most consummately "done." It may well be questioned whether there is any other novel in which the relations between four people are more exhaustively explored or in which such concentration upon a limited area is brought to bear. Add to this the difficulties of James's later prose and the ambiguity of many of the situations and relationships, and it is no wonder that many readers find the book not only exhaustive but exhausting. Max Beerbohm compared the reading of both *Dove* and *Bowl* to a long climb uphill. You are tempted to give it over, he said, "until, when you look back and down, the country is magically beneath your gaze, as you never saw it yet."

It is not only the simpler and more impatient readers who are "turned off" by these books, however. They, and more particularly their heroines, have been viewed with a jaundiced eye by a number of critics who, whatever else they may lack, are certainly not short on sophistication. Both novels have been characterized from time to time as fairy tales, melodramas, morality plays, psychological dime novels, and soap operas, and though their basic plots do not (as James handles them) justify these judgments, they do give occasion for them.

In *Dove*, a pair of English lovers, Kate Croy and Merton Densher, too poor to marry, make the acquaintance of a fabulously rich American girl, Milly Theale, who is also fatally ill. Knowing that Milly loves Densher, Kate persuades him to feign love for her, even if necessary to marry her, so that when she dies, she will leave him her money and he can then marry Kate. The plot succeeds, for though the love-making does not get very far, and Milly is alerted to the true situation by a rival suitor, she rises above her wrongs to the extent of leaving Densher the money; only, having by this time experienced an awakening, he finds himself now more in love with Milly's memory than with Kate's presence; he refuses the money, therefore, and Kate loses him. In the *Bowl* we have another American girl, Maggie Verver, who sustains an unusually close daughterly relationship to her father, a multimillionaire tycoon and art collector. Adam Verver "collects" an Italian prince as a husband for Maggie, but though she loves her husband dearly, her intimacy with her father is not disturbed. Both he and she feel, however, that, now that Maggie is married, it might be well for him to marry also; so they "collect" Charlotte Stant, who had been an old school friend of Maggie's. Unfortunately she had also been an old flame of Prince Amerigo's, and after the marriage their old relationship is renewed and intensified. The whole second volume tells how Maggie saved both marriages by winning her husband away from Charlotte, and the book ends with the departure of Charlotte and her husband for the "American City" in the great West where Verver is establishing a magnificent art center.

It will be well to establish a few basic facts about these two novels before proceeding to the four female characters themselves. The books have many associations in James's work. Though not quite "international novels" in the sense in which *The Portrait of a Lady* is an international novel (as has already been pointed out, both Isabel Archer and Milly Theale pay tribute to James's cousin, Minny Temple[1]), they do involve familiar contrasts between European and American mores and types. Among the many short stories, early and late, which various critics have invoked for comparison are "The Solution" (Carl Maves[2] calls Wilmerding "Milly Theale in trousers"), "De Grey," "Travelling Companions," "At Isella," "The Story of a Year," "A Most Extraordinary Case," "Longstaff's Marriage," "Georgina's Reasons," "The Last of the Valerii," "The Marriages" (when James conceived the idea of *The Golden Bowl*, he regretted that he had "used up" this title), "Maud-Evelyn," and "Miss Gunton of Poughkeepsie."[3]

The title *The Wings of the Dove* comes from Psalm 55, which was also the inspiration of Mendelssohn's "Hear My Prayer": "Oh that I had wings like a dove! for then would I fly away, and be at rest." It is significant that the inspiration for the flight should be the desire to escape from deceit and guile and wickedness. And, as the book develops, Psalm 68 is also important, for here the wings of a dove are "covered with silver, and her feathers with yellow gold." Milly is of course the dove who is done to death by wickedness and guile, but at the end her golden wings "cover" her enemy-friends, so that, as even Kate perceives, "We shall never be again as we were!"

[1] See Lotus Snow, "The Disconcerting Poetry of Mary Temple: A Comparison of the Imagery of *The Portrait of a Lady* and *The Wings of the Dove*," *NEQ*, XXXI (1958), 312–39.

[2] *Sensuous Pessimism: Italy in the Work of Henry James* (Indiana University Press, 1973).

[3] Scott Byrd, "The Spoils of Venice: Henry James's 'Two Old Houses and Three Young Women' and *The Golden Bowl*, *AL*, XLIII (1971–72), 371–84, argues the relevance to the *Bowl* of the chapter indicated in *Italian Hours*.

The Golden Bowl too is biblical: "Or ever the silver cord be loosed, or the golden bowl be broken, or the pitcher broken at the fountain, or the wheel broken at the cistern," which is part of the imagery used to suggest old age in the last chapter of Ecclesiastes, but James may also have been thinking of Blake's

> Can wisdom be kept in a silver rod,
> Or love in a golden bowl?[4]

The bowl symbolism is subtle and, except at one point,[5] effective, so subtle indeed that one critic, John Bayley,[6] refuses to call the bowl a symbol, preferring to consider it a piece of dramatic machinery. Whatever else it may suggest, however, there can be no question that it does represent the flaw in Maggie's marriage, which must be mended at the end. Less developed but equally effective is the book symbolism toward the end. Charlotte has taken the second volume of a Victorian three-decker out into the garden with her; Maggie, desiring a confrontation, follows her with the first as a pretext for approaching her: "*This* is the beginning; you've got the wrong volume, and I've brought you out the right."

As to sources, the original idea for the *Dove*, as described in James's notebooks, was that of

[4]Leon Edel, *Henry James: The Master, 1901–1916* (Li, 1972), 208, points out James's interest in an actual golden bowl, presented to the Lamb family by King George I.

[5]Of course, the smashing of the bowl by Fanny Assingham. This might be effective in either an allegorical tale by Hawthorne or a play by Sardou, but it is out of place here. Moreover, it is impossible to believe that this cautious lady would perform such an act or that she could thus conceive of herself as accomplishing anything. I must add that, though the antique dealer who sells the bowl to Maggie is in himself a teasing figure, I cannot believe in his visit to Maggie, which seems to me artificially contrived.

[6]*The Characters of Love: A Study in the Literature of Personality* (Constable, 1960).

a young person conscious of a great capacity for life, but early stricken and doomed, condemned to die under short respite, while also enamoured of the world; aware moreover of the condemnation and passionately desiring to "put in" before extinction as many of the finer vibrations as possible, and so achieve, however briefly and brokenly, the sense of having lived.

This idea had never really been absent from his mind since the death of Minny Temple. But Milly seems also to have been influenced by Hilda in *The Marble Faun* of Hawthorne, and Leon Edel has suggested the possible influence of *Paradise Lost*, Balzac's *Seraphita*, Ibsen, Maeterlinck (who is twice alluded to in the novel itself), and *The Varieties of Religious Experience*, by William James. Cargill's invocation of the Tristram and Iseult story seems more doubtful, however, and Matthiessen specifically denied Wagnerian influence.[7]

Cargill is more convincing when he argues [8] the influence upon *The Golden Bowl* of two works by the French novelist Paul Bourget, whom James knew—*Cosmopolis* and *A Tragic Idyll*—and Mildred S. Greene is not unreasonable when she studies Maggie against the background of Mme de Merteuil in *Les Liaisons Dangereuses*. Two of George Eliot's novels have also been invoked: Scott Byrd suggests that the bowl may have come from *Middlemarch*, Chapter LXIV, with James taking care to employ the symbol in such a way as to avoid the weaknesses he found in that work, and Miriam Allott adds her discernment of a resemblance between Maggie's Prince and Romola's Tito, though she is careful to specify that Amerigo is "reclaimable," while Tito is not.[9]

[7] *Henry James: The Major Phase* (Oxford University Press, 1944). This was the pioneering and widely influential study of James's three late great novels as a group. See Miriam Allott, "A Ruskin Echo in *The Wings of the Dove*," *NQ*, CCI (1956), 87, for the suggestion that the "Britannia of the Market Place" symbolism for Mrs. Lowder was derived from "Traffic" in *The Crown of Wild Olive*.

[8] *The Novels of Henry James*, 385–89.

Though our novels have, as I have already remarked, their points of resemblance and comparison with James's earlier work, they also contain surprises. They are franker, or at least more direct, in their treatment of sex than James generally is, and certainly the scene in the mountains where Milly is introduced brooding over the kingdoms of this world like Christ at his temptation in the wilderness effectively refutes the common opinion that James could not or did not wish to communicate a physical sensation. Again, the weather in Venice during the sea storm which rages there toward the end of Milly's life proves that, when he chose to do so, James could use nature much as Thomas Hardy did, and it is particularly interesting that calm arrives with the coming of Milly's beloved physician, Sir Luke Strett, who must certainly have been named for Saint Paul's physician, Saint Luke the evangelist. Richard A. Hocks has called attention to the nonrealistic aspects of the *Dove* in connection with the "sense of the presence within" which not only Densher but even the unspiritual Mrs. Lowder experience at the end. "This had, as Poe might say, 'collateral' relations with James's ghostly presences proper, and perhaps more than collateral relations at that."[10] Other influences away from realism are the richly imagistic style, which often comes close to poetry, and the abundance of religious symbolism. But these are over-

[9] Mildred S. Greene, "*Les Liaisons Dangereuses* and *The Golden Bowl*: Maggie's 'Loving Reason,' " *MFS*, XIX (1973–74), 531–40; Scott Byrd, "The Fractured Crystal in *Middlemarch* and *The Golden Bowl*," *MFS*, XVIII (1972–73), 551–54; Miriam Allott, "*Romola* and *The Golden Bowl*," *NQ*, CXCVIII (1953), 124–25. Mildred Greene points out that Maggie resembles Choderlos de Laclos's heroine in that she "has had to learn to control her emotions with her intellect" and that, "like her, she has had to force herself to face her husband with the evidence she hated to recognize herself." But Mme de Merteuil used her power for destruction, while Maggie "uses her insight to preserve her marriage and her father's." James may then have learned from the French novel "that manipulation of others need not always lead to evil consequences: 'goodness' may take some of the strategy but not the attitude of 'evil' to express itself, and virtue, thus sophisticated, triumphs."

[10] *Henry James and Pragmatistic Thought: A Study in the Relationship Between the Philosophy of William James and the Literary Art of Henry James* (UNCP, 1974).

tones, not the warp and woof of the book. Few indeed have been convinced by Quentin Anderson's elaborate interpretation of these novels in terms of a consistent Swedenborgian allegory, based upon the writings of James's father, nor yet by Frederic C. Crews's suggestion that in the *Bowl* Maggie appears as Christ and her father, Adam Verver, as God the Father.[11]

Milly Theale is a "slim, constantly pale, delicately haggard, anomalously, agreeably angular young person, of not more than two-and-twenty summers . . . whose hair was somehow exceptionally red even for the real thing," a "crown of old gold" suitable to "the potential heiress of all the ages" but "'done' with no eye whatever to the *mode du jour*." There is something "helpless in her grace and abrupt in her turns." She has "youth and intelligence and, if not beauty, at least in equal measure a high dim charming oddity" whose appeal is lost altogether on stupid people, for, "expressive, irregular, exquisite" as she is, she has "rather too much forehead, too much nose and too much mouth, together with too little mere conventional color and conventional line." She dresses habitually in black, but on one splendid occasion she appears in dazzling white. Actually we have what amounts to a portrait of her, for, as both she and others realize, she bears a striking resemblance to Bronzino's portrait of Lucrezia Panciatichi, which Lord Mark shows her at Matcham. James characteristically does not name the portrait, which is

---

[11]Quentin Anderson, *The American Henry James* (RUP, 1957); Frederick C. Crews, *The Tragedy of Manners: Moral Drama in the Later Novels of Henry James* (YUP, 1957). It is due Crews to state that he throws out his suggestions as suggestions, hedging them about with restrictions and not insisting upon them as dogma. As for Anderson, it need only be said that James simply did not have the kind of mind he attributes to him. As he himself remarked of his father's system, "I can't be so theological." Francis Fergusson, "The Golden Bowl Revisited," *SR*, LXIII (1955), 13–28, is in agreement with Anderson. Brian Lee, "Henry James's 'Divine Consensus': *The Ambassadors, The Wings of the Dove, The Golden Bowl*," *Renaissance and Modern Studies*, VI (1962), 5–24, rejects Anderson, preferring to see James dependent "on the native intellectual climate" of which both he and his father partook. He was "a descendant of Emerson, Hawthorne, Thoreau and the whole Concord school, rather than . . . his father's disciple."

actually in the Uffizi Gallery, but Miriam Allott has clearly identified it, and it has now been conveniently reproduced.[12] It was wholly suitable that the legend "Amour dure sansfin" should have been carved into Lucrezia's necklace. "Coming after the Watteau image," which precedes it in the novel, writes Viola Hopkins Winner, and "which conjures up a delicious imaginary world exempt from time and pain, good and evil, the Bronzino becomes a symbol of mortality; the elegance and splendor incompletely mask an all-pervading sadness and sense of mutability."

Milly has great wealth, and she brings one faithful friend, the New England magazinist Susan Shepherd Stringham, with her from America and makes another in England in the person of Sir Luke Strett, "a great beneficent being," who makes her feel, after a visit, as if she had received absolution. "You can depend on me for unlimited interest," he tells her at the outset, and nobody ever kept his word with nobler fidelity; he even travels from London to Venice to see her. If Milly herself is, in this novel, a vessel of grace, Sir Luke shares this distinction with her, and surely no novelist ever paid a higher compliment to the medical profession at its best than James pays here.[13] Aside from these persons she has no one. Her family had vanished with her health, for she was a creature "saved," as it were, "from a shipwreck" in which "parents, brothers, sisters, almost every human appendage" had perished.

Death hovers over Milly, then, from the beginning of our acquaintance with her, but, like the crime committed by Kate Croy's father and, in *The Ambassadors*, the identity of

---

[12] Miriam Allott, "The Bronzino Portrait in Henry James's *The Wings of the Dove*," *MLN*, LXVIII (1953), 23–25. See Plate XIII in Winner, *Henry James and the Visual Arts.*

[13] Harold L. Rypins, "Henry James in Harley Street," *AL*, XXIV (1952–53), 481–92, contains an interesting account of a visit James made to Sir James Mackenzie. This was too late for *The Wings of the Dove*, but Rypins suggests that Sir Luke may have derived traits from Dr. William Bezly Thorne and from James himself.

the manufactured article upon which the Newsome family fortunes rest, the nature of her malady is never spelled out for us. Matthiessen seems to be the only critic who ever committed himself to the view that she dies of tuberculosis.[14] The suggestion has plausibility, for "consumption," as it was then generally called, was the great girl killer of the time, and it had taken Minny Temple, who was Milly's confessed original. Moreover, the eager appetence, the almost feverish hunger for life, which Milly manifests is a well-known symptom in tuberculosis patients. Yet the only time tuberculosis is mentioned in the novel as possibly Milly's complaint, Kate Croy dismisses the suggestion. James, heaven knows, needed no excuse for treating anything ambivalently or indirectly, but one cannot but wonder whether he might not sometimes have thought of Winifred Howells, elder daughter of his friend the novelist, whose own personality was as much that of a Henry James heroine as anybody James himself ever created. Winifred's illness was never diagnosed during her lifetime, and her distinguished doctors babbled of "stubbornness" and "hypochondriacal illusions" and subjected her to a regime of which the thought, in retrospect, broke her parents' hearts, for after, in 1889, she had confounded all the wise men by suddenly dying, an autopsy proved that the pain of which she had complained had been all too real. Milly's physician, Sir Luke Strett, is supposed to be the most distinguished doctor in England, but he treats her more like what we should now expect from a psychiatrist than from a physician dealing with a patient afflicted with a mortal disease, and if he ever

---

[14] See *Henry James: The Major Phase*, 43ff. An amusing footnote to *The Wings of the Dove* was furnished by the adventuress Emilie Busbey Grigsby, who was probably the mistress of the Chicago and London traction magnate Charles T. Yerkes. Noted for her red hair, Emilie dramatized herself as the original of Milly Theale, though she did not meet James until after the novel had been published. She appears as Beatrice Fleming in Theodore Dreiser's *The Titan*. In 1906 the *New York Evening Journal* infuriated James with an idiotic story in which it was suggested that he had asked her to marry him. See Edel, *Henry James: The Master*, 174–80.

found out what was wrong with her, he kept his knowledge strictly to himself.

Though Maggie Verver has a number of enemies among Jamesian critics, Milly has only one[15] who really deserves to be called that, though a number of others find fault with her in one way or another or with James's characterization of her. On the one hand, Matthiessen calls her "the most resonant symbol for what [James] had to say about humanity" (incidentally pointing out that he had here employed Poe's most "poetic" subject, the death of a beautiful woman); Crews thinks her "the most romantic and ethereal heroine in all Jamesian fiction"; Edmund Wilson felt her "a personality independent of the novel, the kind of personality, deeply felt, invested with poetic beauty and unmistakably individualized, which only the creators of the first rank can give life to." But writers like F. R. Leavis and Marius Bewley get a very different impression. Leavis finds the novel unsuccessful precisely because the heroine is *not* vividly realized—"she isn't there, and the fuss the other characters make about her as the 'Dove' has the effect of an irritating sentimentality." Bewley, who also feels the imperfect realization of the character, adds that Milly herself lacks animation and wit beyond any other Jamesian heroine. It is interesting to remember

[15]Robert C. McLean, " 'Love by the Doctor's Direction': Disease and Death in *The Wings of the Dove,*" *Papers on Language and Literature*, VIII (1972), Supplement, 128–48. McLean finds Milly homely, extremely jealous of Kate, and possessed by a "pathological egocentricity" and a "neurotic will to exploit the sympathy of others." "Sexually frustrated," she is "the victim of her own warped mind," and she lives in a private world, enacting the roles of princess, dove, and Christian martyr. Her disease is "primarily mental, not organic," and she dies by suicide, "most probably by leaping from the balcony of the Palazzo Leporelli." The value of this article is twofold. It shows (1) that, in dealing with a writer who eschews direct statement to the Jamesian extent, a sufficiently ingenious critic can argue in behalf of even the most absurd hypothesis, and (2) it illustrates the dangers of "close reading" when common sense is not also employed. It is a relief to turn from this to an article like John Carlos Rowe's "The Symbolization of Milly Theale: Henry James's *The Wings of the Dove*, " *ELH*, XL (1973), 131–60, a thoughtful study of the spiritual implications of Milly's life and death against the background of James's memories of Minny Temple and other considerations.

that Stuart P. Sherman was distressed by an impression of
vagueness in James's later characters in general—"rather
presences than persons—dim Maeterlinckian presences glid-
ing through the shadow and shimmer of late Turneresque
landscapes and Maeterlinckian country houses, and rarely
saying or doing anything whatever of significance to the
uninitiated ear and eye." And even the more sympathetic F.
W. Dupee finds that Milly is "not very closely studied" and
real only in a special sense, "a more exquisite Daisy Miller,"
raised above mere questions of manners. Her part in the
novel, he says, is that of a victim, like Ophelia and Desde-
mona, thus ignoring the fact that what she finally does deter-
mines the outcome, though on his next page he points it out.
But all these objections have point only if one is ready to
confess that with female characters he cannot grasp anything
short of a Carmen-like vividness in fiction. Before the real-
istic movement destroyed the older and greater idealistic
mode and tradition in literature, it would never have occurred
to anybody that there was any reason why a character should
not be real, as Dupee says, only in a special sense. For that
matter, so long as art remains one thing and life another, no
fictional character can be "real" in any other sense.[16]

Those critics who find Milly short in intelligence or,
more gently, possessed of "a certain innocence of mind that
is incapable of ironic detachment, with a consequent defi-
ciency in her of critical discernment" are themselves undis-
cerning, all the more so since the whole question is more or
less irrelevant. A certain lack of suspicion, a certain tendency
to trust, is inevitable in a character who was created to be
victimized, and it is difficult to see why she should be held
less worthy of sympathy on this account. Milly is a young and
inexperienced girl; one could hardly expect her to have quite

[16] For Leavis, see *The Great Tradition* (Chatto and Windus, 1948); for Dupee,
his *Henry James*. Wilson's "The Ambiguity of Henry James" and Sherman's "The
Aesthetic Idealism of Henry James" have both been reprinted in Dupee's anthology,
The Question of Henry James.

the insight into the motives of devious people which might be posited, say, of Sir Luke Strett. Actually James not only assures us of Milly's intelligence but goes out of his way to demonstrate it; thus it does not take her long to learn that Mrs. Lowder was "a person of whom the mind might in two or three days roughly make the circuit" and that Lord Mark has no imagination. And if, as she says, she absolutely trusts Kate, this obviously has the dramatic value of deepening the "bad" heroine's treachery toward her. She does realize early that Kate has some secret and senses the potential brutality in her; when Kate paces the room before her, she reminds Milly of a panther. Like all persons who possess reflective power, our young lady, as James would call her, "was for ever seeing things afterwards," and in the long run little was lost upon her. D. W. Jefferson sums it up fairly enough when he calls her "intelligent, ironical, self-reliant," and at the same time "a gentle person, deceived and deeply hurt, and sublimely forgiving."[17]

A number of critics have found Milly's character flawed by Milton's "fatal infirmity" of pride, which Dorothea Krook even sees as causing her to repel the help that might have saved her life. Since she does everything that Sir Luke tells her to do, it is a little hard to follow this, and I know of no other instance in which stoical courage in facing a terminal illness has been accounted a fault. Sallie Sears[18] thinks that "what the book makes so clear and the ending does not is that all three of the principal agents [Milly, Kate, and Densher] played their role in the events that took place, and that all three are at one and the same time responsible and not responsible." But I fear this has never been clear to anybody except this writer, who, though she recognizes Milly's "innocence" and the failure of her "English friends" to appreciate

[17] *Henry James and the Modern Reader* (Oliver & Boyd, 1964).

[18] *The Negative Imagination: Form and Perspective in the Novels of Henry James* (CoUP, 1968).

it, still thinks that the girl should have heeded Kate's second warning and that her "wilful blindness makes her one of the agents" of her catastrophe, though she immediately adds that "the catastrophe would have been inevitable even if she *hadn't* blinded herself to the facts."

It is difficult (or it would be if we had not had the privilege of reading Robert McLean) to see how any critic could be more wrong about Milly than J. A. Ward becomes when he inexplicably permits himself to speak of Milly's excessive reliance upon money and her hesitation "to face life in its fulness." On the contrary, her eager, devouring hunger for life is her most marked characteristic. Her temperament, no less than her money, has made her "the potential heiress of all the ages"; "starved for culture" in her native New York environment, she embarks upon her trip to Europe as her great "fling." As for her money, she has enough so that she need not concern herself about it, like Kate and Densher, who lack it, and Mrs. Lowder, who has enough but would like more; she simply accepts it as an element of "given" in her situation.

Milly manifests "extreme spontaneity" always and gives the impression of great "American intensity," so that it seems from the beginning that "her doom was to live fast" and her "complaint" only "the excess of the joy of life." She lives indeed in "a state of vibration" in which "her sensibility was almost too sharp for her comfort." Susan Stringham realizes much of this in the mountain scene at the beginning, where, dangerously poised though Milly seems to be, Susan is sure that she is not contemplating suicide but rather surveying the kingdom that she has come to possess.

Milly has a passion for self-knowledge also, and, as Dorothea Krook says, she is ready "to suffer pain, confusion and humiliation, and final total deprivation and loss" in order to achieve it. So far from fostering her illness, as McLean thinks, she comes as close to ignoring it and rising above it as flesh can come.

High notes in Milly's appetence are struck at her rhapsodic appreciation of Matcham, culminating in her inspection of the Bronzino portrait; in her glory at the great party she gives in Venice, where, we are told, she practically supersedes Kate, whose handsomeness she herself had always so much admired, and robs her of luster; and, best of all, in the Regents Park scene, where she pauses after her consultation with Sir Luke and feels a sense of mystical union with the humanity that surrounds her.

It seems odd that so many of the critics who muster an infinite charity toward the "bad" characters in James's last books should be so eager to cast all the "good" ones into the outer darkness the moment they sense any limitation in them. This point of view, I suppose, has its counterpart in another area in the tendency of some sociologists to shed bleeding-heart tears over criminals while apparently remaining perfectly indifferent to the sufferings of their victims. For that matter, it would not require much ingenuity to defend the thesis that, even in the New Testament, the publicans get rather more charity than they deserve and the Pharisees relatively less.

Though Milly Theale has, as I have indicated, her affinities with the ideal characters of the older romantic literature, *The Wings of the Dove* is still not quite indistinguishable from *The Legend of Good Women*, and James has therefore taken pains to "humanize" Milly by indicating that she did possess limitations; as Crews says, "she is sacrificed as a martyr, but the choice of martyrdom is not her own." If she is a religious symbol at the end of the book, she is far from having been a devotee, unless of love and pleasure. Her hunger for life being what it is, she "goes in" for pleasure indeed as determinedly as the heroine of *La Traviata*, though her particular choice of pleasures differs considerably, and when she resents Kate's superior attitude toward Susan Stringham because "it just faintly rankled in her" that a person whom she had accepted should not be good enough for Kate, her attitude, though completely understandable, or even justifiable, is certainly not saintly. But those who object that the characterization is imperfect because the girl who at the end embodies a Christ-like forgiveness has also been hungry for all the good things of this life, and even, perhaps, at times, somewhat complacent in accepting the real or feigned admiration that is showered upon her, would seem somewhat to have confused Spaceship Earth with the New Jerusalem. Of course Milly passionately desires to live. If she did not, she would be a repulsive masochist. Her spiritual conquest at the end is an achievement, not an inheritance, and this is the only kind of spiritual conquest that has meaning for human beings. It does not on that account follow that, as Charles Thomas Samuels believes, her end is only "the sentimental death in Venice of a young girl who couldn't get her man." Milly's turning her face to the wall when Lord Mark reveals Kate's and Densher's treachery to her manifests her mortal weakness, but her forgiving her betrayers and leaving her money to them shows her rising above it.

Since it has become the fashion with some modern critics to call every character in fiction who lives nobly and sacrificially a "Christ-figure," it is not at all surprising that this label should have been pinned upon Milly and, with even less justification, upon Maggie Verver too. In an age in which Jesus Christ has become a "superstar" as the hero of a "rock" musical and has also been presented on the stage as a clown, it may be a little late to protest against this kind of thing; perhaps one ought rather to hail it as a sign of lingering spiritual sensitiveness on the part of those who seem to manifest it nowhere else. But though the New Testament exhorts us to "fill up the sufferings of Christ," those who have come closest to doing this seem always the least inclined to wipe out the distinction between themselves and Him, and however one may admire the "Christ-figures" in modern literature, it is still, I think, in order to recognize that Christ was something more than any of these.

As I have already pointed out, the scene in the mountains where we first glimpse Milly inevitably recalls Christ's temptation in the wilderness, and James must have intended that it should; nevertheless, the circumstances and conditions in the two scenes are very different. The dove is certainly a Christian symbol, and the token of Milly's forgiveness is made to reach Densher on Christmas morning. He feels "forgiven, dedicated, blessed," and even if he is, as some feel, a little complacent about it, and more severe in his judgment of Kate than of himself (which is not what Christian humility requires), we must still, I think, believe that Milly's act had blocked the future he had planned for himself and raised his life to a higher plane. For all that, I believe it is enough for Milly's glory to say that she forgave her enemies as Christ commands and practiced a perfect nonresistance.

Densher refuses to accept Milly's bequest or to accept Kate unless she will have him without it; thus the effect of the dead girl's forgiveness and surrender is to redeem him and simultaneously punish and deprive Kate, who is clearly not redeemed.

> Returning good for evil [Milly] has proved her superiority but she has also had her revenge: without intending it she has heaped coals of fire upon the heads of those who tried to wrong her. It has turned out that Susan Stringham was right and Kate Croy was mistaken; Milly was not a helpless dove but a princess magnificent in power.[19]

A few critics have given the impression that they think this was intentional but this is altogether wrong. It is part of Milly's innocence that she did not foresee these effects. That they should have occurred shows more about James than it does about her, and what it shows about him is that he believed in the fundamental decency of life itself.

Maggie Verver, the heroine of *The Golden Bowl*, has been called everything from an avatar of Divine Love to a heartless Machiavellian. Like Milly, she is an American and

---

[19] Ernest Sandeen, "*The Wings of the Dove* and *The Portrait of a Lady*: A Study of Henry James's Later Phase," *PMLA*, LXIX (1954), 1060–74.

like her she is betrayed by those she trusted; unlike her, she triumphs over them for her profit in this world, wins the one she wishes to hold to her side, and banishes her enemy; hence Matthiessen says of her that she "combines Milly Theale's capacity for devotion with Kate Croy's strength of will." Like Milly, again, she is very wealthy; unlike her, she has a devoted father. Before the Prince came into her life and Charlotte into that of her father, Adam Verver, Maggie playfully thought of herself as being "married" to her father (whose marriage to her mother had obviously been a pretty tepid affair), as Pierre was "married" to his mother in Melville's novel. It is difficult for post-Freudian readers to avoid reading unpleasant implications into this. None such were intended, and none such play any part in James's novel; Joseph J. Firebaugh's statement that Maggie does everything "she can short of actual incest to keep her father for herself" and again that marrying him afterwards to her friend Charlotte is "a symbol of incest"[20] is about as wrong in both aspects as anything any critic ever permitted himself to write. James was fully aware that the close tie between Maggie and her father was a menace to both her marriage and his, and this is what *The Golden Bowl* is largely about, but the matter has no sexual overtones. Her "marriage" to her father is a childish game, a part of her immaturity at the beginning of the novel. She is as yet playing at life, and her father is playing with his child; she does not really begin to live until she becomes aware of the intrigue between Charlotte and her husband, whereupon she proceeds to move into her tortured and and finally triumphant maturity.[21]

As we meet her, Maggie is a "funny" little person by sophisticated European standards, lovable but lacking in

[20]"The Ververs," *EIC*, IV (1954), 400–10. I may add that I find no evidence to support J. A. Ward's view that the "spiritual love" between Maggie and her father makes her insensitive to Amerigo's sexual love. But Ward himself is as wildly romantic as Maggie herself ever was when he declares that the Prince and Charlotte "ennoble what James treats most often as mere lust, so that their sin shares somewhat in the rich sensuousness of Renaissance Italy, to which both have ties."

poise, not "smart" or wise in the ways of the world, ignorant of evil and the bewildering complexities of life and not wanting to know about them, "a small creeping thing" who "lives in terror." Her father's wealth and his love have always protected her—she herself tells him that she has never had a blow and might be abject under it—and Colonel Assingham sums her up coldly but not altogether unfairly when he says that, though she is very nice, he always thinks of her primarily as a young person who has a million a year. Her being drawn to Prince Amerigo because his name recalls Amerigo Vespucci and the tie between the Old World and the New is a little like Marilyn Monroe's interest in Arthur Miller because she thought he looked like Abraham Lincoln, and if the existence of romantic, faraway violence and crime in Amerigo's Italian family background does not repel her, we must not hold this against her, for she has no understanding of such matters. As she tells him at an early stage, she has divided her faith in him into watertight compartments.

James's ignorance of the American businessman was equaled only by his lack of interest in his doings, and the usual view of Maggie's father, among those who have been brought up on Theodore Dreiser's novels about Frank Cowperwood (who was Charles T. Yerkes), is that his thrusting his hands into his pockets, sucking on cigars, and occasionally using slang do not suffice to make him a convincing portrait of the American as either tycoon or art collector, suggestive in various ways of William Randolph Hearst, John D. Rockefeller II, or even James's friend Isabella Stewart Gardner. Verver's apparent youthfulness and innocence are often emphasized; if he is, at the outset, Maggie's play-husband, he

---

[21] See Edel, *Henry James: The Master*, 211, for the possible influence upon *The Golden Bowl* of Lizzie Boott's relations with her father, Francis Boott, and her husband, the painter Frank Duveneck. Did James also possibly think of Marian Hooper (Mrs. Henry) Adams, who also sustained an unusually close relationship to her father, and whose suicide in 1885 seems to have been caused, at least in part, by physical and spiritual exhaustion after having helped nurse him through a harrowing final illness?

is also her little boy—"a great and deep and high little man" who can be imaged as a doll or a lamb or an infant king. After his second marriage Mrs. Assingham calls him "Charlotte's too inconceivably funny husband," but though she thinks he may be stupid, she also admits the possibility that he might be "inconceivably great" and "sublimer even than Maggie herself."[22]

If we read *The Golden Bowl* as most novels are read, this view of Verver is probably fair; only perhaps it is not quite safe to read a James novel in that way! Since James is known to have shared with Hawthorne a horror of using human beings as things, it now seems very unlikely that Matthiessen was right in his impression that James missed the sinister side of Verver's "collecting." Maggie and Amerigo are of course jesting when she tells her husband that he is "a

[22]Among the writers who have commented illuminatingly on the complexities of Adam Verver are Edwin T. Bowden, *The Themes of Henry James*, 103ff.; Crews, *The Tragedy of Manners*, 89–90; Laurence Bedwell Holland, *The Expense of Vision*, 352ff.; Maves, *Sensuous Pessimism*, 126–29; Donald L. Mull, *Henry James's "Sublime Economy": Money as Symbolic Center in the Fiction* (Wesleyan University Press, 1973), 138ff.; Tony Tanner, "*The Golden Bowl* and the Reassessment of Innocence," *London Magazine*, n. s. I (October, 1961), 38–49; Winner, *Henry James and the Visual Arts*, 154ff. On James's businessmen in general, see Blair G. Kenney, "Henry James's Businessmen," *Colby Library Quarterly*, Series IX (1970), 48–58. Caroline G. Mercer, "Adam Verver, Yankee Businessman," *NCF*, XXII (1967–68), 251–69, first summarizes the various views that have been taken of Verver, all the way from "an emblem of wisdom and father of the American Redeemer" to an image of "American irresponsibility toward Europe" and a demonstration that since writing *The American* James had learned to understand "the corrupting power of an acquisitive life," then develops the interesting idea that Verver has been colored from the traditional "smart" Yankee in popular American humorous story and drama. Caroline Gordon, "Mr. Verver, Our National Hero," *SR*, LXIII (1955), 29–47, stands alone in seeing Verver as James's "arch-creation." "Charlotte's evil practices have turned her into a monster," representing "the terrible woman of the future," but "James seems to have hoped that Uncle Sam could subdue even her!" Mildred E. Hartsock, "Unintentional Fallacy: Critics and *The Golden Bowl*," *Modern Language Quarterly*, XXXV (1974), 272–88, has a useful corrective review of various ideas that have been expressed concerning Adam Verver, as well as other aspects of the novel. A. R. Gard, "Critics of *The Golden Bowl*," *Melbourne Critical Review*, VI (1963), 102–109, advances the thesis that James's treatment of the Ververs is deliberately ambiguous.

rarity, an object of beauty, an object of price," to which he replies that "I cost a lot of money," but many a truth is spoken in jest, and James was certainly not less aware of this than we are.[23]

It is almost impossible to describe what Maggie does to break up the affair between Charlotte and the Prince, thus preserving both her own marriage and her father's. Dorothea Krook, whose study of the novel, in *The Ordeal of Consciousness in Henry James*, is not only the longest we have but one of the very best, says it as well as it can be said:

Maggie's task, we gradually come to see, is accomplished precisely by not insisting; by not pressing or harassing her husband the Prince but, instead, simply letting him alone—to see for himself the shamefulness of his act of betrayal, to come by his own effort to the knowledge of good and evil, and so to supply himself in the end with that moral sense which . . . he so lamentably lacked.

In James's pages the description of this process develops in the reader a nervous tension almost comparable in kind to that experienced by the people in the novel, but this kind of thing cannot be communicated in a critical summary. Up to the time the Prince walks in on the fragments of the shattered bowl, Maggie tells him nothing but pursues instead a simple policy of watchful waiting; at this point she merely lets him understand that she knows and refuses to go a step beyond that. When she becomes convinced that Amerigo has not

---

[23] The Assinghams are used to supplement Amerigo's view of the action of *The Golden Bowl* in the first volume and that of Maggie in the second. The fullest study of them is in Sister M. Corono Sharp's *The Confidante in Henry James*, where, incidentally, a much severer attitude is shown toward the Prince than most critics manifest, though not more so, than John R. Theobald, "New Reflections on *The Golden Bowl*," *Twentieth Century Literature*, III (1957–58), 20–26, who calls "that sensitive exquisite" dilettante, gigolo, and wastrel. Theobald also, oddly, finds Charlotte "a negative enigma who trembles on the verge of reality only towards the end of the tale." Ora Segal, *The Lucid Reflector*, 207–10, is correct in pointing out that Edith Wharton failed to grasp the full use James had made of the Assinghams, but I regret that I must still agree with Mrs. Wharton that they are bores.

confided in Charlotte, she begins to believe that she is winning, but the situation is not brought to a head until her rival, strained beyond endurance, goes through the empty form of saving her face by seizing the initiative through boldly accusing Maggie of personal hostility and desperately opting for the removal of Verver and herself to America, ostensibly in order that she may there finally have her husband to herself.

All this has inspired some of the most rhapsodic and some of the most hysterical passages in contemporary critical writing.[24] To Sallie Sears "the last part of the book, under Maggie's sponsorship, resembles a sado-masochistic nightmare worthy of the dark dreams of Poe" and Maggie's treatment of Charlotte "a *tour de force* of masochistic self-manipulation and disguised sadism," a statement which at least manages to employ all the fashionable words. Firebaugh agrees but adds philosophical, political, and sociological considerations. To him *The Golden Bowl* is "a gigantic horrified protest against the manoeuvering of appearances to favor a priori concepts of the good, the true, and the beautiful; against the use of knowledge to preserve the specious appearance of innocence" and thus "a criticism of the very basis on which the notion of the absolute stands," but Maggie's wealth also makes her a "politico-economic monster" and a symbol of the "cartelized, totalitarian state." Somewhat similarly but more reasonably, Tony Tanner, who is much more sympathetic toward Maggie, reads the novel with one eye upon American postwar imperialism, hypocritically masquerading as world benevolence; Tanner speaks of "the spirit of conquest" in Maggie and her father and quotes Graham Greene in *The Quiet American*: "Innocence is a kind of insanity." Anything which calls attention to a muddleheaded foreign policy which has already brought untold

---

[24] For a sensible mediating view, see Walter Wright, "Maggie Verver: Neither Saint nor Witch," *NCF*, XII (1957), 59–71. But Ronald Wallace's "Maggie Verver: Comic Heroine," *Genre*, VI (1973), 404–15, though ingenious and not without insight in matters of detail, is as a whole forced and in its alleged parallelism between *The Golden Bowl* and *A Midsummer Night's Dream* absurd.

misery into the world is useful, but since the situation was very different in James's time, he cannot really be supposed to have intended any of this.

Criticism of Maggie at the end generally centers upon her treatment of Charlotte, who is separated from her lover and sent into the American West with a husband whom she does not love and who, in all probability, knows that she has been unfaithful to him with his daughter's husband, though on the other hand, her guilty partner, the Prince, is rewarded by being enabled to establish a new, close relationship with a loving wife, now detached from her father, while the Ververs themselves suffer not at all.

None of this is strictly accurate. It *is* true that the Prince gets off lightly, for he loses only Charlotte, and since he, by this time, believes her "stupid," this is, for him, probably rather a relief than a loss.[25] She has been the aggressor in their affair from the beginning, and it has always been Mrs. Assingham's view that he had never loved her because she was too easy to get. It is also true that he has now suffered a change of heart while she has not. But it is simply not true that the Ververs have paid no price to save the marriages. Both have gone through a great deal of silent suffering. Ellen Leyburn comments rightly that "the extravagance of [Maggie's] images throughout her reflections has been one of the ways in which James has revealed her as romantic," and this is true, but it has also revealed the terrible tension under which she has lived. If Charlotte's situation in America is unenviable, why should Adam Verver's be considered much

---

[25]Personally I am free to admit, however, that Amerigo's coldness toward Charlotte at the end does not make him any more attractive to me. He causes her great suffering by turning away from her after the smashing of the bowl without giving her any explanation of his conduct. She, on the other hand, has been guilty of nothing worse than she was guilty of all the while they were lovers, and in the sin committed they both shared. Some loyalty may be reasonably regarded as a moral obligation even in illicit connections, and it is the tragedy of such relationships that they tend to box people in so that they cannot do right toward one person without harming another.

more so? She has been compelled to give up a lover she had no right to have, and her husband has had to agree to be separated from his beloved daughter.

Critics who see Maggie indifferent to Charlotte's pain at the end ignore the fact that such images as that of the silken halter around her neck (which so shocked Matthiessen) come from Maggie herself. "It's always terrible for women," she says. She even refuses to call Charlotte's bluff when the latter pretends that her departure is voluntary. Short of simply acquiescing supinely in the liaison, it is difficult to see what course she could have adopted under which Charlotte would have suffered less.

There has been rather too much talk about how the Ververs "collected" both Amerigo and Charlotte and rather too little realization that if these persons were bought they themselves were fully consenting partners to the transactions involved. I do not believe that Charlotte will be happy in American City, but nobody is forcing her to go; if she decides to do so, the reason obviously is that she prefers to live in American City as the wife of a multimillionaire rather than in London as a divorcee, however well she might be provided for. Leon Edel, to be sure, sees a comparatively comfortable future for her: "We know she will ultimately be free, like James's other American wives, to travel, to build houses, to acquire art treasures, or other lovers. She can become Mrs. Touchett [in *The Portrait of a Lady*] or resemble the real-life Mrs. Gardner." But this is again the unfortunately familiar error of confusing literature with life. John Bayley makes the same mistake, though reaching quite the opposite conclusion, when he sees Charlotte becoming a true wife in America. Charlotte does not exist outside the pages of the novel, and at its end she has been definitely "put down." Ferner Nuhn, who must be the only reader who ever wanted *The Golden Bowl* longer than it is, and who sees Maggie as "crafty-innocent, smugly virtuous, coolly victorious," longs for another part called "Charlotte's Revenge."[26] But all this kind of speculation about fictional characters should be confined to those like Gordon Bottomley (*King Lear's Wife*), St. John Ervine (*The Lady of Belmont*), and Robert Nathan (*Juliet in Mantua*) who are capable of making entertaining literary capital of their own out of it.

I agree with those who feel that Maggie would be more attractive at the end if she showed some realization that she and her father do share the responsibility for the situation which developed between Charlotte and the Prince. Certainly her statement to Fanny Assingham that she and her father are the real losers, "lost to each other really much more than Amerigo and Charlotte are; since for them it's just, it's right, it's deserved, while for us it's only sad and strange, and not caused by our fault," though not wholly incorrect, has an unpleasant smugness about it, and if Charlotte is to be condemned for her stupidity and regarded as having incurred the Dantean damnation upon those who have lost "the good of the understanding," then surely the Ververs have been stupid too. But whatever may be said of Adam, we must still remember that for Maggie at least there is much more excuse than there was for Charlotte, since she was so much less knowing and also that ignorance is a mortal sin only when it is willful.[27]

Some critics take a dim view of Maggie's interest in preserving forms and appearances, but we may feel sure that James would not have agreed with this. Though he always

[26] *The Wind Blew From the East: A Study in the Orientation of American Culture* (Harpers, 1942).

[27] Though the Ververs are Catholics, James does not give the Church any share in saving the marriages. A priest appears at their table, but he does nothing but eat and drink, and we are specifically told that Maggie did not confide in him but fought the battle to save her marriage on her own. The portrait, though it does not seem to be motivated by any animus against the Church as an institution, is devastating. For further discussion of the religious aspect, see Michael T. Gilmore's fine chapter on *The Golden Bowl* in *The Middle Way: Puritanism and Ideology in American Romantic Fiction* (RUP, 1977), which appeared some time after my manuscript had been completed.

refused to make an idol of form, his respect for it in its place was considerable; one feels that he must have agreed with Ibsen and with Conrad about vital illusions and that he would have approved of Stuart Sherman's comment that *The Golden Bowl* throbs "with the excitement of [his] imaginative insight into the possible amenity of human intercourse in a society aesthetically disciplined and controlled." As a matter of fact, he himself once advised Edith Wharton, during a crisis of her own, to "sit tight" and "go through the motions of life."

Actually Maggie preserves considerably more than form; she respects the dignity of others as well as her own. Thus the satisfaction craved by those who long for one good bang-up scene to clear the air is precisely what she wishes to avoid. She demands no confession from either Charlotte or Amerigo; neither will she force her father into an admission of having been cuckolded. "I live in the midst of miracles of arrangement," she says, "half of which I admit are my own; I go about on tiptoe, I watch for every sound, I feel every breath, and yet I try all the while to seem as smooth as old satin dyed rose-colour." Fanny Assingham calls her "amazing" and "terrible," and even Amerigo says she is "deep" (he had, to his cost, never known it before). Maggie herself feels that she can bear anything for love. "When . . . you love in the most abysmal and unutterable way of all—why then you're beyond everything, and nothing can pull you down."

At the same time she is a much weaker candidate for sainthood than Milly Theale, and she makes a much less overwhelming appeal to the imagination. It is the lost causes which continue to hold their purchase upon the imaginations of men, and the martyrs are remembered long after the conquerors have been forgotten. Milly's is the martyr's victory, and hers is the shining example of perfect forgiveness and nonresistance. It was, to be sure, not of her own will that she won this glory—she would have preferred to live and marry the man she loved—but she accepted it when it confronted her as her destiny, and it is for this that she is loved.

Maggie is a faithful, loving wife who uses every means in her power to hold two families together. In itself this is wholly virtuous, but though her detractors have made much too much of the lies she tells (as when she denies to Charlotte that she has a grievance) or what they call the capacity for manipulating others that she develops, which is closely tied up with the development of her insight and maturity, and away from the naïveté which had given occasion for her husband's transgression, it is neither saintly nor Christ-like, and she has her reward here.

One question remains: Was the Prince worth the fight that Maggie made for him? I must admit that my own inclination would be to answer that he was not, but fortunately I was not the one who was married to him. As H. L. Mencken once observed, it must be a terrible thing to be a woman and compelled to marry a man! Nevertheless, it is clear that James intends us to believe that Maggie loves Amerigo passionately and considers him worth winning and holding. "He could do what he would with her; in fact what was actually happening was that he was actually doing it." And again: "A single touch from him—oh she should know it in case of its coming!—any brush of his hand, of his lips, of his voice, inspired by recognition of her probable interest as distinct from pity for her virtual gloom, would have her over to him bound hand and foot." And it is equally clear, I think, that James intended his readers to feel that, in spite of both his sins and his limitations, Amerigo, unlike Gilbert Osmond in *The Portrait of a Lady*, is both redeemable and capable of growth.

James's original notebook entry for *The Golden Bowl* imaged the character corresponding to the Prince as a more or less stock, typical European "villain," but this is not the characterization presented in the novel itself. More than one critic has compared Amerigo as we first encounter him to Hawthorne's Donatello. A frank hedonist, he is out to do the best he can for himself, but, as he specifies carefully, without injuring others. He is inclined to be passive rather than active: "He had done nothing he oughtn't—he had in fact done nothing at all." Unlike Kate Croy's Densher, he has had wide experience with women, and he can be fatuous enough to reflect solemnly that "he had after all gained more from women than he had lost by them," which brings him within hailing distance of that actor of the past generation who called his autobiography *Women Have Been Kind*, yet he shows some understanding when, upon Charlotte's asking him whether he does not think they are alike, he replies that he cannot tell since they are not married to each other. An aristocratic snob, he does not so much look down upon those whom he considers beneath him as simply fail to see them. But his greatest limitation is probably his inclination to stop with aesthetic, rather than moral, judgments, applying to everything only "the touchstone of taste."

The hopeful element is that he himself clearly recognizes his limitations and hopes, after his marriage to Maggie, to overcome them. If the Ververs have bought him, the bargain has not been cynical or coldhearted on his part, and he is eager to "be much more decent as a son-in-law than lots of fellows he could think of had shown themselves in that character." Self-conscious enough to realize that there is something in him that cannot be wholly accounted for in terms of his heredity, he cultivates humility, admitting frankly not only that he lacks the Anglo-American moral sense but also that he is stupid and often fails to see things until they have been pointed out to him. He sincerely wishes to move out of the past and establish himself firmly in his wife's modern and moral world.

Amerigo has "amenity, urbanity, and general gracefulness," and he "understood and practised every art that could beguile large leisure." Unfortunately, like most traditional unimaginative aristocrats, he is completely useless and has no business in the world. Colonel Assingham, often only a straight man for his wife, is clear-sighted enough when he perceives that he is in danger because he has nothing to occupy him, and this is an important part of Charlotte's opportunity. Nevertheless, it must be understood that the fight Maggie puts up for him would have availed her nothing had there not been something in him which responded to it. Once he has come to appreciate her, he understands also her superiority to Charlotte, who has so sadly underestimated her, and as a result Charlotte's charm is lost for him and her hold upon him broken. If Prince Amerigo married Maggie for her money, he certainly does not stay with her for that reason alone.

Much has already been said or implied about our two "bad" heroines in connection with the "good" ones; it is now time to turn to them directly. Kate Croy and Charlotte Stant are both handsome, extremely capable, sophisticated young women (Kate, dark-haired, "slender and simple" and "frequently soundless," has "stature without height, grace without motion, presence without mass"), but Charlotte's gifts are probably greater, and she achieves her dominance over Amerigo partly because the Ververs show a tendency to shift the "public relations" aspect of their lives to her capable shoulders while they remain comfortably and quietly at home and enjoy each other. Both Kate and Charlotte are "humanized" by being placed in circumstances where they are strongly tempted, but James does not permit us to hold them guiltless on that account.[28] Like Amerigo, Kate is considerably more sympathetic in the novel itself than in James's notebook entry; even as a finagler she is subject to flashes of honesty, as when she warns Milly to "drop us while you can." In Dante's inferno both girls would have landed in the lowest circle nevertheless, since both betray those who trusted in them, and the kiss which Charlotte exchanges with Maggie on the terrace after the card party is a Judas kiss. In the last

[28] Milton Kornfeld, "Villainy and Responsibility in *The Wings of the Dove,*" *TSLL*, XIV (1972), 337–46, has an effective refutation of the view of Stephen Spender and others that the actions of Kate and Densher are determined by their circumstances.

analysis, too, both are defeated, despite their intelligence, because the "sinner" is never able to understand the "saint."

The first two books of *The Wings of the Dove* are almost wholly devoted to Kate and Densher, and in them Kate's behavior is admirable. The decency and sincerity of her love for Densher is unquestionable; her father is as worthless a "dead beat" as can be found in literature, a man with "charisma" and nothing else; her whining, widowed sister is a millstone around her neck; her well-to-do aunt, Mrs. Lowder, that "Britannia of the Market Place," one of James's most appalling embodiments of the materially minded woman, will help her only on condition that she can control her life (Kate's "fall" might indeed never have occurred if Mrs. Lowder had been more sympathetic toward her love affair). Her loyalty to her dreadful family runs, at the beginning, far beyond the call of duty; as Sallie Sears says, her offer to live with her father is her "first and last unequivocally moral gesture." Moreover, "it is no empty offer, but an effort to redeem herself in advance from herself, from what she so clearly senses she might do, and by doing, become." As she herself tells her lover, "I do see my danger of doing something base." Croy rejects her suggestion because he would rather have her cold-bloodedly "work" Mrs. Lowder in her behalf and in his own. Kate discourages Lord Mark, the "desirable" suitor favored by her aunt, and continues to see as much of Densher as she can, but she does not wish to live in poverty either; instead she chooses to try carrying water on both shoulders and begins her career of finagling. There is some justification then for Louis Auchincloss' charge that she is even more greedy than her Aunt Maud (James specifically tells us that material things "speak" to her), for she wants everything that corrupt woman can give her and her own true love besides. In an early chapter she remarks that her father's dishonor is a part of her, and before we have finished with her, we learn that this is true.

Unlike Charlotte, Kate does not try to steal another woman's man; on the contrary, she proposes "lending" hers to another. Milly is known to be in love with Densher, without knowing that he is pledged to Kate, and all, including those who love her best, are agreed that to be loved would be the best possible therapy for the sick girl. "I don't like it," says Kate, "but I'm a person, thank goodness, who can do what I don't like." Under some conceivable circumstances, this might be generous and self-denying; in Kate's case it is vitiated by the treachery involved and the cold-blooded greed for gold which inspires it. Worse still, Kate shares in the direct responsibility for Milly's death, for she tells Lord Mark that she and Densher are secretly engaged, and it is when he treacherously passes this on to Milly that the invalid "turns her face to the wall." "Would you have liked me," Kate asks Densher afterwards, "would you have liked me . . . to give him an answer that would have kept him from going?" This has been called part of her honesty, and the spiteful Lord Mark, rejected by both Milly and Kate, has been called the only person in the book who tells the truth. But in *The Wings of the Dove* the truth does not set free, except from life itself.

The relationship between Kate and Densher has been compared to that between the two Macbeths, and the comparison has point in that she instigates his "crime" and appears at the outset much "stronger" than he is. "Dear man, only believe in me, and it will be beautiful. . . . Ah leave appearances to me! I'll make them all right. . . . You won't be able to say I haven't made it smooth for you." As the novel proceeds, however, the comparison becomes a contrast. Once Macbeth has killed Duncan, he and his wife draw apart, and she has no share in his succeeding activities. Her great failure was an inability to forecast the effect which their crime would have upon either her husband or herself, and ultimately the burden of her guilt grows so heavy that she kills herself. It would be an overstatement to say that she repents; rather she dies in despair, but even this is better than dying defiantly as he does, having piled crime upon crime:

> I am in blood
> Stepp'd in so far that, should I wade no more,
> Returning were as tedious as go o'er.

Macbeth stakes everything upon the vain conviction that "things bad begun make strong themselves by ill," and Kate has a hint of this when, upon Densher's wavering in the campaign of deceiving Milly, she eggs him on with, "Do you want to kill her?" For at the end, with Milly dead, Kate can still call the outcome of their machinations "quite ideal," and she could probably have lived happily ever after with her lover if he had not drawn back from her in horror, shocked by her "brightness" and "lucidity" and redeemed, one hopes, by the memory of Milly's love and forgiveness.

From the beginning of their relationship it is made abundantly clear that Densher is a more sensitive person than Kate, and we are made to think more of her because of her love for him and her loyalty to him despite his poverty. To her he represented "all the high dim things lumped together as of the mind," and James tells us that "it was to the girl's lasting honour that she knew on the spot what she was in presence of." Certainly the pledging of their troth in Book Second is quite as beautiful as they believe it to be, and even in Volume II Densher still thinks all other women stupid compared to Kate, even though he does not pretend that he understands her. "You're a whole library of the unknown, the uncut." If they had married, hers would have been the practical efficiency in their partnership, while his idealism would have uplifted her, which is probably another way of saying that they might have complemented each other and made a pretty successful marriage.

J. A. Ward sees Densher as "a forerunner of a dominant character type of modern literature," comparing him to

Eliot's Prufrock, Conrad's Heyst, and Graham Greene's Sco-
bie. But the man who is weaker in practical matters than the
woman is common in James, who speaks frankly of Densher's
"incapacity for action," as he is also in the novels of James's
friend Edith Wharton. Densher rebels effectively (before the
end) only at the point where he insists that he will not go on
with Kate's plan unless she will attest her commitment by
spending the night with him. This is the first time they have
been together and apparently the only time they ever will be,
and James is far more direct in his handling of it than he is in
indicating the precise relations between Charlotte and the
Prince. But the primary shock value of the incident lies not
in the act of copulation itself but because it takes place as a
part of all their scheming. Kate surrenders her body because
she wants something from Densher besides love, and despite
the genuine affection these people feel for each other, this
introduces an element of prostitution into their contact and
sex itself is soiled. Densher's delicacy is shown again, however, in his feeling how the memory of Kate's presence glo-
rifies his room long after she has departed from it: "He
couldn't for his life, he felt, have opened his door to a third
person."

Since Kate had begun to suspect that Densher might
love Milly as early as Book Eighth, her obtuseness at the
end, when the dead dove's wings—now wings of power—
"cover" the lovers and separate them, may seem a little odd.
Actually, however, her intelligence does not fail; she is merely
trapped and betrayed by her old moral insensitiveness. To
the end Densher tries his best to find a common meeting
ground with her. She can have him or she can have Milly's
money, but she cannot have both.[29] It is she who perceives
that this is impossible. He has grown away from her to such

[29] Maxwell Geismar's *Henry James and the Jacobites* (HM, 1963) seems to me
an almost deliberately perverse book and certainly a convincing proof that nobody
should go to the trouble of writing about an author he hates, but I admit that Geismar has a point when he asks, "For what right has Densher to assign a fortune
which he has never earned, which has come to him in fact as a direct reward (or
rebuke?) for his moral perfidy; how can he assign this fortune, as a noble gesture,

an extent that he now prefers Milly dead to her alive. "Her memory's your love. You want no other." And, "We shall never be again as we were!"

Densher had come away from his final interview with Milly (arranged through the good offices of the all-comprehending Sir Luke) feeling that "something had happened to him too beautiful and too sacred to describe." "Like the hero in any great tragedy," says Matthiessen, "he has arrived at the moral perception of the meaning of what has befallen him." But this means nothing to Kate, for it lies beyond the range of her experience and understanding. To the very end she remains satisfied with her course (though dissatisfied with its outcome), and this is her infinitely pitiful damnation. "We've succeeded," "She won't have loved you for nothing. And you won't have loved *me*." And when she begins to grasp that she has lost him, she can only wail, "We've been going on together so well, and you suddenly desert me?" Holland compares her tossing Milly's farewell letter into the fire unread, on the ground that Densher will "have it all" from New York, with Hedda Gabler's burning Lövborg's manuscript. The parallel, while not perfect, is suggestive. What Densher will have from New York is the money, and that to Kate is everything. The spiritual and emotional overtones of Milly's bequest interest her only to the extent that she knows she must do her utmost to prevent him from feel-

---

precisely to the woman whose criminal plot has caused, or at least hastened, the death of the fairy-tale princess?" For further reference to Densher and his experience, consult R. W. B. Lewis, "The Vision of Grace: James's *The Wings of the Dove*," *MFS*, III (1957-58), 33-40; R. Christian Brown, "The Role of Densher in *The Wings of the Dove*," *Moderna Sprak*, LXV (1971), 5-11; Sr. Stephanie Vinec, "A Significant Revision in *The Wings of the Dove*," *Review of English Studies*, n. s. XXIII (1973), 58-61. But Joseph J. Firebaugh's "The Idealism of Morton Densher," *Texas Studies in English*, XXXVI (1957), 141-54, is a fierce attack upon Densher as a "solipsistic modern man" who finds it easier "to love the memory of a dead woman than the actuality of a live one" because "he finds it impossible to accept the fact that life is a very mixed thing, in which people do take advantage of one another for the sake of experience, for the sake of a sense of life." Evidently this critic achieves no closer meeting of minds with James than does Geismar; certainly he does not "read each work of Wit/With the same spirit that its author writ."

ing their influence. What wonder that James writes of him: "He had brought her there to be moved, and she was only immoveable—which was not moreover, either, because she didn't understand. She understood everything, and things he refused to; and she had reasons, deep down, the sense of which nearly sickened him."

Charlotte Stant is tall, strong, handsome, and always smartly and beautifully dressed, in sharp contrast to Maggie, who has little taste in such things. She has thick, brown hair; her face is long and narrow, her mouth large, her eyes comparatively small. Her arms remind the Prince of the great Florentine sculptors. A partly Europeanized American, she was born in Florence, and her background gives her, in some aspects, more consanguinity with the Prince than Maggie herself can boast. Like Kate Croy, she is upon her own resources and commands no great means. She has not had a sheltered life, and her circumstances have taught her boldness and aggressiveness. She can face danger and is confident of her ability to swim, not sink, in almost any sea. Maggie, who loves her, is also somewhat afraid of her and regards her as much "greater" than herself; but Charlotte thinks Maggie "quaint" and "funny." She is intelligent, poised, lithe, and terribly efficient; we are told that she plays the piano as if she were playing tennis! She is often compared to beasts of prey; when she leaves the card table and comes out to face Maggie on the terrace in one of the great "scenes" of the book, she seems like a "splendid shining supple creature" that has burst out of its cage. "Inordinately handsome" at the Ververs' social affairs, where she is generally called upon to do the honors, she holds high "the torch of responsive youth and the standard of passive grace."[30]

After parting from Amerigo before his marriage to Mag-

---

[30] In his illuminating study *The Melodramatic Imagination: Balzac, Henry James, Melodrama, and the Mode of Excess* (YUP, 1976), Peter Brooks describes the card scene as constituting both "the threat of melodramatic outburst and its transcendence." Cf. his comment on Fleda's asking Mrs. Brigstock whether she has come to "plead" with her "as if I were one of those bad women in a play" as "a typically Jamesian procedure of ironizing dramatic conventions all the while

gie, she had tried hard to find a husband in America but without success. When Mr. Verver proposes to her, she plays her cards extremely well. She doubts that he knows her well enough to marry her, wonders whether there is room in his life for her, and asks whether he wishes to marry her for Maggie's sake. When, in response to the announcement of betrothal, the Prince sends a separate telegram addressed to her, she offers to show it to Verver, but she well knows that he is too much the gentleman to take her up. One of her most interesting confidences to the Prince after their intimacy has been resumed is that she very much wanted to have a child by Verver but could not manage it. However, she immediately adds that she does not believe ten children could have kept Verver and Maggie apart.

It is not possible to believe that Charlotte's motives are innocent when she comes back to England on the eve of Maggie's wedding and at once resumes seeing the Prince. All she wants is to have one hour alone with him, she tells him, to choose a wedding present, but she also informs him that "you're not rid of me." Later, after the wedding, she manages to get Maggie to persuade her father to invite her for a visit.

Despite Charlotte's aggressive efficiency, there is an element of fatalism in her, and she likes to pose as a passive creature whose circumstances have placed her in a position where she can do nothing except—well, except just what she wishes to do. The interesting thing is that the Prince *is* quite as passive as she would like to make herself appear, espe-

---

suggesting their imaginative appropriateness: a way of having one's melodrama while denying it" and his study of *The Wings of the Dove* as an illustration of James's ability to "subtilize and complicate the terms of melodrama, their relation to individual character and their conflict, while at the same time preserving their underlying identity and nourishing the drama from their substratum." Carl Maves seems a little extravagant, however, when he compares Charlotte on one occasion to Satan "high on a throne of royal state" in *Paradise Lost*. See also Elizabeth Owen's excellent article, "The 'Given Appearance' of Charlotte Stant," *EIC*, XIII (1964), 264–74.

cially when he is in the hands of so clever a manager as she is. Her comparative "hardness" is well brought out in the differences between their respective attitudes toward Mrs. Assingham after their affair has got under way. Amerigo worries about what Fanny may think of them, but Charlotte is interested only in the fact that she is not in a position to do them any harm. It is no wonder that he calls her "terrible."

"There is only one kiss in *The Golden Bowl*," wrote Jacques Barzun, "but it is as fully expressive and adulterous as would be a juridical account of the lovers' every assignation."[31] Nevertheless, I think those critics at fault who speak of them as adulterers with no more qualification than they might have pinned this label upon them if James had furnished that "juridical account." Some even state or imply that they had copulated during their romance before Amerigo's marriage, though Fanny Assingham categorically denies this. To be sure, Fanny was not there, but were the critics? However, since Charlotte and Amerigo are certainly guilty of spiritual infidelity to their *sposi*, the question of whether or not they went to bed together is not of very great interest.

Like Kate Croy, Charlotte betrays trust; unlike her, she has no motive except affection for the man she loves. Dorothea Krook believes that she and Amerigo are bound by lust, not love, but this seems a little severe. In its final phase their love was unlawful, but this does not prove that it was unclean in itself. If Charlotte and Amerigo had married before he met Maggie, which they probably would have done if both had not been too greedy, I see no reason why they should not have established an at least reasonably successful and respectable union.

Leavis, Nuhn, Jean Kimball, and John Clair have all defended Charlotte, Miss Kimball going to the fantastic length of seeing her as the true heroine of *The Golden Bowl*, with her transgressions existing only in Maggie's imagination, which

---

[31] Barzun's "Henry James, Melodramatist" is included in Dupee's *The Question of Henry James.*

is about as reasonable as the attempt of other critics to make the governess the evil force in "The Turn of the Screw"; and John Clair is equally though mercifully more briefly astray when he sees her and Amerigo acting together out of pure benevolence "to prompt a twinge of jealousy in the 'simple' Maggie which will effect her separation from her father and permit each of the married couples to live more comfortably apart."[32] As Bernard Shaw is said to have replied to the "Mr. Kipling, I presume?" with which a passer-by had hailed him, "If you can presume that, you can presume anything." If it would be foolish to believe that there will never be any problems involved in interpreting James, perhaps we might at least make a beginning if we would agree to give up the notion that what he meant was exactly the opposite of what he says.

As we have already seen elsewhere, though Maggie finally pushes Charlotte to the wall, she does understand her position and is capable of feeling some sympathy for her; but Charlotte, on her part, never accomplishes either of these things in relation to Maggie. Neither does she ever acknowledge fault or guilt. All she can do when she is cornered is to try to brazen the thing out by pretending that she is the person who has been wronged, and Maggie's final generosity is to allow her the empty pretense of the name now that she has lost the game.

[32] Jean Kimball, "Henry James's Last Portrait of a Lady: Charlotte Stant in The Golden Bowl," AL, XXVIII (1956–57), 449–67; John A. Clair, The Ironic Dimension in the Fiction of Henry James. Harry Hayden Clark's "Henry James and Science: The Wings of the Dove," Transactions of the Wisconsin Academy of Sciences, Arts, and Letters, LII (1963), 1–15, has little relevance to the particular matters discussed in this volume, but it is too significant a study not to be listed. Clark sees James's knowledge of contemporary science reflected in the Dove, though his own attitude toward it emerges as ambivalent.

[33] Ruth Bernard Yeazell's Language and Knowledge in the Late Novels of Henry James (UCP, 1976) did not appear until after this book had been completed, but her climactic chapter, in which all that she has perceived and superbly set forth concerning James's style and method in his last novels is applied to the study of The Golden Bowl, must be cited here, despite its specific emphasis upon technique rather than character study, as one of the most penetrating studies in the field.

X. THREE HELPMATES

MAY BARTRAM, ALICE STAVERTON
& THE FRIEND OF GEORGE STRANSOM

IN THESE DAYS of "women's lib," the title of this chapter must be expected to give offense in some quarters. However else the "modern woman" may like to think of herself, she tends to be cold to the nineteenth-century notion of the *Ewig Weibliche* who leads men upward for their good. And insofar as she is protesting against the disabilities under which women have suffered or the notion that one half of the human race ought somehow to be subordinated to the other half, she is abundantly justified. Yet there can be no question that men need women even beyond the sense in which women need men, and except for the unisex fanatics, who, as J. M. Barrie used to say, devote themselves to championing the equal right of women with men to grow beards, there can be little question that this fact is, or has been, as important to women as to men. For men and women alike, self-abnegation has a place in human development, not instead of but beside self-assertion, though this is no excuse for those who impose it upon others. As May Bartram tells the impercipient John Marcher in "The Beast in the Jungle," she has had her man as he has had his woman.

So far as this chapter is concerned, however, our concern is not with what the relations between men and women "ought" to be but rather with what they are and how James portrays them. The three women considered in this chapter

are by no means his only helpmates.[1] But in "The Altar of
the Dead," "The Beast in the Jungle," and "The Jolly Corner"
at least, one would think the most ardent feminist might find
it difficult to cavil at James's treatment of the sex. All three
of these women have to do with a man who is in some measure obsessed, and each is, in some measure, sacrificed to
her man. No one of the women is the man's wife. One, in
"The Altar of the Dead," is not even given a name. One woman and presumably one man[2] die. Only one couple (in "The
Jolly Corner") seem to find their way at last into harbor, as
"harbor" is commonly conceived in love stories. John Marcher's moment of truth does not arrive until after May Bartram's death and George Stransom's, apparently, only when
he himself stands upon the brink. But in every case the woman is the eyes or the conscience of the man, and it is through
her that he comes to himself and achieves the best of which
he is capable. Yet in no sense does any one of the women,
in the usual sense, "dominate" her man or impose herself
upon him. What they give is measureless love and understanding, leaving him to work out his own salvation because they
are wise enough to know that this is the only kind of salvation there is.

Stransom's obsession in "The Altar of the Dead" is less
abnormal, certainly less devastating, than that of the others;
perhaps indeed it is only from a worldly, "practical" man's
point of view that these adjectives can apply at all. "The
Altar of the Dead" has always been not only my favorite
among James's stories but, to my way of thinking, one of the
most beautiful stories in the language, and when I learned
that, upon at least one occasion, James himself had singled

[1]See especially Sister M. Corona Sharp, *The Confidante in Henry James,* and
Ora Segal, *The Lucid Reflector,* on this point.

[2]George Stransom in "The Altar of the Dead." Though James does not specifically say that Stransom dies, his last paragraph would be seriously misleading
upon any other hypothesis.

it out as the work with which "he was least dissatisfied,"[3] I felt very much as the possibly apocryphal Boston policeman must have felt who escorted the writer across Copley Square during his last visit to that city, for we are told that this gentleman startled his charge by abruptly asking him which of his novels he preferred, and that, when James chose *The Golden Bowl*, he received the reply, "Oh, thank you sir! That is my favorite too."

After what one gathers has been a fairly distinguished career in government service, George Stransom finds his religion in an almost Chinese reverence for the dead. Securing permission to decorate and illuminate an altar in a Roman Catholic church, he sets up a lighted candle for each of the friends who, as he puts it, had died in possession of him, and here he finds increasing comfort in the presence of what seems like a mountain of light. In the course of time, he finds his rites shared by an unknown lady in deep mourning, with whom, very gradually, he first becomes acquainted and then establishes a deep friendship and to whom he confides the care of his altar after his own candle shall have been added to it.

Two discoveries follow: first, that all her dead are one, and, second, that her dead is the late, great Acton Hague, the closest friend of Stransom's youth and early manhood, who later betrayed him and for whom no candle can glow on any altar of his. This, of course, spoils both the rites and the friendship, and the ensuing misery endures until the very end of Stransom's life.

The lady impinges upon the reader's consciousness almost as gradually as upon Stransom's own. Her singleness, her devotion, is the first thing he notices about her. She is more constant in her attendance than he is; he envies her ability to sink, rapt and motionless, into prayer; she convin-

[3] H. Montgomery Hyde, *Henry James at Home* (Farrar, Straus & Giroux, 1969), 287.

ces him that women have more of the spirit of religion than
men. At first she looks "faded and handsome," and he is sure
she has no fortune. When they meet and speak for the first
time at a concert, he decides that she is prettier and more
interesting than he had supposed. Though she is much younger than he is, she is no longer in her first youth, and he feels
sure that her youth has been "sacrificed." "She might have
been a divorced duchess—she might have been an old maid
who taught the harp." Later he learns that she writes (fiction,
presumably) for the popular magazines, but they never speak
of her work, and he never reads anything she has written.
"She knew too well what he couldn't read and what she
couldn't write, and she taught him to cultivate indifference
with a success that did much for their good relations." Still
later he finds that, though she has lived apart from public
affairs, there has been one great, in the end result unhappy,
experience in her life which, beyond all others, has shaped
and colored her character.

Their intimacy develops very slowly. When Stransom
first becomes interested in her, he even feels hesitation in
going to the church freely, as if disloyalty to the dead were
involved in coming for anybody besides them. It takes him
"months and months to learn her name [which is more than
the reader ever does], years and years to learn her address."
At first it seems to both that "her debt . . . was much greater
than his, because while she had only given him a worshipper
he had given her a splendid temple." Later, however, this
indebtedness is reversed. He never enters her home until after the death of the old aunt with whom she has been living;
then he feels at last "in real possession of her." But this, like
many touches in the tale, is deeply ironical. If he had never
entered her home, he would never have seen Acton Hague's
photograph there or learned of his old friend-enemy's connection with her. When he had done that, "it struck him that
to have come at last into her house had had the horrid effect
of diminishing their intimacy."

Nothing could more interestingly mark the difference between Henry James and the sex-obsessed novelists of our own time than his failure to tell us just what the lady's connection with "their terrible friend" had been. Once Stransom asks her what Hague did to her but she only replies, "Everything!" He asks himself whether he is in love with her "that he should care so much what adventures she had had" and even, with a grim laugh, "why the deuce" she liked Hague "so much more than she likes me." But the only thing either we or he are ever sure of is that she had loved Hague deeply and that in some way he had betrayed her. Stransom knew that "a woman, when wronged, was always more wronged than a man, and there were conditions when the least she could have got off with was more than the most he could have to bear. He was sure this rare creature wouldn't have got off with the least. He was awestruck at the thought of such a surrender—such a prostration."

After their rupture, if one can call it that, both persons are entirely logical in the positions they take up and completely true to themselves. Indeed it is not a rupture in the usual sense of the term, for "she was not vindictive or even resentful. It was not in anger she had forsaken him; it was in simple submission to hard reality, to the stern logic of life." She continues to see him at her home, but they can no longer meet at the church and share their worship there, because with Acton Hague the only one of Stransom's dead to whom he had deliberately refused a candle, he had specifically excluded her from all share in his rites and thus made her attitude "all wrong." With Stransom the case was different. "He had had his great compassions, his indulgences—there were cases in which they had been immense"; in his own way, he had even thought he had forgiven Hague. But "to provide for him on the very ground of having discovered another of his turpitudes was not to pity but to glorify him." Yet he knows almost from the beginning that his forgiveness cannot match hers. "Women aren't like men," she tells him. "They can love even when they've suffered," and, beyond the mere meaningless statement that he has forgiven, he can only reply, "Women are wonderful."

We shall not judge the situation fairly unless we keep it steadily in mind that we are intended to think of Hague as a rich, gifted, fascinating, but evil man. He filled the life of everyone "who had the wonderful experience of knowing him," but there can be no question that Stransom's judgment of him is just. This is made absolutely clear by the woman's unprotesting acceptance of Stransom's statement that "he did me—years ago—an unforgettable wrong." She accepts his words in silence, tears fill her eyes, and she reaches out her hand to take his. "Nothing more wonderful had ever appeared to him than . . . to see her convey with such exquisite mildness that as from Acton Hague any injury was credible." Yet all this is oddly irrelevant. Nothing is more striking in these three tales than the fact that in them women love men as God, in the Christian Gospel, loves His sinful children, seeing all their sins clearly, but with no abatement of love and willing, if need be, to die for them; we shall see this wonder emerging even more clearly if anything in "The Beast in the Jungle" and "The Jolly Corner" than it does here.

When the ghost of Acton Hague steps between Stransom and his friend, it does more than disturb their personal relations however; it also destroys Stransom's worship. The fires of his shrine are quenched, and the church becomes a void. James is completely in harmony here with the Sermon on the Mount: "Therefore if thou bring thy gift to the altar, and there rememberest that thy brother hath ought against thee; Leave there thy gift before the altar, and go thy way; first be reconciled to thy brother, and then come and offer thy gift." Perfect worship, in other words, can only exist in an atmosphere of perfect harmony and adjustment; exclusion and irreconcilability are wholly incompatible with it. J. A. Ward says it all very well: "Not until he forgives Hague is Stransom's altar of the dead complete, for he still shares in the self-destroying egotism of the world he rejects." And Walter F. Wright adds a comment which shows that (since life is one) this had the same validity for art as for religion: "The introduction of Hague has revealed a flaw in Stransom's spiritual world, and it is obvious that, if the story is to be artistically complete, this flaw must cease to exist."[4]

The problem cannot be solved, then, until Stransom rises to the spiritual condition of his friend, and it is her great service to him that she shows him this, not by preaching to him but simply by being what she is. The barrier is in him, not in her, and only he can remove it. He does not achieve this until after his health has broken, weakening, it would seem, his own stubborn, divisive will, and (quite as if he had been reading Walter Wright!) he goes at it first like an artist. "There came a day when, for simple exhaustion, if symmetry should demand just one he was ready so far to meet symmetry." But he does not remain merely an artist. When he goes to church for the last time, after his illness, and before he ought to be out, it seems to him "he had come for the great surrender," and when he finds her there, it seems that God must have sent her and him too. But she meets him halfway, for she too has grown; through "the sweetest of miracles" she has lost all sense of their difference. Suddenly what had hitherto been impossible has become not only possible but inevitable. If she could no longer come to the church for "her own," she could come "for them," and, though she does not say it, for him. Love has superseded logic or subsumed it. The perfect acceptance which she had already achieved in her forgiveness of Hague has now been extended to take in Stransom also, and the circle is whole again.[5]

Leon Edel says that James was reading *The Varieties of*

[4] J. A. Ward, *The Imagination of Disaster*, 89; Walter F. Wright, *The Madness of Art* (UNP, 1962), 325.

[5] It may be remarked in passing that Stransom's friend has been shown in "The Altar of the Dead" in comparison with Stransom's dead love, Mary Antrim, whose death, before their contemplated marriage, had left him her perpetual mourner,

Religious Experience when he wrote "The Beast in the Jungle." He might well have been reading the Grimms' story of "The Youth Who Could Not Shudder" also. John Marcher, who enjoys "a modest patrimony," a library, and a garden in the country and who holds "a little office under Government," had first met May Bartram a decade before the story begins, when she was twenty and he five years older, and had then confided in her his "sense of being kept for something rare and strange, possibly prodigious and terrible, experience." Sooner or later the Beast would leap upon him out of the Jungle, perhaps to overwhelm him, and there was nothing he could do about it save to wait and endure. One of the first striking manifestations of his self-centeredness we encounter is that when he meets her again at Weatherbee, at the beginning of the tale—handsome, but "ever so much older" than before and, like the lady in "The Altar of the Dead," marked by suffering—he should have a vague memory of their former interchange but with all the details wrong and the confidence he had reposed in her having completely escaped him. May, on the other hand, has forgotten nothing. Instead of laughing at him, she had accepted his communication with perfect sympathy and understanding, and so she has kept it in her mind through the years. She believes in him and agrees to "watch" with him, and this gives him a wonderful sense of no longer being so "abominably alone." But both irony and the hint of future developments are involved in

---

and, to a lesser extent, in comparison with the first Mrs. Paul Creston, the only woman he had known since "for whom he might perhaps have been unfaithful," and, by way of contrast, her indelicate successor, whom he meets only once and is determined never to see again. If Hague's hold upon the woman is, in a sense, loosened in the final chapter, it might be supposed that Stransom too is, in a degree, liberated from the much more benevolent spell of Mary Antrim, but James evidently did not intend this, for he has the glory of the altar gather itself into "human beauty and human charity" and "the far-off face of Mary Antrim." Mildred E. Hartsock's "Dizzying Summit: James's 'The Altar of the Dead,'" *SSF*, XI (1974), 371–77, is a rewarding study, which involves a review of criticism and attempts to place the story in relation to the author's own beliefs and spiritual attitudes.

the consciousness of both persons that they have already missed something and in Marcher's rejection of her suggestion that perhaps what he expects may be simply the experience of falling in love.

It must be clearly understood that Marcher is not a "bad" man. It is true that in effect May is sacrificed to him, but this is not his intention; he never deliberately exploits or victimizes anybody. He is "tremendously mindful" of all she does for him and worried over whether he is not taking more than he gives. He escorts the lady to the opera and observes her birthday with more expensive gifts than he can really afford. He even thinks of asking her to marry him, and in a way it is only his consideration for her which prevents this: he is a man marked by destiny, but he is also a man of feeling, and he cannot believe that a man of feeling would ask a lady to accompany him on a tiger hunt. His egotism coexists with a naïveté which almost makes it seem innocent; when she praises his attitude toward his ordeal, he asks, "It's heroic?" and again, "I *am* then a man of courage?" Nevertheless, it is appalling. When May is stricken at last by mortal illness, he wonders momentarily whether her death might be the leap of the Beast for which he has been waiting, but he rejects this idea as he had previously rejected the idea of the love experience (it would be, for him, "a drop of dignity") and even goes to the length of pitying the "sphinx," the "lily" that May has become, because she may have to die without finding out what is going to happen to him!

What we must never forget in dealing with Marcher is that his failure in this matter is a failure in *understanding* rather than a failure in good intentions, but it is equally important to remember that this does not completely exonerate him. That "the devil is an ass" has never been more impressively demonstrated upon a national scale than during recent years, and few of us are happy enough to be sure that we have never demonstrated it ourselves in our private lives. Mrs. Gummidge believed that, though life was hard for everybody, she felt it more than other people, and I believe it was Tolstoy who perceived a species of immorality in making oneself an exception in any aspect. The consciousness of being set apart, even for misfortune, can easily become a force for distortion, especially when, as in Marcher's case, you do not see it as entailing any obligation or requiring any action. Gamaliel Bradford remarked of Cowper, who thought he had committed the unpardonable sin, that he preferred being damned to being convinced that he had been mistaken, and theologians have always realized that the sinner who supposes his sins to have been so uniquely great as to lie beyond the boundaries of God's forgiveness is guilty of monstrous selfishness as well as the sin of despair.

May Bartram achieves the near miracle of knowing Marcher thoroughly and yet viewing him objectively; at the same time, she protects him by trying to help him "to pass for a man like another." As for him, he realizes nothing except through her (he has not even grasped his own aging until he observes with the eyes of his flesh that *she* is visibly growing older!), and it is a tragedy for both of them that she is powerless to communicate to him the most important piece of knowledge she has about him for the simple reason that this is one of those things which a man must learn for himself or else die without knowing. For the Beast in Marcher's jungle is not imaginary, but he is different from anything Marcher has imagined. Marcher is the Empty Man with whom literature since James's time has become so tiresomely preoccupied, the embodiment of what Hemingway called "Nada," the man "to whom nothing on earth was to have happened," and this he became through his inability to love. Life offered her best to him, and he passed it by, not because he did not value or desire it but simply because he did not recognize it. As the children get "warm" from time to time while searching for a companion or an object in a game of hide-and-seek and then veer off again, he experiences flashes of prescience which give us moments of hope for him: the fear of being too late; the thought that not to be anything would be worse than to be bankrupted, hanged, or dishonored; but he fails to follow up these clues because he cannot really believe that such a thing could happen to so marked and exceptional a being as himself.

May, on the other hand, learns the truth as early as the end of the second of the six divisions of the tale, where Marcher accuses her of knowing what is to happen and of withholding her knowledge from him because it is too terrible to tell. She will only tell him that he will never know and never suffer. During her final illness she adds that it has already happened and that he has not recognized it. Why should he seek to know that which he need not know? It is enough that *she* knows and that she can be grateful for having lived to learn what it is not. He continues to experience flashes of perception. He feels that she has something more to give him than he has yet received. Once he even asks her if she is dying for him, and though we are not told the cause of her illness, in a sense she is, as Milly Theale dies for her friends (or enemies) in *The Wings of the Dove*. But since he also accuses her of deserting him and leaving him alone to meet his fate, it is suitable enough, in a sense, that he should be left stranded on the periphery as he is at her funeral.

For if he is often perceptive, he is more often blind. He can charge her with withholding information from him and, almost in the same breath, tell himself that, except for her feminine intuitions, she has no more knowledge than he has. Yet her own love and understanding never falter, and some hope remains to the end. "The door's open," she tells him. "It's never too late." She is right when she says, "I've shown you, my dear, nothing," but this is merely because he has no eyes, and she is right again when she says, "I haven't forsaken you" and "I'm with you—don't you see?"

But she is mistaken about one thing. Ultimately Marcher does "know" and suffer too, though this is not until after her death, when everything has become "vulgar and vain" without her, through a chance encounter near her grave, which has become to him something like Stransom's altar, with a desperately bereaved, "deeply stricken" husband, visiting his wife's grave near by. This man is one of those who, as Henry Adams, glancing obliquely at his own never-healing wound, once expressed it, "suffer beyond the formulas of expression — who are crushed into silence and beyond pain," and Marcher envies him! "What had the man *had*, to make him by the loss of it so bleed and yet live?" And, by the same token, what had Marcher himself missed? "No passion had ever touched him, for this was what passion meant; he had survived and maundered and pined, but where had been *his* deep ravage? . . . He had seen *outside* of his life, not learned it within, the way a woman was mourned when she had been loved for herself." This man had lived, and May had lived, but Marcher had escaped living, and "*she* was what he had missed." The Beast had sprung at last, and we leave Marcher, in his awakened anguish, flung, face downward, upon her grave. Knowledge has come at last. But May has had to die to give it to him.[6]

"The Jolly Corner" differs from our other tales in that it alone is one of James's stories of the supernatural. It is

[6] Jessie R. Lucke, "The Inception of 'The Beast in the Jungle,' " *NEQ*, XXVI (1953), 529–32, argues plausibly for Hollingsworth in *The Blithedale Romance* as a possible source for Marcher. Edward Stone (*The Battle of the Books*) also speaks of *Blithedale* in his commentary on James's use of names and seasons in the "Beast"; see further George Monteiro's sensitive study, "Hawthorne, James, and the Destructive Self," *TSLL*, IV (1962–63), 58–71. Of the three stories considered in this chapter, the "Beast" has drawn the largest amount of commentary (especially from Freudianly oriented critics), and the "Altar" the least: Robert Rogers, "The Beast in Henry James," *AI*, XIII (1956), 427–53, for example, interprets the tale autobiographically in orthodox Freudian style; like many articles of its kind this might almost have been turned out by a Freudian computer. Courtney Johnson, "John Marcher and the Paradox of the 'Unfortunate' Fall," *SSF*, VI (1968–69), 121–35, sees the "Beast" as "a story of frustrated romantic love, more specifically. . . about frustrated sexual love," with much reference to the Sphinx and the Oedipus story. See also David Kerner, "A Note on 'The Beast in the Jungle,' " *UKCR*, XVII (1950–51), 109–118, who sees May as both a person and a hallucination ("like the ghost in 'The Jolly Corner,' May is the Road Not Taken"); James Kraft, "A Perspective on 'The Beast in the Jungle,' " *Literatur in Wissenschaft und Unterricht*, II (1969),

also of course one of James's late and very difficult stories, and there are things in it which one cannot afford to be dogmatic about. The heroine, Alice Staverton, is comparable in her devotion and understanding to the other women; she listens without chattering and knows how to encourage without scattering abroad "a cloud of words." But, as befits the heroine of a ghost story, she is more "psychic" in her divinations, and she knows what the ghost will be like before Spencer Brydon encounters it, for she has seen it in dreams. She is also, I think, more sophisticated than the other women, and one suspects her of greater executive competence. One cannot imagine either of the others speaking ironically of Spencer's "ill-gotten gains" and his sentimentality or telling him frankly at the end that she intends to "keep" him. She is the only one of the three women who does "keep" her man, and she may well have planned this from the beginning, for she tells him at the outset that the old house would make a very different impression "if it were only furnished and lived in."

He is fifty-six years old when the story opens and after thirty-three years abroad has returned to his native New York and the old deserted house on the "jolly corner" where he had lived as a child. Alice is in the "afternoon of noon," "the delicately frugal possessor and tenant of the small house

---

20–26; Peter J. Conn, "Seeing and Blindness in 'The Beast in the Jungle,' " *SSF*, VII (1970), 472–75. The idea of seasonal and nature symbolism in the story is further developed by Joseph Kau, "Henry James and the Garden: A Symbol Setting for 'The Beast in the Jungle,' " *SSF*, X (1973), 187–98, and by Joel R. Kehler, "Salvation and Resurrection in James's 'The Beast in the Jungle,' " *Essays in Literature* (University of Denver), I (1973), 13–28, who sees May enacting three roles: "as spring goddess, as archetypal sufferer and redeemer, and as a species of Madonna." Betty Miller, "Miss Savage and Miss Bartram," *Nineteenth Century and After*, CXLIV (1948), 285–92, compares the situation in the story with Samuel Butler's relations with Eliza Mary Anne Savage, though without claiming influence. Stephen Reid, " 'The Beast in the Jungle' and 'A Painful Case': Two Different Sufferings," *AI*, XX (1963), 221–39, compares the "Beast" with the story named by James Joyce. See also Ronald Beck, "James's 'The Beast in the Jungle': Theme and Metaphor," *Markham Review*, II, 2 (February, 1970), unpaged.

in Irving Place to which she had subtly managed to cling through her almost unbroken New York career." A "pale pressed flower (a rarity to begin with)," she confronts the strain and stress of the "awful modern crush" and all its "public concussions and ordeals" without fear and with such "a slim mystifying grace" that it is difficult to tell whether she is "a fair young woman who looked older through trouble, or a fine smooth older one who looked young through successful indifference," but her heart is with the "memories and histories" of an older New York which she shares with Brydon. Her impregnable stability is one of the things about her that he admires most. Nothing, he thinks, could have altered her fundamentally; she must have been what she is anywhere or under any circumstances; here was a "perfection" which nothing could have "blighted."

His own options were much more varied; if he had remained in New York, for example, he might have developed into something altogether different from what he is, might even have manifested executive powers "quite splendid, quite huge and monstrous."[7] She feels this quite as strongly as he does (the phrase indeed is hers), but when he asks her if she would have liked him thus, she simply replies, "How should I not have liked you?" Yet here again, as with the other women, James makes it quite clear that Alice does not "idealize" Brydon, for when he asks her whether she thinks him "as good as I might ever have been," she replies, "Oh no! Far

[7] Since Henry James himself left America to live abroad for many years, he inevitably wondered, from time to time, what differences continued American residence would have meant for his destiny. This is not the only point at which speculation has been inspired concerning possibly autobiographical passages in all three of our stories, but most of this has been inconclusive and ill-advised. Obviously there must be many points of connection between the experience and the work of any writer, but in James's case most of the keys have been lost. Though Leon Edel has a disarming way of assuming the factuality of everything that suits the particular hypothesis he may be developing at the moment, nobody knows positively whether the death of Constance Fenimore Woolson was suicide or accident; consequently what Edel has to say about "The Altar of the Dead" cannot carry full conviction.

from it! But I don't care." True, clear-sighted understanding coupled with generous acceptance—once again this appears as the only love worth having and the only kind that can survive the shocks of life.

Alice Staverton is certainly no less important to Spencer Brydon than the other women with whom we have been concerned are to their men, but in a sense she is less directly involved in his ordeal, for she is absent from the scene through the whole second chapter of "The Jolly Corner" (there are only three, and the last is very short), while Brydon prowls through the midnight hours at the Jolly Corner, first stalking and then being stalked by his alter ego, the Spencer Brydon who might have been. For this is Brydon's obsession: "He found all things come back to the question of what he personally might have been, how he might have led his life and 'turned out,' if he had not so, at the outset, given it up." James's description of the double stalking is a brilliant tour de force, but when Brydon is confronted at last by the hideous maimed monster he thinks he has been seeking, the shock nearly kills him (indeed he afterwards believes that he had died and come to life again), and he knows no more until the next morning, when he finds himself lying in the hall with his head in Alice's Madonna-like lap.[8]

The last chapter of "The Jolly Corner" is as profound as it is brief, and the critics have been considerably stimulated

[8] The usual interpretation of "The Jolly Corner" is that Brydon confronts what he has been seeking—the ghost of himself as he might have been had he remained in New York. But Floyd Stovall, "Henry James's 'The Jolly Corner,' " *NCF*, XII (1957–58), 72–84, thinks that the ghost which frightens Brydon in the hall is not the one whose confrontation he had funked upstairs but rather the ghost of himself as he actually is, after having been false to himself for thirty-three years. Stovall's article, which is persuasively developed, contains valuable insights whatever we may make of its central thesis, but it seems doubtful that we need two ghosts in the story or that, had he intended to provide them, James would have indicated it so obscurely than nobody would have grasped his intention before 1957. In "The Beast in 'The Jolly Corner': Spencer Brydon's Ironic Rebirth," *SSF*, XI (1974), 61–66, Allen F. Stein denies that Brydon is redeemed by his encounter with the monster. "His much vaunted awakening love for Alice is simply a shift from a bare acknowledgement of her existence as a friend who will tirelessly listen to his talk of him-

by it. Thus Dorothea Krook tells us that Brydon is saved because he learns just in time the lesson Marcher fails to learn
until it is too late. In *The Ambassadors*, she believes, James
entered a claim for "the redeeming power of consciousness
alone," while "The Jolly Corner" "points directly toward
James's last, and perhaps most poignant story, 'The Bench
of Desolation,' in which the redeeming power of the mere
capacity to receive love shows as the last flickering pin-point
of light in the dark night of a world sunk in helpless, hope-
less suffering." The religious element in all three of these
stories is sufficiently strong to cause the reader to wonder
whether those who find no religion in James's work may not
be pointing to a lack in what they bring rather than in what
they find. William A. Freedman[9] compares Brydon's symbolic
death and resurrection with relevant passages in Dante, Plato
(the "Allegory of the Cave"), and especially the New Testament story of the raising of Lazarus. But when we speak of
what Brydon learns in the last chapter, we need to tread
warily. He does not seem to have any settled conviction concerning the ghost, for the very violence with which he pro-
tests that the thing is not himself shows that he is not sure.
Peter Buitenhuis[10] thinks that when Alice tells him, "No,
thank heaven, it's not you!" she does not really mean it but

---

self to a complete dependence on her as a buffer to shield him from having to face
the harsh facts of life." He remains what he has always been and "perverts Alice's
potentially redeeming love." On the other hand, Ernest Tuveson, " 'The Jolly Corner': A Fable of Redemption," *SSF*, XII (1975), 271–80, interprets the story in
terms suggested by his subtitle and involving a comparison with F. W. H. Myers's
Human Personality and Its Survival of Bodily Death (1903), in which we know
William James was greatly interested. Still another interpretation of the story, in
terms very different from those which have been employed in this chapter, and
which to me seems oversubtle, appears in John A. Clair's *The Ironic Dimension in
the Fiction of Henry James*.

[9] "Universality in 'The Jolly Corner,' " *TSLL*, IV (1962–63), 12–15.

[10] *The American Writings of Henry James* (University of Toronto Press, 1970).
See pp. 10–21 for a sensible interpretation of "The Jolly Corner" in general and
a thoughtful critique of views previously presented.

is merely comforting him as one might comfort a frightened child. Such at the moment she might well do, but she is surely more interested in removing his blinders than in fastening them upon him. Is it not much more likely that what she is saying is more like what we mean when we tell somebody who must be rebuked for an unworthy action that this is not "like him" or that he is "not himself"? A careful reading of the last few pages of the story makes it abundantly clear that Alice (who has twice seen the horror in her dreams) does not deny the monster element in Brydon; as we have seen, she has already specifically told him that she does not think him as good as he might be. But because she knows and cherishes his best potentialities as well as his worst, she knows too that he cannot be *identified* with the monster, and, because she loves him, she can accept even the "unhappy" and "ravaged" horror that has so terrified and revolted him along with the other elements which make up his personality. For of course we must not think of the Brydon who might have developed in New York as "bad" or of the Brydon who had returned from abroad as "good." He himself has told Alice that his life has not been "edifying," that in some quarters at least it has been considered "selfish frivolous scandalous" and "barely decent," while she herself tells him bluntly that "you don't care for anything but yourself," and if he might have difficulty in accepting this as the whole truth, he does know that his experience has been defective and incomplete and admit the need of cultivating "his whole perception" and bringing it "to perfection, by practice." His search for his other self is a search for integration or wholeness, or, in more conventionally religious terms, a search for salvation, and at the end of the story we may have good hope that he will achieve it at last through a woman's unselfish, all-comprehending love.

INDEX